Messages of Reconciliation and Hope

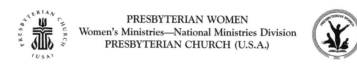

PRESBYTERIAN WOMEN
Women's Ministries—National Ministries Division
PRESBYTERIAN CHURCH (U.S.A.)

Messages of Reconciliation and Hope

75 Years of Birthday Offerings 1922-1997

Catherine Stewart Vaughn

PROVIDENCE HOUSE PUBLISHERS
Franklin, Tennessee

Copyright 1997 by Catherine Stewart Vaughn

All rights reserved. Written permission must be secured from the publisher to use or reproduce any part of this book, except for brief quotations in critical reviews and articles.

Printed in the United States of America

01   00   99   98   97   5   4   3   2   1

Library of Congress Catalog Card Number: 97–68105

ISBN: 1–57736–060–5

Unless otherwise noted, Scripture quotations and photos are supplied courtesy of the Presbyterian Archives, Horizons magazine, various Presbyterian publications, field missionaries, and Birthday Offering benefactors. Scripture is based on Revised Standard Version of the Bible. Copyright © 1946, 1952 Division of Christian Education of the National Council of the Churches of Christ in the United States of America. Used by permission.

Back cover photos: top left, Entrance Gate, Montreat, North Carolina; top right, Stillman College, Tuscaloosa, Alabama; bottom, Miss Dowd's School for Girls, Kochi, Japan (circa 1922). Front cover photo: modern chapel, Seiwa University (originally Miss Dowd's School for Girls), Kochi, Japan.

Cover by Bozeman Design

Photo of Catherine Vaughn on page 254 is courtesy of Olan Mills Portrait Studios.

PROVIDENCE HOUSE PUBLISHERS
238 Seaboard Lane • Franklin, Tennessee 37067
800-321-5692

With Love

To Si Vaughn, my husband and companion for forty-four years, a true partner who has supported me in ways too numerous to list.

To our children—Stewart and Laura Vaughn and Andrew and Amy Vaughn—who have brought great joy to our lives and who have now become treasured friends as well.

To our much-loved grandchildren, Christopher, Matthew, and those yet to be born—who have made growing older fun and who have filled our lives with many serendipities.

To Presbyterian women everywhere with whom I have journeyed through the years, from whom I have learned much, by whom I have been inspired and challenged, and in whose faces I have seen the compassion, zeal, and caring that is exemplified in the ministry of our Savior, Jesus Christ.

Contents

Foreword	ix
Preface	xi
Acknowledgments	xiii
Introduction	xv

Part I The First Fifty Years in Summary: 1922–1972   1

    1. The Woman's Auxiliary (1922–1947)
       The Board of Women's Work
       Presbyterian Church, U.S.   3

    2. The Women of the Church (1948–1972)
       The Board of Women's Work
       Presbyterian Church, U.S.   35

Part II The Years before Merger: 1973–1988   71

    3. The Women of the Church (1973–1988)
       Office of Women—Division of National Mission
       Presbyterian Church, U.S.   73

Part III The Years since Merger: 1989–1997	153
4. Presbyterian Women (1989–1997) Women's Ministries—National Ministries Division Presbyterian Church (U.S.A.)	155
Appendixes	215
A. Birthday Gifts through the Years (1922–1997) Arranged in Chronological Order	217
B. Birthday Gifts through the Years (1922–1997) Arranged by Destination/Recipients	225
C. Board of Church Extension (PCUS) Correspondence (1966)	233
D. Board of Women's Work (PCUS) Excerpts from Minutes (1972–1973)	237
E. Board of World Missions (PCUS) Excerpts from Minutes (1972–1973)	239
F. Board of World Missions (PCUS) Correspondence (1973)	243
G. Creative Ministries Offering Committee	245
H. Criteria for Birthday Offering Proposals	247
Resources	249
Index	251
About the Author	254

Foreword

The first edition of *The Birthday Book* traced the history of fifty years of birthday gifts of women of the Presbyterian Church, U.S. After 1988, an intimate relationship developed when United Presbyterian Women and Women of the Church formed a new organization called Presbyterian Women in the Presbyterian Church (U.S.A.).

Bound by this historical merger, the Churchwide Coordinating Team of Presbyterian Women is grateful to Cathy Vaughn for volunteering her services to write an updated history of seventy-five years of birthday offerings. The first section of the history summarizes the first fifty years of birthday offerings. She conducted an extensive research by reviewing proposals from 1973 on, poring over records in the Department of History (Presbyterian Historical Society) in Montreat and in the Louisville office of the Associate for Mission Participation, discovering in files how the contributions have been used over the past twenty-five years.

Our profound thanks to the Creative Ministries Offering Committee for their encouragement and cooperation along each step of this project.

The intention of this book is to celebrate the rich history of women of faith, their unfailing belief that God has and will continue to bless the givers and the receivers with an abundance of God's grace, love, and mercy through the birthday gifts given worldwide.

—Gladys Strachan
Coordinator for Presbyterian Women

Preface

Do you remember your first Birthday Party? Most of us do not; however, many of us do remember our first Women of the Church or Presbyterian Women Birthday Party. My first celebration was in 1955. I was a young bride, and my husband and I had moved to a town where we did not know anyone. We joined the local Presbyterian Church, and I became part of a Circle of young women. That Circle became the nucleus of my friendships. It was also the place where I first participated in a Birthday Celebration—the Yodogawa Christian Hospital in Osaka, Japan. At that time, I did not dream that I would one day chair the Birthday Selection Committee, nor did I realize that forty-two years of joyous celebrations would follow and that it would be my happy privilege to write a history of the first seventy-five years of Birthday Celebrations.

In her excellent history, *The Birthday Book, The First Fifty Years*, Patricia Houck Sprinkle begins with these words, "Like wisps of clouds across an evening sky, memories of former Birthdays drift across the minds of most Women of the Presbyterian Church, U.S." Janie W. McGaughey, in her book, *On the Crest of the Present*, writes of the motivation behind women's involvement in these annual offerings, "Because there is entrusted to Christians the message of Reconciliation through Jesus Christ for all people, Christian women through the years have felt the responsibility for their share in the discharge of the world mission of the Church."

As I have read updated accounts of what has happened in mission at home and abroad as a result of seventy-five years of Birthday Offerings and the ongoing influence many of them continue to have, I rejoice in the vision, sacrifice, and faithfulness of Presbyterian women across the years. These offerings are, indeed, as Patti Sprinkle said, "more than memories." Oscar Wilde wrote, "Memory is the diary that we all carry about with us" (*The Importance of Being Earnest*). The succession of Birthday Celebrations is, for me, like a diary, putting faces on people and bringing to life places throughout the world, for these gifts through the years have met many needs and have witnessed to Jesus Christ all over the world.

By some measurements these gifts may not seem very significant, but to me, the gifts carry images of reconciliation, hope, and love to hurting people in our own country and throughout the world. Women have contributed more than $23 million through the seventy-five years of Birthday Gifts. Through the Depression they brought their pennies, through recessions they gave what they could, in times of prosperity they shared generously. The story of why each of these gifts was given and of what has happened because of them, the needs they met and continue to meet, makes for fascinating reading.

A statement of Oscar McCloud's in *Concern* seems a fitting introduction to this history: "To mark a birthday is to honor what has been and to hope for what is yet to be." Happy Birthday, Presbyterian Women! May we have many more.

Acknowledgments

I am indebted to the Creative Ministries Offering Committee of Presbyterian Women, who made it possible for this history of an important part of the heritage of women in the Presbyterian Church (U.S.A.) to be recorded, and especially to Una Stevenson, the Chair of the Committee. The Churchwide Coordinating Team of Presbyterian Women—Women's Ministries, Presbyterian Church (U.S.A.), the successor to the Board of Women's Work, Presbyterian Church in the United States, has given permission to quote from the history of the first fifty years of Birthday Offerings. I am deeply indebted to Patricia Houck Sprinkle, the author of that book, *The Birthday Book, First Fifty Years*, which was published by the Board of Women's Work. Her book provided the basis of the abbreviated accounts of the first fifty offerings, and I quoted frequently from the book, summarized, chose essential facts, and updated the information. Her book is a valuable resource for background information about these offerings and a wonderful supplement, in general, on mission during those fifty years.

I owe a special word of thanks to Jean Cutler, Associate for Mission Participation, Presbyterian Women, and her administrative assistant, Cindy Goodman, for their assistance in gathering information, in spite of overcrowded schedules. I am indebted to Diane Sanderson, of the Department of History, Montreat, for assistance in searching out scattered files. I am also indebted to *Horizons* magazine for its excellent articles and information on Birthday Offerings since 1989. Other information was gathered from files, minutes, and copies of *Presbyterian*

Women, a publication of Women of the Church, and their articles about the offerings, and the interpretive materials prepared by the staff in Atlanta. Unfortunately, the files are not complete, so some components are missing. Diane Sanderson, Jean Cutler, and I were unsuccessful in finding some photographs that would have enhanced this history.

I am grateful for first-hand information from many persons like retired or former missionaries Jule Spach, Kitty and Lyle Peterson, Dot Hopper, John Moore, Frank Arnold, Dr. Herb Codington, G. Thompson Brown, Jessie Junkin McCall, and Jack Crawford. The Rev. Arthur Kinsler, serving now in Seoul, Korea, was very helpful. Several persons on the staff in Louisville were interviewed, including Harrell Davis, Hunter Farrell, and Ben Gutierrez. Miss Janie McCutchen, former Secretary of the Board of Women's Work (now ninety years young), shared her memories, as did Bluford Hestir, formerly with TRAV. Dr. Cordell Wynn of Stillman College, the presidents and staff of Austin Theological Seminary, Columbia Theological Seminary, Presbyterian Theological Seminary in Louisville, Union Theological Seminary in Richmond, and Presbyterian School of Christian Education also provided information. Dr. Bernard Wagner, President of Evergreen Presbyterian Ministries; Anne B. Earle, Director of VEFC; Dr. Henry C. Simmons, Director of the Center on Aging, PSCE; Bill and Carol Schlesinger of Project VIDA; W. Blake Davis, Administrator of Duvall Home; Harry F. Petersen, Executive Director of Villa International; David Batlle of Manos de Cristo; and David Dearinger of Goodland Presbyterian Home for Children were also very helpful. Numerous others responded to my request for information including a number of Presbytery and Synod Executives (especially Angela Abrego, Associate, Synod of the Sun) and others too numerous to list.

The author is indebted to each person who helped to make this history possible. I also wish to thank Providence House Publishers, especially Mary Bray Wheeler, for their patience, support, and invaluable assistance.

Most of all, I am grateful for the support of my husband, Si Vaughn, for without him, this work would never have been completed.

Introduction

How Did It Begin?

By 1997, the seventy-fifth anniversary of Birthday Offerings, Presbyterian Women and one of its predecessors—Women of the Church—had joyfully and sometimes sacrificially given over $23 million to worthy causes both at home and abroad. How did this tradition begin?

In 1912, the Woman's Auxiliary of the Presbyterian Church, U.S. was organized. As the tenth anniversary of its founding approached, the leaders of the Auxiliary wanted to make an offering to some definite cause in the Church as a Birthday Gift. At the same time, the Stewardship Committee of the Presbyterian Church, U.S. was meeting and was charged to raise money, through the Every Member Canvas, for the regular support of the Church and its missions, and, at the same time, to raise $5 million for sorely needed equipment and facilities in the home and foreign mission fields. Lists of greatly needed items had been presented by both Home and Foreign Mission.

The following summer at a meeting of the Stewardship Committee in Montreat, the Secretary of the Stewardship Committee discussed with Mrs. Hallie Paxson Winsborough, Superintendent of the Woman's Auxiliary, the possibility of the Auxiliary assuming the responsibility for raising a definite part of the Equipment Fund. One of the items on the Foreign Mission list was Miss Dowd's School in Japan. The superintendent had just returned from a visit to the Orient and had spent two days in the dilapidated building that housed the school, the Carrie MacMillan Home, and knew from her experience the urgent need for a new home for the school. This led to a solution that would accomplish a twofold goal—give a

Birthday Gift to Miss Dowd's School and at the same time take care of one of the items on the Equipment Fund list. No definite amount was promised, but the women said they would do their best. "If we may be left entirely free to promote the offering as we think best, we will provide as liberal a gift as we can raise toward one item on the Foreign Mission list of needs, namely, Miss Dowd's School," was their response to the request.

The Stewardship Committee accepted this decision, and the first campaign began for a Birthday Gift. The idea was a new one, and budgets were already taxed to their limits; therefore, every woman in the Church was urged to bring an offering that would equal "A penny for every year you have lived and if that is a secret, bring a dollar!" The Birthday Offering amounted to more than $28,000.

At the very inception of the campaign, the Synodical Presidents had announced that a small part of the money given would be used as a gift for the birthplace of the Woman's Auxiliary, Montreat, and $2,000 of the first offering was used to erect the Memorial Gateway there. Twenty-six thousand dollars was given to erect a new home for Miss Dowd's School. It was reported that "the birthday celebration was very joyous." The tradition of annual Birthday Parties had begun.

The next year it was taken for granted that there would be another Birthday Party, and for several years the Birthday objectives were selected from the list of equipment needs of these two committees, alternating between "Foreign" and "Home" objectives. In 1997, Presbyterian Women mark seventy-five years of "very joyous" Birthday Celebrations.

About This Book

The history is arranged in three sections. The first section summarizes the first fifty years, using data from the first history and updated material from various sources. The second section covers the period from the fiftieth year through 1988, when Women of the Church and United Presbyterian Women united to become Presbyterian Women. The third section covers the years, to date, of Presbyterian Women's involvement since 1989 in Birthday Offerings. The history is presented in chronological order. There is an additional listing arranged according to geography—the international separate from the United States. Observe, as you scan the lists and read the histories, the changes through the years.

In the April 1997 issue of *Presbyterians Today*, Eva Simpson writes about the changing face of mission:

Introduction

xvii

> If you think global mission is just about sending missionaries, think again! . . . Gone is the era of once-a-year slide shows about U.S. Christians ministering in far-off lands. . . . A new era is dawning, marked by an increased variety of models for mission involvement at every level of the denomination. . . . Sometimes the Presbyterian Church helps meet a need overseas by supporting a mission worker from another denomination or by working through an ecumenical agency such as Church World Service or the World Council of Churches. In other cases a partner church in another country might be able to supply personnel to do a particular [ministry].

Indeed, missions *have* changed from the days of Miss Dowd, Maria Fearing, Charlotte Kemper, and many others. In her book, *Pioneer Women*, Mary Irvine says, "History, in the making, is unconscious of itself. While the issue is on, the chief concern is with its outcome, leaving the future to reveal, in proportionate outline, its true perspective and color." The scope of the history of Birthday Offerings over the past seventy-five years is coincident with the life of Presbyterian women. While the history was being made, women were not so much aware of its scope. The future, which is now, has revealed its incredible importance and impact.

As we look back through the pages of this particular method of caring and sharing, there is revealed to us not only the changing face of mission but the emerging and more active role of women in the Church since 1922. Just as most of the overseas projects supported by women in the Church have reached maturity and are responsible for their own management and direction, so too have the roles of women changed.

Presbyterian Women rejoice in bonds that hold them together, in the ways they are nurtured through these bonds, and in their commitment to ministry as manifested through offerings like the Thank Offering, including Health Ministries and the Birthday Offerings. Someone has said, "History is prelude to the future." Look back at your history, Presbyterian Women, and be thankful; look ahead to the future and be filled with excitement and expectation.

PART I

The First Fifty Years in Summary
(1922–1972)

CHAPTER ONE

The Woman's Auxiliary
(1922–1947)

*The Board of Women's Work
Presbyterian Church, U.S.*

1922

Seiwa School (Miss Dowd's School), Kochi, Japan *(See also Introduction; see also 1947, 1975)*

Seiwa School, known for many years as the Carrie MacMillan Home because it was housed in a building by that name, was founded in the city of Kochi, Japan, by Miss Annie Henrietta Dowd, who went to Japan as a missionary in 1887. About 1901, according to *The Birthday Book* (a book by Patricia Houck Sprinkle published by the Board of Women's Work on the fiftieth anniversary of Birthday Offerings), Miss Dowd "became concerned about the plight of poorer girls in Japan." Taxation was oppressive, and farmers and others often hired out their daughters as servants or sold them as prostitutes. Two of these girls were sent to Miss Dowd, and she took them into her home. Soon so many others followed that Miss Dowd appealed to the Japan Mission for financial help. "The Mission agreed to pay their rent but had to insist that the girls work to support themselves. Thus was founded the Industrial School of Kochi." Domestic science courses formed the bulk of their studies, with Bible study the centerpiece. To earn money, Miss Dowd taught the girls to make lace, and American women agreed to buy all they could make.

Miss Dowd legally had to adopt every girl whom she took in and even buy some of them; otherwise, the fathers would turn up when the girls were older and claim them. Space was also a problem, and when the number of girls reached forty-five, she moved them into a house rented for her by the mission. Soon that house, too, was terribly overcrowded.

Miss Annie Dowd.

When she was on furlough, Miss Dowd related her worries to a girlhood friend (not a Presbyterian), and the friend and her relatives gave enough money to buy land and build the Carrie MacMillan Home in memory of their aunt. The building was cheaply built, and when Miss Winsborough (see also Introduction) visited the school, she found deteriorating, crowded conditions but a high quality of education and work; thus was born the idea of a "love offering" in celebration of the tenth anniversary of the Woman's Auxiliary. The rest is history.

An attractive yellow stucco building was built with $25,699 of that first Birthday Offering, and for five years it housed the school. Then, in 1927, the building burned, and, due to an oversight, the mission had allowed the insurance policy to lapse. With no funds to rebuild, Miss Dowd began again. Contributions poured in from Japanese Christians, students from throughout the province and from the Presbyterian Church, U.S. until enough funds

Miss Dowd's School for Girls, Kochi, Japan.

The First Fifty Years in Summary

Carrie MacMillan Home.

were available to build once again. In 1933, the Depression caused a loss of funds for maintaining the school. Almost miraculously, the First Church of Kochi, with 1,900 members, celebrated its fiftieth anniversary by taking on the support of Miss Dowd's School in honor of its birthday. In the spring of 1934, the congregation assumed responsibility for the school, and the Carrie MacMillan Home became the Seiwa School, which means "pure peace."

Mrs. Hiroe Ueno, a teacher at Seiwa Gakuen for nearly thirty years, wrote in a letter to retired missionary Catherine Peterson dated November 26, 1996:

> We enclose with this letter a number of photographs, including a picture of the Carrie MacMillan Home which was built in 1924 with the first birthday offering. As you can see from the photos, the school has certainly come a long way in the last 100 years. We thank the Lord for all his blessings and especially the blessings of all the support (both financial and spiritual) that our friends in the United States have given us.

Montreat Gate
At the very beginning of the campaign for the first Birthday Offering, the Synodical Presidents had announced that a small part of the objective that year would be used as a gift for the birthplace of the Woman's Auxiliary, Montreat. Two thousand dollars was designated to construct the stone gate that marks the entrance to Montreat. The Auxiliary, which was organized in 1912, continued under that name until 1948 when the plan of organization and the program were revised and the name was changed to Women of the Church. The gate still stands today and serves as a reminder to all who enter Montreat of the rich heritage of first the Woman's Auxiliary, then the Women of the Church, and today, Presbyterian Women.

1923

Presbyterian-Mexican (Pres-Mex) School, Taft, Texas [Now Presbyterian Pan American School, Kingsville, Texas] (*See also 1938, 1944, 1950*)

The year after the first Birthday Offering, it was taken for granted that there would be another Birthday Party, and this time an objective was selected from the "Home Mission Committee" list. One of the important mission efforts of the Presbyterian Church, U.S. had been among the Mexicans who constantly crossed and recrossed the border between Mexico and the United States. Texas was a part of Mexico until 1836 when it became an independent country. Texas was an independent country until the year 1845 when it was admitted as a state to the United States. The Birthday Offering in 1923 was directed to those Texans who remained, after statehood, essentially Mexican in speech and custom. The Presbyterian School for Mexican Girls in Taft, Texas, was founded with the second Birthday Offering. The Synodical of Texas challenged the other synodicals to match their gift of $25,000. The women accepted the challenge, and a total of $52,928, plus an individual contribution of $10,000 and 200 acres of land given by the city of Taft, made it possible to establish the school. On October 1, 1924, the school officially opened with nineteen students. The goal of Pres-Mex, as the school came to be called, was to train leaders and teachers for the Mexican people, both in the United States and Mexico, rather than to educate the mass of Mexican young people. Between 1924 and 1944, more than 700 girls attended the school.

1924

Assembly's Training School, Richmond, Virginia [Now Presbyterian School of Christian Education] *(See also 1948, 1958—Part of 1940, 1977)*

As a result of studies made by members of the faculty of Union Theological Seminary and members of the Presbyterian Committee of Religious Education and Publication, the Assembly's Training School (ATS) was established in 1914. The purpose of the school has always been to prepare women and men for service in church vocations, with emphasis upon the educational work of the church. For the third Birthday Offering in 1924, the women chose to provide funds for the President's Home at ATS. A total of $23,388 was given, and the handsome, red-brick dwelling featuring two gables, is still in use today.

1925

Charlotte Kemper School, Lavras, Brazil

The Charlotte Kemper School is the girls division of Gammon Institute. Charlotte Kemper, at the age of forty-five, left her teaching position at Mary Baldwin Seminary (now College) to apply as a missionary to Brazil. She served as teacher, housemother, treasurer, and evangelistic visitor for a mission school in Campinas. In 1891 and 1892, three severe epidemics of yellow fever struck Campinas. Miss Kemper was one of the few missionary survivors. The mission decided to move the school to another climate and chose the city of Lavras in a mountainous region. On February 1, 1893, the first classes opened in Lavras. At fifty-five, Miss Kemper became known to the Brazilians of that city as "the little lady who walks too fast." In 1908, the East Brazil Mission decided to honor the girls school by officially naming it the "Charlotte Kemper Seminary."

In 1925, the Gammons took a long overdue furlough, and Miss Kemper, now eighty-eight, went with them. They appealed to the Woman's Auxiliary for the Birthday Offering to construct a new building "that will not leak when it rains." The 1925 Birthday Offering, $39,251, was designated for the Kemper School. The money was used to build an impressive white building with towering columns for classrooms and a temporary auditorium/chapel. Over the door of the new building is written in large letters: *Collegia Carlota Kemper*. Miss Kemper was still living in 1927 when the building was completed. Ninety years old, she toured the entire building. Ten or twelve days later she was taken ill and could not attend the dedication on April 2, so a private dedication service was held in her room. Two weeks later she died.

Note: The Brazil Mission was dissolved in 1985 and facilities turned over to the national church.

1926

Oklahoma Presbyterian College, Durant, Oklahoma *(For related projects, see also 1938, 1954, 1976, 1993)*

For almost seventy-five years, a school in Durant, Oklahoma provided a solid foundation in Christian education for generations of Native American, Anglo, and international students. The Woman's Auxiliary gave two Birthday Offerings to Oklahoma Presbyterian College (OPC), the first in 1926. The school was founded in 1894 as Calvin Institute by C. J. Ralston, a pioneer missionary to the Choctaw, Chickasaw, Cherokee, Seminole, and Creek tribes that live in that part of Oklahoma. In 1900, the school changed its name and narrowed its mission, becoming Durant Presbyterian College. In 1910, the school changed again, becoming Oklahoma Presbyterian College for Indian Girls, to educate the most promising Native American girls in the region. The college offered a B.S. or a B.A. degree. Until 1915, the federal government had paid tuition and fees for "Indian students" at both private and public schools. At that time the government decided to pay for the students only at public institutions. The decision put a financial strain on the school. The college combined some of their courses with Southeastern Teachers College, located in the same town. In order to continue their mission, which included Bible study and Christian education, OPC requested the 1926 Birthday Offering to provide salaries for Bible teachers and to strengthen the Christian education program on campus. That year's offering, initially $41,892, was used to establish an endowment fund and increase library offerings in the Bible field. The interest from the fund was used to employ a second Bible teacher. The gift was formally dedicated in December 1926 as the Mary Semple Hotchkin Bible Chair. For forty years the income from that 1926 offering provided Christian education teachers at OPC.

In 1951, the college decided to become coeducational, and the name was shortened to Oklahoma Presbyterian College. However, OPC was, in reality, more of a "hostel" than a college. By 1957, the only courses offered were Bible, music, and kindergarten. OPC did offer its students a

Christian place to live and opportunities to study Bible and the Christian faith while attending the local state college. The student body included a number of international students. Even so, the future did not look very bright. The school closed in 1966, and income from the Mary Semple Hotchkin Bible Chair was transferred on action of the Board of Women's Work and the Board of Church Extension to Goodland Presbyterian Children's Home in Hugo, Oklahoma, where Ms. Hotchkin is buried (see Appendix C). For some time, the funds were used to employ someone in Christian education; however, the home has not received income from the fund for some years. At the time of publication, officials at Goodland and the author of this book are still trying to learn where the corpus is located and how the income is being used.

Income from another fund, the Janie W. McGaughey Endowment (see Appendix C), was transferred in 1966 to the Presbyterian School of Christian Education (PSCE) in Richmond on action of the same boards to be used primarily for scholarships for international students. PSCE received income from the fund until the eighties but has received no income in the past decade or so. At the time of publication of this book, officials at PSCE and the author are still trying to find where this corpus is now located and what use is being made of the income.

1927

Jennie Speer School for Girls, Kwangju, Korea *(See also 1947, 1975)*

The first Birthday Gift to Korea in 1927 met a crucial need. Education had always been a priority for the PCUS Korea Mission, and every mission station had established schools for Christian students who came primarily from the lower classes and could not afford Japanese schools. After the Independent Movement in the country in 1919, laws were enacted to give private schools designated (accredited) standing, which would give graduates approximately the same privileges as graduates of government schools. The law forbidding the teaching of religion was also relaxed. The mission could not afford to upgrade all ten of its schools to meet "designated" standards, so the mission decided to upgrade two schools for designation, one in Chunju (capital of North Chulla Province) for boys, and one for girls in Kwangju (capital of South Chulla Province). Education for women was a problem in Korea because most parents saw little need for it, and little or no provision for it was made in public schools.

The Jennie Speer School in Kwangju, chosen as the girls school to be upgraded, was founded in 1908. Facilities and equipment were totally inadequate, so the mission requested help from the Woman's Auxiliary. The 1927 offering ($58,875) was given to the Jennie Speer School, and with those funds the mission built Winsborough Hall for classroom and administrative purposes. There was enough money to build an additional classroom building and gymnasium, with enough leftover funds for seven acres of rice and garden lands and for the grading of a playground and athletic field! Speer School is now, as Patti Sprinkle says, "a grown daughter," able to determine the direction of her own life.

For an update on Speer School, see 1947 for quote from Kinsler letter dated April 1997.

1928

Stillman College, Tuscaloosa, Alabama, Emily Estes Snedecor Nurses Training School (*See also 1938, 1942, 1952, 1960, 1972, 1988*)

No Birthday objective was closer to the hearts of Women of the Church than Stillman College, which received seven Birthday Gifts, the latest in 1988, the year before Presbyterian Women came into existence. Stillman even received an offering from the women in 1921, a year before the first Birthday Offering. Altogether, Stillman College has received all or part of seven offerings, more than any other recipient. The entrance gates to Stillman proudly proclaim "Stillman College, Founded 1876, By The Presbyterian Church, U.S." Stillman College is listed as one of the historically black Presbyterian Colleges that is in sound condition, financially and academically. Women of the Church were always proud of Stillman, and proud of the small part they were able to play in helping Stillman maintain its high standards. Stillman describes itself as:

> . . . a flagship institution of a select group of historically black colleges and universities. . . . Stillman College began as a training school for Negro ministers. Today, its programs, resources, and support services create an educational climate that is both Christian and intellectual . . . multicultural and global.

Stillman is a four-year, coeducational, liberal arts college. It is accredited by the Southern Association of Colleges and Schools and by the Alabama State Department of Education. The average enrollment is 950 students. There are sixteen majors plus preprofessional programs in engineering,

The First Fifty Years in Summary 11

law, medicine, ministry, and social work. There are fifty-eight full-time professors as well as a number of part-time faculty. Forty-seven percent of the faculty hold doctoral degrees.

The women in the Presbyterian Church, U.S. were involved in Stillman College even before the days of the first Birthday Gift. In 1916, when a Conference for Negro Women was held at Stillman, the school still only accepted men. Concerned about the lack of quality education opportunities for Negro females and spurred on by the Superintendent for Women's Work, Miss Hallie Winsborough, and by her maxim that "no race will ever rise higher than its womanhood," the women began a campaign to make Stillman coeducational. No doubt you can guess the outcome. In 1921, the General Assembly granted approval, and the women raised funds to build the first women's dormitory, Hallie Paxson Winsborough Hall. The building is still in use today.

In a letter dated March 4, 1997, Dr. Cordell Wynn, President of Stillman College, wrote:

> Hallie Paxson Winsborough Hall is the oldest building now on the Stillman Campus. It was completed in 1922 and fully renovated in 1987 for $1,400,000. Winsborough's renovation in 1987 was one of the high points in my first five years at Stillman, and a major aspect of our campaign which was completed that year. It serves as a residence hall for upper-class women with higher grade point averages. Winsborough occupies a prominent position on the main quadrangle next to Stillman Boulevard.

Winsborough Hall, Stillman College.

Snedecor Hall, Stillman College.

At the time of the first Birthday Gift to Stillman in 1928, hospitals in the South were segregated. There was no hospital in Tuscaloosa that would admit blacks as patients nor was there an infirmary on the Stillman campus. Furthermore, there was not even a program to train "Negro nurses" in the area. The University of Alabama, also located in Tuscaloosa, volunteered to conduct a nurses training program at Stillman if facilities could be made available. In response, the Woman's Auxiliary designated their entire Birthday Offering, $41,875, to build a combination training school/hospital/infirmary on the campus. With these funds, a two-story brick building was constructed. It was named in honor of Emily Estes Snedecor, Dean of Women Students. Mrs. Snedecor was the widow of the first Secretary of Colored Evangelism for the Presbyterian Church, U.S.

For twenty years, the hospital served as college infirmary and was the only medical care available to blacks in the community. The end of World War II brought unexpected changes when an army hospital was turned over to the city with the stipulation that it accept patients of all races and creeds. By 1948, the hospital and nurses training school at Stillman were closed. The upper floor of Snedecor was converted to a library in 1948,

The First Fifty Years in Summary 13

with the kitchen below. Eventually, the upper floor was converted into science laboratories and classrooms; when a new library was completed in 1956, the lower floor was converted to office space.

In the letter dated March 4, 1997, Dr. Wynn, wrote:

> Emily Estes Snedecor Hall (1929) is certainly still in use! . . . Snedecor Hall has had many uses . . . and at one time was the only hospital open to African-Americans in West-Central Alabama. Many people in our area were born in Snedecor. . . . Snedecor now houses Humanities Divisional offices and our Teacher Education Department. When the new Humanities Center is built . . . Snedecor will serve entirely for Teacher Education, a field which is rapidly growing and which has an almost 100 percent placement rate for our graduates. The U. S. Department of the Interior has allocated a $250,000 matching grant for the restoration of Snedecor as a historic building.

1929

Two Schools for Mexican Girls, Chilpancingo and Zitacuaro *(See also 1957)*

Until 1857, no religion was permitted in Mexico except Roman Catholicism. A constitutional amendment that year officially separated church and state, and Presbyterians from Texas established a school at Matamoros. Until 1934, very few government schools were accessible to rural students. A primary focus of Presbyterian mission in Mexico was education. In 1929, the mission asked the Woman's Auxiliary for funds to enlarge their facilities and reopen an elementary and secondary school with boarding homes and a chapel. The women gave their Birthday Offering, $52,015, for schools at Zitacuaro and Chilpancingo. A school had begun at Chilpancingo in 1923, only to be closed by the state on the grounds that it taught religious education. With Chilpancingo's share of the offering, $26,000, they purchased a beautiful site of 123 acres, bounded on one side by a river, with farmland, pastureland, and an orchard already bearing fruit. The first building was constructed. Because of government restrictions, the chapel was erected across the river, in easy walking distance, apart from school and homes.

At Zitacuaro, the school already had 200 pupils by 1929, forty of whom boarded. The school was renting a building for classes and a house for the boarders. Their share of the offering was used for new facilities. Two days after the cornerstone was laid for the new building, word came

that the school would be accredited and graduates were encouraged to establish schools in rural areas. Then new developments shook the mission. In 1934, a constitutional amendment changed the nature of *all* schools to state-owned institutions, and buildings and facilities were confiscated from Roman Catholic and most Protestant missions. The Presbyterian Church, U.S. was more fortunate. The government bought the Chilpancingo school, and the proceeds from the sale, $19,506, were put into an endowment fund for religious education for women and girls. The story continues in 1957.

1930

Hallie Paxson Winsborough Foundation in the Endowment Fund for Ministerial Relief

The Birthday Offering in 1930 represented the women's participation in a denomination-wide campaign to establish an endowment fund and to use the annual income for retirement salaries and pensions. The Birthday Offering of $55,137 was considerably more than in any previous year. The women were challenged to give by the knowledge that their beloved Secretary, Mrs. Winsborough, was retiring and that her salary would be paid for her lifetime with the income from that gift. That money, called the Hallie Paxson Winsborough Foundation in the Endowment Fund for Ministerial Relief is still used today, its income pooled with others.

1931

Girls Homes and Women's Work Buildings at Five African Mission Stations *(See also 1939)*

The first gift to Africa was in 1931 when the Woman's Auxiliary designated the Birthday Gift for Girls Homes and a school for children of missionaries. Today, we read about droughts, political instability, tribal wars, cruel dictatorships, economic crises, refugees, and the human struggle to provide for families in various countries of Africa. Where do we find images of hope in all this suffering?

Perhaps the images began back in 1889, when William Sheppard, son of a former slave, and Samuel Lapsley, son of a former slave owner, established the first mission station in the Congo (now Zaire). When Sheppard graduated from Stillman College in 1887, he applied time after time to go to Africa as a missionary but was always turned down. He turned down offers to go with the "Northern Presbyterian Church" because he really wanted to go from his own church in the South. Finally, white professors from Tuscaloosa overtured the General Assembly to send him along with Lapsley, and the two men set out together in 1889. Letters indicate that the two cared for each other like brothers through all the dangers and joys of their pioneer work. They set about building the site for what was to become the American Presbyterian Congo Mission. Sadly, Lapsley fell ill with fever and died in 1892. Sheppard, left alone in grief and loneliness, continued the work of exploring, learning the language, and building relationships with the African people.

In 1894, while on furlough, Sheppard married his fiancee, Lucy Gantt, a teacher. Later that year, three persons went as missionaries with the Sheppards on their return to Africa. One of these was a small black woman, Maria Fearing, of Talladega, Alabama, who had volunteered to go to Africa with the Sheppards. However, the Board of Foreign Missions would not send her because she was fifty-six years old and had less than a high-school education. Undaunted, Ms. Fearing sold all of her possessions and paid her own way. She set about learning the language, and like Miss Dowd in Japan, was appalled at conditions for young girls. Sold as slaves or to cannibals, turned out as prostitutes, traded for goats and other foodstuffs, they were commodities rather than persons. She began to persuade families to permit their daughters to visit her overnight and, later, to let her buy these girls whom the families insisted on selling. With her own income, she supported up to forty girls at one time—housing them and teaching them to cook, to mend their own clothing, and to keep themselves clean, all the while sharing with them her Christian love. Her idea was picked up by women missionaries across Congo, and by 1931, homes existed in five stations in crude huts or in missionary dwellings.

A major portion of the Birthday Gift, $45,000, was given to be divided equally to build, on these stations, five "permanent and adequate" Girls Homes, each equipped for one hundred girls.

One of Miss Fearing's Girls Homes.

One of the women who helped Miss Fearing was Althea Brown Edmiston, another black woman who had grown up in Russellville, Alabama. The author of this history is indebted to Mrs. Edmiston's biography of Miss Fearing in *Glorious Living* and is also indebted to *Lest We Forget, Racial Ethnic Profiles*, edited and compiled by Vera Swann.

Central School for Missionary Children, Lubondai, Congo (Zaire) *(See also 1945)*

In 1926, Congo missionaries began Central School in an effort to provide education for their children near the stations they served rather than sending them back to the United States to boarding school. The enrollment in 1931 was twenty-two. The facilities were quite primitive, leaking badly in the rain, and so, in 1931, an appeal was made to the Woman's Auxiliary, and a portion of the 1931 Birthday Gift ($5,148) was given to construct permanent facilities. By the fall of 1931, the first dormitory was built, then another across from it. In 1938, a new classroom building was built with the remaining part of the gift plus interest and some additional contributions. A large room in the new addition was set aside as a chapel and study hall.

The First Fifty Years in Summary

Central School was closed in 1973 and its facilities turned over to the Congolese Girls School. For some years after that, children of missionaries in Zaire attended the International School in Kinshasa, Zaire.

In a conversation with Dorothy (Dot) Longenecker Hopper, daughter of missionaries in Congo (Zaire), she told of her days as a student at Central School. Dot entered the school just short of nine years of age in 1928 when the buildings consisted of mud and sticks. She left after eight years, in 1936, to go to school in the United States. Dot was at Central at the time the Birthday Offering provided money to construct the permanent buildings. She remembers those years as very happy ones. Her older sister, Alice Longenecker Vail, was a student there also, so she did not feel deprived of family. Dot says Virginia Gray Pruit, who taught at the school, was her very favorite teacher of all time. Later Dot married Joe Hopper, and they served as missionaries in Korea until retirement in 1988.

1932

Christian Home Training Departments in Two Mountain Schools in Appalachia—Stuart Robinson School, Blackey, Kentucky, and Highland Institute, Guerrant, Kentucky [Successor: Lees College] *(See also 1966)*

"In 1932, in the depths of the Depression, the Birthday Offering was given to women and girls for whom financial depression was a way of life," writes Patti Sprinkle in *The Birthday Book*. The total offering that year, $42,331, went into an endowment fund to be used for Christian Home Training Departments at Stuart Robinson School in Blackey, Kentucky, and the Highland Institute in Guerrant, Kentucky. When Dr. Guerrant established Highland in 1908 and Stuart Robinson in 1914, there were no public schools accessible to most mountain children, and in most locations, students had to board at school. The goal was to teach girls sewing, cooking, household arts, care of the sick, how to live on a budget, child training, and how to have a Christian home. By 1934, Christian Home Training Departments were functioning in both schools.

Over the years, changes came to the mountains, public schools were built, and the need for the two schools was not so urgent. In the mid-fifties the two schools merged. In 1960, Letcher County, where the school was located, built a new consolidated high school. For four years Stuart Robinson-Highland functioned only as a boarding facility, and in April 1964, Guerrant Presbytery voted to close the school and make Lees

College in Jackson, Kentucky, its legal successor. The Presbytery and Board of Church Extension transferred all financial assets of the school to Lees College. The following month the Board of Women's Work concurred with the Board of Church Extension "in transferring the corpus and accrued income of the 1932 Birthday Offering to the Trustees of Lees Junior College for investment in the endowment fund of the college."

According to a telephone conversation with Ms. Marcia Myers, Interim Executive Presbyter of the Presbytery of Transylvania, the Presbytery of Transylvania and the Board of Trustees of Lees College, in July 1996, voted to cease operating Lees as a church-related college, and Lees became a part of the University of Kentucky system. At the time of publication, the Governor of Kentucky and state officials were debating a change in the higher education system whereby colleges like Lees would no longer be a part of the University system but become a part of another state system. Also, at the time of publication, the author has not been able to find information from Duncan Ferguson, Coordinator and Associate for Colleges and Universities, in Louisville, or Presbytery of Transylvania officials about the 1932 Birthday Offering, which was transferred to the Lees College Endowment Fund or the Chair of Appalachian Sociology at Lees College that was endowed by the 1966 Birthday Offering.

1933

China Bible Institute, North Kiangsu and Mid-China Missions (*See also 1947, 1991; redesignation of 1933 and 1947 funds in 1973*)

During the first ten years, the designation of Birthday Gifts abroad had been following a sort of rotation system or cycle. The first gift went to Japan, then Brazil, Korea, Mexico, and Africa. The 1933 gift went to the sixth mission field—China—to establish a trust fund. The income from this fund was to be used for conducting Bible institutes, or Bible schools, for women in North Kiangsu and Mid-China Missions. These "institutes" were conferences that trained women and girls so that they were equipped to serve as volunteer workers in their churches and among the women in their communities. North Kiangsu had eight mission stations and had held Bible institutes annually for several years but were concerned about women who lived in small towns and rural areas who were not reached in this way. Part of the money was used to take Bible schools to them. Another part of the offering helped to finance the regular schools and to subsidize the cost to the women. The institutes were held in the seasons when farm work was light; they were inexpensive, and the curriculum was full. Inquirers as well as Christians came, and the schools lasted ten days or longer. The women often brought their own food, fuel, and bedding. Schools were designed with classes for beginners, second-year students, and third-year students. They worshiped together twice daily.

Income from the 1933 Birthday Offering supported these schools for many years. When the China Mission was closed in the late forties, the fund that had been invested by the Board of World Missions had increased to $115,118.89. In July 1972, the Board of Women's Work voted to redesignate funds from the 1933 offering and $34,475.22 from the 1947 offering. They voted to consolidate the two offerings into a new "Fund for Christian Mission Among the Chinese People . . . be held, with accumulated interest, until such time as opportunity should arise for its use in Christian Mission on the Mainland of China" (see Appendix E).

At the board meeting on October 1, 1972, the board voted to communicate to the Board of World Missions their decision (made in February 1972) that the Birthday Selection Committee be charged with redesignating unused Birthday money with the Board of Women's Work and Women's Advisory Council approval. Then they invited the Board of World Missions to consult with them. After several exchanges of communications between the Board of Women's Work and the Board of World Missions, a check for $155,665 (which included $6,071.02 in interest) was sent on October 25, 1973, by J. A. Halverstadt, Treasurer, to Miss Janie McCutchen, Secretary of the Board of Women's Work. This was in response to an action of the Board of Women's Work on October 24, 1973: "That the undesignated Birthday Offering plus accrued interest be used to supplement the 1973 Birthday Objective" (see Appendix F).

It is interesting that the women designated the 1975 Birthday Offering to the three causes recommended by the Board of World Missions for the China Fund designation at their October 1973 meeting (see Appendix E), but with the apportionments changed from one-third for each to one-fourth for Seiwa School (Japan), one-half for Hanil Women's Seminary (Korea), and one-fourth for Ho Nam Theological Seminary (Korea).

1934

Emergency Relief Fund for Home Mission Families, Retired and Deceased Ministers' Families

"In 1934, in the aftermath of the depression, the women again gave their Birthday Offering for Ministerial Relief" (*The Birthday Book*). Sixty percent of the gift ($31,506) was administered through the Executive Committee of Home Missions "to relieve the distress of home mission families of ministers serving churches supported by the Executive Committee of Home Missions." Forty percent ($21,004) was administered through the Executive Committee of Christian Education and Ministerial Relief "to relieve the most pressing emergencies and to prevent another cut in the monthly checks of retired ministers and the widows of those who were deceased." All the monies were used for these purposes.

1935

Kinjo University (Golden Castle School), Nagoya, Japan *(See also 1947, 1967)*

Kinjo Gakuin, which means Golden Castle (the name by which the school was known when it received the Birthday Offering in 1935), received three Birthday Offerings. Founded by Christian missionaries in 1889, today Kinjo University is the oldest and largest women's university in Japan. It is located in Nagoya, a large metropolitan city. Mrs. Annie E. Randolph was the founder, and the Rev. R. E. McAlpine was the Board Chairman.

The offering in 1935 was used to build Glory Hall, a steel and concrete auditorium that would seat 1,500 people and was used for chapel, graduation, and other gatherings. Glory Hall still stands today. Also, in 1936, a Kinjo student, Miss Tamiko Okamura, came to the United States as the first "Women of the Church Friendship Student" to study at Agnes Scott College in Decatur, Georgia. That was the beginning of the practice of bringing young women from other countries to the United States for study with money from voluntary offerings of women to the Friendship Student Circle. This practice continued until 1973.

Today, according to a pamphlet from Kinjo, the school is made up of Kinjo University, Kinjo Senior High School, Kinjo Junior High School, and Kinjo Kindergarten, the only coeducational division of Kinjo Gakuin. The enrollment of the combined kindergarten, junior high, senior high, university, and graduate school totals more than 6,000 students.

In a news item in the Presbyterian *News Brief* in 1989, Marj Carpenter wrote:

> A missionary named Mary Smythe many years ago went from the Makemie Church in Accomac, Virginia, to Japan. Recently, Kinjo University in Nagoya, Japan [as a part of their centennial celebration, 1889–1989], sent a $10,000 check back to the church to express appreciation for the missionaries who helped begin the work at that school.

The First Fifty Years in Summary 21

Kimono from cover of Kinjo Gakuin booklet.

According to information from Kinjo University:

> The school provides a quality Christian education for women. The school is rooted in the firm belief that only in the context of faith in Jesus Christ can young women develop their potential. . . . The school seeks to maintain an educational system that integrates faith and academic achievement.

During its first one hundred years, more than 75,000 students graduated from Kinjo Gakuin.

1936

Fellowship Hall, Montreat, North Carolina [Since 1984 the Winsborough, Montreat Conference Center]
In 1936, the entire Birthday Gift went to Montreat to construct the World Fellowship Building, a stone building overlooking Lake Susan. There was not enough money to both construct the building and furnish it, so Montreat College (later Montreat-Anderson College) agreed to provide the furnishings if the female students at the college could use the

building as a residence during the winter months. The Mountain Retreat Association (which operates the Conference Center) also contributed $1,000. The building was dedicated at the Women's Conference in 1938, when, for that week, the building was reserved for use by the women. During the fifties, Fellowship Hall was used in the summer by board and staff members of the Board of Women's Work along with missionaries and minorities who were not allowed, due to segregation, to reside in the other accommodations. Later, when these barriers no longer existed, the building was used less and less. In 1970, the building was remodeled by the Mountain Retreat Association for office space.

In 1976, Montreat-Anderson College purchased Fellowship Hall and Howerton Dormitory and Cafeteria from the Mountain Retreat Association and carried out extensive renovation of all three facilities. Fellowship Hall was renamed Groseclose Hall. Groseclose Hall continued in use as a college residence hall until 1984 when Montreat-Anderson College Foundation purchased the Winsborough Building from the Mountain Retreat Association and returned title of the former Fellowship Hall to them as part of the exchange. The association then named the facility "the Winsborough" and uses it as a conference residence hall. Montreat-Anderson College built the present Belk Campus Center on the site of the old Winsborough.

1937

Agnes Erskine School, Recife, Brazil; Work among the Caiua Indians, Dourados, Brazil; Training Christian Women and Girls for Service to Brazil

On the silver anniversary of the birth of the Woman's Auxiliary, the entire Birthday Offering ($48,861) went to three objectives in Brazil. The first part of the gift, $16,000, went to the Agnes Erskine School for Girls in Recife. The school was founded in 1904 and enjoyed the reputation of an outstanding school. The original buildings were deteriorating, and the request was made for the 1937 Birthday Offering. With the gift, the school was able to restore and decorate the inside of the main building, complete the second wing by constructing a second floor above the auditorium, build a laundry, and landscape the grounds.

The Caiua Indian Mission was located in Dourados in 1937, and they received $2,000 of the Birthday Offering that year. The mission was an ecumenical one, made up of four denominations, including the

The First Fifty Years in Summary 23

Presbyterian Church, U. S. It provided a ministry of teaching, preaching, healing, and farming among the remote tribe, and a very successful ministry was carried on for several decades. In the early seventies, the Caiua Mission was independent.

The largest part of the 1937 Birthday Offering, $30,861, was put into an endowment fund for leadership training of Brazilian women and girls. The lack of training was due in large part to great distances, lack of funds, and need for people to train them. The mission used the money to provide small scholarships, to pay a portion of the salary of the Executive Secretary of Women's Work in Brazil, to finance Bible schools on mission stations and in outposts, to hold conferences, to pay travel expenses, and to provide music lessons for girls attending the Charlotte Kemper School (see also 1925). Later, all work and funds of the mission were turned over to the Presbyterian Church of Brazil as a matter of policy of the Presbyterian Church, U.S.

1938

Women and Girls of Other Races in the Homeland *(See boldface entries below for gift disbursements; see also 1923, 1928, 1944, 1946, 1956, 1958, 1993)*

"During the depression and the following years, home mission churches badly suffered, especially many of the ethnic missions" (*The Birthday Book*). In 1938, a special Birthday Offering of $45,714 was given for the benefit of women and girls of "other races in the homeland." According to Sprinkle's research, a small portion of the gift was used to encourage the **First Czecho-Slovakian Church, Prince George, Virginia,** whose savings account for the completion of a Sunday school and social room had been lost in an earlier bank failure. Another small part was given to the **Hungarian Mission, Hammond, Louisiana,** to complete a Sunday school and social room for women's meetings. The largest part of the gift was divided among groups who had received earlier Birthday Gifts or who would receive later ones.

The **Chinese Presbyterian Church, New Orleans,** began in 1882 with five young Chinese men. By 1938, the number had grown to 120. The Chinese population was scattered throughout the city, and transportation was difficult. A portion of the 1938 offering was used to buy a Chevrolet Carryall Suburban, a forerunner of the station wagon or mini-van, and a small car for the director. The mission received two more Birthday Gifts, in 1946 and 1958.

A part of the 1938 offering was given to **Indian Presbyterial in the Synod of Oklahoma** (now part of the Synod of the Sun) to erect women's buildings. At that time Choctaw and Chickasaw Presbyterians belonged to a separate presbytery, Indian Presbytery. The women played a large part in the life of the church and by 1937 had eleven auxiliaries with ninety-seven members. For travel convenience, women's meetings were held at the same time as those of the men, and the women had to meet outside the main building in a tent or hut. With their portion of the Birthday Gift, Indian congregations built one-room houses beside their churches where the women could come together for Bible study, prayer, and sewing. These buildings lasted until Sunday school rooms were built, and then they were torn down.

The 1938 offering assisted in a ministry to **Italian Americans** living in **Kansas City, Missouri**. A little more than a third of the offering was given to help the Presbyterian Italian Mission construct a community center and gymnasium. The mission began as a project of Central Presbyterian Church among the 6,000 Italians located in the Little Italy section of the city. The mission used the $16,500 from the Birthday Offering to go with other funds to build a community center and gymnasium, costing $38,000, in its Northeast location. This mission received another Birthday Gift in 1946.

Another recipient of the 1938 offering was the **Ybor City Mission** in **Tampa, Florida,** which ministered to Americans of Cuban, Spanish, and Sicilian descent. Ybor City is a distinct section of Tampa with a large population of persons for whom English was, in 1938, a second language. The Mission was founded in 1904 as a Sunday school, and in 1909 Presbytery established the Ybor City Presbyterian Mission. In 1915, the Ybor City Presbyterian Church was officially organized. Assembly Hall of the Ybor City Mission was partially built with the 1938 Birthday Offering. See 1956 for an additional Birthday Gift to Ybor City.

A portion of the 1938 Birthday Offering was the second Birthday gift received by the **Presbyterian School for Mexican Girls** in **Taft, Texas**. The school was founded with the 1923 Birthday Offering. Pres-Mex's share of the 1938 offering was used to provide floor covering, roofing, water-proofing and painting to maintain the buildings. An additional room for the infirmary and quarters for the dietician were also built with the 1938 Birthday Gift. See 1923 and 1944 for additional Birthday Gifts to Pres-Mex.

A part of the 1938 offering was given to **Stillman College** to build a nurses home on campus. In 1938, the Nurses Training School had grown from two students to thirty-seven and from twenty-five beds to fifty-eight,

The First Fifty Years in Summary 25

Knox Hall, Stillman College.

and a nurses home was badly needed. The Woman's Auxiliary gave part of the 1938 Birthday Offering to Stillman College to build **John Knox Hall**, a home for nurses on campus.

Dr. Wynn, President of Stillman College, wrote in a letter dated March 4, 1997:

> John Knox Hall was built in 1939, and it is the nurses' home you mention in your letter. John Knox Hall housed nurses for many years, then became our Student Health Center, with a residence hall for male students on the second floor, following the discontinuation of the Stillman Nursing Department. Knox Hall was rededicated in March of 1995 following a comprehensive renovation as a male residence hall.

1939

Edmiston-Fearing Memorial Fund for Girls Homes *(See also 1931)*

In 1894, Maria Fearing paid her own way to go to the Congo (Zaire) as a missionary. It was due to her vision and efforts that the Girls Homes, which received the 1931 Woman's Auxiliary Birthday Offering, were established. One of the women who helped Miss Fearing was Althea Brown Edmiston. Althea Brown was sent alone as a missionary to the Congo in 1902. There she assisted Miss Fearing in the homes, serving as matron and also as teacher and principal. Highly educated, she developed

Mrs. Edmiston.

a written form of the Bakuba language and wrote the first grammar and dictionary in Bakuba. In 1905, she married fellow missionary Alonza Edmiston.

Soon after the permanent homes were built with the 1931 Birthday Offering, it became apparent that upkeep and operating costs would be more than the mission could afford. Another source of funds would need to be found. Then in 1937, within three weeks of each other, Mrs. Edmiston and Miss Fearing (at age ninety-nine) died. The Birthday Committee decided to designate the next "abroad" offering as a memorial to them. The entire 1939 offering, $49,659, was named the Edmiston-Fearing Memorial Fund for Girls Homes, to be used for maintenance and operation. It was a fitting memorial to two remarkable women—missionary pioneers.

Miss Fearing and Girls Home residents.

1940

Vacation Bible School Movement

The Birthday Offering ($47,306) in 1940 was given to supplement the Vacation Bible School Movement. The movement called for the Church to go to the children, not wait for unchurched children to come to the Church. The plan was for carefully worked out courses to be taught for three, four, or five hours a day for a period ranging from two to four weeks. To provide the needed trained personnel, the women gave the Birthday Offering so that the entire junior class at Assembly's Training School was trained and sent out to hold Bible schools in several churches each summer. College students also were trained and sent out. Each church was expected to provide room and board for the worker, and the Birthday money provided for transportation and a small weekly stipend for incidentals. The offering was used over an eleven year period and supplemented an already existing program.

Between 1939 and 1940, the number of Vacation Bible Schools increased by 586, and the enrollment by 47,130 (*The Birthday Book*). In 1947, nearly 160,000 children attended Vacation Bible Schools in churches and centers all over the General Assembly. The program picked up many children who were not in the habit of attending Sunday school or any form of church activity. Between 1940 and 1951, the Birthday money sent Bible schools to thousands of children.

1941

Pioneer Evangelistic Work, Brazil

All but $10,000 of the 1941 Birthday Offering was given for Pioneer Evangelistic Work in Brazil. Brazil's share of $50,025 was used for churches, ministers, and lay workers to reach people in an area as large as the United States west of the Mississippi. Part of the money supported a home missions project for the Brazilian Church in western mission sites and to help the National Church of Brazil keep up with the national slogan, "March to the West." The Brazilians took up their own offering, and the encouragement of the women's Birthday Offering caused them to surpass their goal. Bill Moseley, missionary evangelist, was quoted in *The Birthday Book*, "We have dipped into this fund for just about every new thing we have done in North Brazil for at least thirty years."

The work included the training and support of a large force of Brazilian evangelists, the establishment of centers and outposts, and the erection of a radio broadcasting station. A mission was established among the Portuguese-speaking people around Dourados (see the Caiua Indians, 1937). By 1966 the fund was exhausted.

Collegiate Home, Montreat *(Redesignation of funds to Villa International)*
In 1941, during an "abroad" year for Birthday Offerings, the Executive Committee of Foreign Missions requested and received $10,000 as an endowment to help with the upkeep of Collegiate Home in Montreat. Collegiate Home represented a home away from home for missionary children sent to the United States for education, who were unable to return home to their parents for holiday season. Instead, they went to Collegiate Home.

Collegiate Home was started by Presbyterian women in the Montreat Woman's Club. In a house and a shed rented for a small amount of money, two women hostesses and several students spent two summers. In the third year, the Executive Committee of Foreign Missions bought a building known as Hickory Lodge, and between 1937 and 1940, enrollment was usually one hundred students. Over the Christmas holidays in 1940, a group of missionary children stayed at Collegiate Home for two weeks, happily playing in the snow, being entertained by Montreat residents, playing Monopoly, and sharing each other's loneliness.

Collegiate Home continued to serve the purpose for which it was founded until the late fifties when the decreasing need for such a facility caused the Board of World Missions to close the home. The property was sold to the Presbyterian Historical Association, and the Board of Women's Work held the Birthday endowment.

In 1972, the Board of Women's Work voted to redesignate the $10,000 endowment fund plus accrued interest (nearly twenty-five years of interest) to Villa International in Atlanta to help with furnishings for the building that the 1970 Birthday Offering had built.

1942

Training Christian Black Leaders for Work among Their Own Race
(See also Stillman College 1928, 1938, 1952, 1960, 1972, 1988)
In 1942, the women gave a Birthday Gift to "Train Christian Negro Leaders for Work Among Their Own Race." Part of the offering was designated to pay the salary of Field Worker Miss Louise Miller, a missionary on enforced leave from Korea during World War II, to train Negro women leaders of the Presbyterian Church, U.S. She worked with the women in the All-Negro Snedecor Memorial Synod, visited all four presbyterials, taught Bible and methods, and consulted with Negro

Presbyterian leaders. In 1943, she took all four presbyterial presidents to the Woman's Auxiliary Training School in Montreat. The next year the Snedecor Synod held its own synod-wide training school at Stillman. Miss Miller also made sure that white Presbyterian women were made aware of the capabilities and needs of their Negro sisters. When money was transferred in 1950 to Stillman College (see below), $5,000 was held back to continue field work until the money ran out in 1956.

In 1951, the General Assembly voted to dissolve Snedecor Memorial Synod as soon as its four presbyteries could be combined into three and absorbed into the synods of Georgia, Alabama, and Louisiana. The synod was officially dissolved on March 31, 1952. The women remained for some time as the "Women of the Snedecor Region" with a regional rather than a synod council.

The largest part of the 1942 offering (see below) was designated for Stillman, but held in reserve until a specific need should be realized. In 1948, Stillman had begun the process of seeking accreditation by the Southern Association of Colleges, but several improvements had to be made. The men's dormitory was unsafe, and the Executive Committee on Women's Work gave permission to have the nurses home converted into a men's residence hall. Another imperative for accreditation was a gymnasium and auditorium. In 1950, the Board of Church Extension's Division of Negro Work transferred the $46,864 held in reserve from the 1942 Birthday Gift to Stillman College to assist with the construction of Birthright building, about one-third of the cost.

Dr. Cordell Wynn, President of Stillman College, writes in a letter dated March 4, 1997:

> Birthright Hall, built in 1951, continues in use as our gymnasium and provides offices for our coaches and physical education staff. We also use Birthright for banquets, commencement, and other special events. It is interesting to note that Mr. and Mrs. Charles Birthright were former slaves who had a large farm in Missouri; they died in 1912 and bequeathed their property to Stillman Institute. *The Birthrights' bequest was the largest gift received by Stillman until the Women of the Church gift for Winsborough* [in 1921].

1943

Christian Literature in Mexico

In 1931, 62 percent of the people of Mexico were illiterate; by 1967, nearly 60 percent were literate due in large part to the government's emphasis on literacy and its insistence that each person who could read should teach someone who could not. The Presbyterian Mission had recognized for some time that as the country became increasingly literate, Christian literature would become more and more important. The mission requested that the 1943 Birthday Offering be given to the Presbyterian publishing house in Mexico, Casa de Publicaciones EL FARO, S.S., and to the publishing of Christian literature in Mexico. Representatives of the Board of World Missions wrote that there was a "deplorable lack of Christian literature" in Mexico. Miss Janie McGaughey had observed on a trip to Mexico that when she shared literature with the women, she saw longing in their eyes. There were no family periodicals, no Bible commentaries, few reference books, no Sunday school teaching helps—in fact, lay people had little or no Christian reading matter. As someone said, "Literature can often go where a missionary cannot or stay when she/he must go."

Two thousand dollars of the 1943 gift of $68,029 was spent each year from 1943 to 1947. At that time, the amount left, $60,896, was frozen and only the interest was used for publications. In 1957, it was decided that principal could be used because $2,000 was no longer sufficient. In 1957, a hymnbook was published with $3,500 from the fund. In 1961, $10,000 of the fund was used to buy and renovate a building that would provide more space, and another $15,000 was approved as a loan for working capital. Casa EL FARO also petitioned the Board of World Missions to allow them to pay interest on the loan from the interest on the remaining capital in the fund. Permission was granted.

With the changeover from mission to Mexican control in the early seventies, the mission turned over the endowment fund to Mexican ownership and control.

1944

Presbyterian School for Mexican Girls, Taft, Texas [Now Presbyterian Pan American School, Kingsville, Texas] *(See also 1923, 1938)*

By 1944, Pres-Mex was running a kindergarten and nursery for the many Mexican children who lived in housing surrounding the school. This project provided day care for the previously unattended children while their mothers worked and, at the same time, taught child care to students at Pres-Mex. A major portion of the 1944 Birthday Offering, $57,641, was given to construct a building to house the kindergarten, nursery, and a clinic for community children. Another part of the money was used to build a library and recreational facilities for Pres-Mex students and to purchase a school station wagon to carry the high-school students to attend the public Taft High School. By 1952, half of the graduating seniors were going on to college.

Defense Service Council

During World War II, Birthday objectives recognized new priorities. The Defense Service Council was set up in 1941 as an agency of the General Assembly to further the spiritual life of men and women in the armed forces and to help them maintain ties with their home churches. The council approved the appointment of chaplains, oversaw the purchase and distribution of materials, and had oversight of aid to churches that served men and women in the armed forces. A portion of the 1944 offering, $28,005, went to the Defense Service Council to purchase field communion sets and devotional materials for chaplains, to assist small churches near military bases to carry on programs for service men and women, and to help the Service Men's Christian League publish and distribute *The Link*, an interdenominational Christian magazine especially for servicemen and servicewomen.

1945

Varied Work in the Congo Mission—Evangelistic, Educational, Medical *(See boldface entries below for gift disbursements; see also 1931)*

Central School, Lubondai—The first really large Birthday Gift to Africa came in 1945 when $110,033 was given for varied evangelistic, educational, and medical work. Part of that offering benefitted Central School once again. Money from the offering provided funds to install electric lights in 1943 and a water system a few years later. In 1950, a guest house and a house for teachers were built from the Birthday Offering. Central School was closed in 1973 because too few children of missionaries were the age to attend. However, it served its purpose well, and the facilities were turned over to the Congolese Girls School, which is part of the Girls Home that was built with a portion of the same Birthday Offering that built Central School in 1931.

According to some missionaries, the 1945 Birthday Offering made possible the "great forward surge the work in the Congo experienced after World War II." Among the beneficiaries were medical dispensaries; a Rescue Home for elderly in **Luebo**; dormitories in **Bilanga, Bulape, Moma,** and **Mutoto** for student evangelists; wards for men and women as well as a Pediatrics Department at Bulape; missionary residences; facilities for a whole new station at Luluabourg (**Kananga**), which was to become business headquarters for the entire mission; and water and sanitation for mission stations. All of this, as well as the projects at Central School, was accomplished with $109,421. In 1961, the mission station at Luluabourg (name changed to Kananga in 1972) was turned over to the United Theological School, a joint school between the Presbyterian Church and the Disciples of Christ. At the time of publication, the successor of the United Theological School, the Faculty of Reformed Theology of the Kasai (Kasai is the name of the province in which the school is located) still exists, according to Dr. John Crawford, former missionary in Zaire, in spite of fighting between government forces and rebels in that area. He said, "Some missionaries are still present, living a few miles away in the Good Shepherd Hospital [see also 1969], and the school property is still standing although pilfering has occurred."

1946

The Italian Mission, Kansas City, Missouri *(See also 1938)*

In 1946, the Italian Mission in Kansas City requested and received $41,250 of the Birthday Offering to help pay for the construction of a sanctuary adjoining the community center. The total cost of the building was $112,000. Construction did not take place until 1950, and by that time interest had increased the Birthday Gift to $45,977. The new church came to be known as Christ Presbyterian Church. One young man from this congregation, Walter Passigalia, served the Ybor City Mission in Tampa, Florida (see also 1938 and 1956).

The Chinese Presbyterian Church, New Orleans, Louisiana *(See also 1938, 1958)*

The Chinese Mission in New Orleans received $26,250 of the 1946 Birthday Offering to help build an educational building. Completed in 1953, the building also served for nearly ten years as a sanctuary for the congregation, converting to a fellowship hall and Chinese school during the week. The Chinese Mission was organized into the Chinese Presbyterian Church in 1957 with eighty charter members.

The First Fifty Years in Summary   33

Relief of Christians and Reestablishments of Church Life in Europe and Asia

In 1946, recognizing the awful devastation caused by World War II, $57,608 of the Birthday Offering was channeled through the General Assembly's Permanent Committee on War Relief and the interdenominational Church Committee on Overseas Relief and Reconstruction to assist in bringing relief to Christians abroad and to help them reestablish their Church life.

The two committees shipped supplies to help keep people alive and to provide some measure of spiritual comfort to them. Provisions of clothes, food, hospital supplies, Bibles, and toiletries for women in a tuberculosis hospital and assistance with building temporary worship structures were some of the ways assistance was provided.

1947

Mission in the Orient—Japan, Korea, China *(See boldface entries below for gift disbursements; see also 1922, 1927, 1935, 1967, 1975)*

In 1947, the offering was given to repair damage done to missions during World War II.

During the war in **Japan**, Christian schools were oppressed. After the war, at **Seiwa School** (Miss Dowd's School) nothing remained, not even a chair. The Women of the Church contributed $5,000 from the 1947 Birthday Offering for equipment. With its share of $33,125, **Kinjo University** (Golden Castle School) was able to repair Glory Hall and erect two classroom buildings. Glory Hall was the only auditorium left standing in Nagoya at the end of the war; the school rented space to civic groups and used the income for restoration of the campus.

In **Korea** after the war, one high priority for the mission was to reopen its schools and provide Christian literature to offset propaganda from other sources. An appeal was made to the Woman's

Drawing of a Japanese family.

Auxiliary, and Korea received $38,000 of the 1947 Birthday Offering. The first share ($15,000) went to the **Jennie Speer School** for major repairs and a Chair of Bible. The mission decided to upgrade the Jennie Speer School to meet designated (accredited) standards, but the facilities were inadequate, so the first share of the offering went to the Jennie Speer School for major repairs, equipment, and a Chair of Bible. Another share, about $15,000, was equally divided between Women's Bible Schools on five stations for equipment. Bible Schools at **Soonchun** and **Mokpo** received a share of the gift, but the part for **Choong Nam** was held until after the Korean War. By that time the Choong Nam Presbytery had divided into the Taejon and Choong Nam Presbytery and each received $1,500 of the 1947 Birthday Offering. **Taejon** Presbytery bought a building in 1957 and Choong Nam Presbytery began a Bible school in 1959. Two of the schools—**Neel Bible School** in **Kwangju** and the **Ada Hamilton Clark Bible School** in **Chunju** were merged in 1960. Arthur W. Kinsler, PC(USA) missionary in Seoul, Korea, wrote on April 16, 1997: "The two Bible Schools which joined are now Hanil University . . . " (see 1975). He also wrote regarding the Jennie Speer School: "The Speer Girls Middle and High Schools are still Presbyterian with 1,293 in the Jr. Hi and 1,457 in the High School. Winsborough Hall [see 1927] is now used as the main and admin[istration] building for the Jr. Hi."

One share of the offering was used for several years to prepare and publish Christian literature for the training of children and the development of Christian homes, making it possible for Christian literature to be prepared and printed in a critical time.

One-half of the 1947 Birthday Gift for China ($76,463) was designated to the Presbyterian China Mission to build two missionary residences in **Kiangyin**, to rebuild the Woman's Bible School in the same city, to establish one or more "mothercraft" schools, and to establish a fund for the translation, printing, and promotion of phonetic work. War had torn China apart, and the missionaries who had returned in 1946 had to leave again before 1951. According to Board of World Mission records, $41,988 of China's share of that year's offering was disbursed. Of the 1947 offering, $34,475 remained in the bank awaiting redesignation by the Board of Women's Work in consultation with the Board of World Mission. (See 1933 and Appendix D for final redesignation of the funds.)

CHAPTER TWO

The Women of the Church
(1948–1972)

*The Board of Women's Work
Presbyterian Church, U.S.*

1948

Mountain Retreat Association, Montreat, North Carolina *(See also 1922, 1936, 1941)*

In 1948, the women gave $40,000 of the Birthday Offering to Mountain Retreat Association (Montreat Conference Center) to help with the completion of Howerton Hall and Cafeteria. The stone building overlooking Lake Susan, known fondly as "the Castle," replaced the old, wooden Alba Hotel, which was destroyed by fire. Construction of Howerton took several years, and during that time the summer conferences were handicapped by lack of hotel space. The Birthday money helped to complete the facility, which was ready for service during the conference season in 1948.

In 1976, Montreat-Anderson College purchased World Fellowship Hall (see also 1936) and Howerton Dormitory and Cafeteria from the Mountain Retreat Association. Extensive renovation and upgrading was done to all three facilities, including an entire new kitchen in Howerton.

Assembly's Training School, Richmond, Virginia [Presbyterian School of Christian Education] *(See also 1924, 1940, 1958, 1977)*

The Birthday Gift of $95,378 to Assembly's Training School in 1948 came at an important time in the life of the school. With the money from the gift, an administration building was built. For several years, the school had turned away students because dormitories and classrooms were crowded and they had no more space. At the same time, the Church was begging for additional trained Christian workers. The graduates promoted the Birthday objective with the appeal, "Help us take the offices out of the bedrooms, the classrooms out of the basement, and the dining hall out of the chapel!" (*The Birthday Book*). The handsome building stands across Palmyra from the President's Home, also built with a Birthday Gift (1924).

1949

Varied Mission Work in Brazil *(See boldface entries below for gift disbursements; see also 1925, 1937, 1941, 1959, 1963, 1973, 1994)*

In 1949, the Brazil Mission received about $116,040 of the Birthday Offering to use in various ways. Some of the money, $10,000, was used toward the publication of the **official paper of the Presbyterian Church** in Brazil. Another $5,000 helped publish a **monthly youth magazine** and provided **leadership training** for young people and their leaders. With another $10,000 of the offering, a **missionary residence** was built. The largest parts of the offering went to the **Presbyterian Seminary of the North in Recife** ($25,000) and the **Bible Institute of the North in Garanhuns** ($45,000). The money to the seminary was used, along with funds from other cooperating churches, to build new facilities—a chapel, dining hall, men's dormitory, two faculty residences, and an entrance to the campus.

The Bible Institute of the North used its share of the money to purchase land and construct buildings in a new location. Among the buildings built with the offering were an administration and classroom building, a women's dorm, and a chapel. The Institute was founded to meet the urgent need for teachers and religious education workers in the churches and evangelistic fields of Brazil. Graduates were sent to open parochial schools in the interior of North Brazil.

The American Bible Society *(See also 1972)*

The American Bible Society was founded in 1816 to translate, print, and distribute Bibles around the world, and since 1861, the Presbyterian Church, U.S. has participated in that work. In 1949, the American Bible Society received the first $26,000 of the Birthday Offering. The funds were channeled through a special emergency fund set up to supply Scriptures to China, Japan, Korea, South America, Mexico, Africa, and many other parts of the world recovering from a devastating war. In Germany alone, 12 million Bibles were needed to meet the annual needs of those joining churches and to supply families who had lost their homes or were displaced. Similar requests came from Korea, Japan, the Philippines, and other countries. Birthday money helped to fill the needs.

1950

Texas-Mexican Industrial Institute, Kingsville, Texas [Now Presbyterian Pan American School *(See also 1923, 1938, 1944)*

The Women of the Church gave one Birthday Gift to the Texas-Mexican Industrial Institute for Mexican boys. The gift of $60,000 in 1950 was the largest single gift the school had received to that time. It was used to endow a Chair of Bible, the first endowed position at the school. Tex-Mex, as it was called, was chartered in 1911 as a coeducational school but decided in 1912 it would no longer admit girls. Henrietta King, wife of Captain King of King Ranch, gave 660 acres of land on which to establish a school for Mexican boys; the land was about five miles out of Kingsville. The boys built most of the buildings, worked in the machine shop, helped run a large farm, and learned many trades.

As a result of a study, the two schools, Tex-Mex and Pres-Mex, were merged into the **Presbyterian Pan American School** by an act of the Synod of Texas in July 1955. The National Church of Mexico was confused about the mission of the two schools and felt the emphasis should be on Christian leadership training. Furthermore, at that time there was no longer a strong need for industrial training. The study committee recommended, and Synod adopted, a plan for the merger of the two schools into one which would be "thoroughly Christian, Pan American in policy, coeducational and international, with one board and one campus." There was a provision in the plan that each student should work his or her way through school, and that each student should be required to take one course each year in Bible, Beliefs and Church History.

The new school was located on the Tex-Mex site. Former Birthday Gifts to Pres-Mex helped because property at Taft was sold and the funds used at the new school to construct the Homer McMillan Dormitory for boys. The Presbyterian Pan American School is still in existence today. The Interim President, Mr. Jerry Tompkins, wrote in a letter dated April 8, 1997, that the school "is a preparatory school in the mainline U.S. tradition . . . fully accredited by the Southern Association of Colleges and Schools. Its student body remains international and still primarily Mexican." In their promotional literature, the school states that it:

... seeks to be an international Christian community of worship, study, and work. Its primary concern is to help students of good character strive to reach their full intellectual, spiritual, social, and physical potential within an atmosphere that accentuates the Christian concepts of dignity of the individual, love of God and neighbor, and responsibility for one's actions. . . . The 1994-95 student body consists of 99 boarding students, 11 day students. Most of the students are from Mexico and Texas.

The school is incorporated as a not-for-profit institution, governed by a board of trustees—nine elected by the Synod of the Sun, Presbyterian Church (U.S.A.), two by the National Presbyterian Church of Mexico, and the remainder by the board.

In a response to an inquiry concerning the endowed Women of the Church Chair of Bible ($60,000 given in 1950), Mr. Tompkins writes, "My research regarding the Endowed Chair in Bible is disappointing. The endowment does not, apparently, exist as a formal fund. (However, you have sparked my interest, and I plan to try to trace the fund's history. . . .)"

Ecumenical and Training Opportunities for Students and Student Workers

The 1950 Birthday Offering provided ecumenical or additional training for students and campus workers for twenty-two years—1950–1972. The first part of the gift of $83,800 was used to provide students with study trips abroad during summer vacations. The second part of the offering was given for ministers who served as chaplains or pastors on campus. Many of these persons felt a need to continue their education, and this money provided study grants ranging from $1,000 to $3,000. The third part of the offering was used to provide ecumenical experiences at home and around the world for students and student workers. As the students learned from their experiences, they also provided services; for example, salaries were paid for Christian women workers to start and maintain Westminster Fellowship groups at schools like Florida State University. Other experiences included projects like working with the Inner City Church Council in San Francisco or providing for a study/work trip behind the Iron Curtain or participating in Operation Crossroads Africa. Twenty-two years! Quite a return on an investment of $83,000.

1951

Chapels and Christian Centers, Congo

The 1951 Birthday Offering of $160,406 was a turning point for the American Presbyterian Congo Mission, according to Patti Sprinkle in *The Birthday Book*. It opened the way for Presbyterian urban mission work in the Congo, providing funds to construct chapels and Christian centers in the heart of urban areas. With the Birthday money, the mission built nine churches in seven rapidly growing towns: three in the city of Luluabourg (now Kananga), two in Bakwanga (now Mbujimayi), diamond capital of the world, and one each in at least seven railroad towns—Muene Ditu, Luhuta, Tshimbulu, Mweka, Kasha, Kakenge, and Ilebo.

The offering also represented a turning point for the Congo Church. Contributions to help with the construction of these churches were solicited from African Christians, and the World Day of Prayer offering from African churches that year was designated for their share in that work. Even more important, large congregations developed that would go on to be self-supporting.

The mission stipulated that each station receiving chapels from the Birthday Gift should erect in connection a "room of adequate size, specifically for Women's Activities, such as classes in mothercraft, cooking, sewing, hygiene, reading, and homemaking" (*The Birthday Book*). This led to involvement of the women and eventually to their service as deacons and elders.

1952

Chair of Bible, Stillman College *(See also 1928, 1938, 1942, 1960, 1972, 1988)*

The women (see also 1942) had previously released funds to Stillman College to help upgrade facilities to assist with efforts for accreditation. In 1952, one year after Stillman received accreditation by the Southern Association of Colleges, the first part of the Birthday Gift, $75,000, went to Stillman to endow a Chair of Bible. Dr. Cordell Wynn, President of Stillman College, wrote in a letter dated March 4, 1997:

> The chairman or chairwoman of the Department of Religion and Philosophy bears the title of Janie W. McGaughey Professor of Bible, and at present this is Dr. Neil Jones, who was also the first recipient of the John and Phyllis Todd Award for Excellence in Teaching.

Sunday School Extension Work

The 1952 Birthday Offering was divided into two parts, the first to Stillman College and the second, $76,160, through the Board of Church Extension for Sunday school Extension work. The purpose of the Department of Sunday School Extension was to take Sunday school to those who might not otherwise be exposed to the Church and its teachings—into trailer parks, for example, or mining camps, or suburban areas where churches were scarce—and through Sunday schools to begin new churches.

When the 1952 Birthday Offering was given, seven workers were already involved in this type of program throughout seven synods. The offering was to help the Department of Sunday School Extension increase that number. In the year following the offering, three more workers were added, and the year following that, a fourth.

This part of the 1952 Birthday Offering initiated no new program, but it strengthened the work already being done.

1953

Furlough Homes for Missionaries

The 1953 objective for the Birthday Offering was a new kind of overseas gift—provision for a place for missionaries to live, study, and work while on furlough for a year. Mission Court, next to Union Theological Seminary (UTS) in Richmond, Virginia, was established in 1920 to provide a place for missionaries to be "refreshed" and "restored" during furloughs. Mission Haven, at Columbia Theological Seminary (CTS) in Decatur, Georgia, built its first building in 1950. In 1953, the Board of Directors of Mission Court proposed that the Birthday Offering be used to build furlough homes at the two other PCUS Seminaries, Louisville Presbyterian Theological Seminary (LPTS) and Austin Theological Seminary (ATS) and to expand facilities at Mission Court and Mission Haven. The money from the Birthday Gift, $177,504, was divided equally into four parts, with each facility receiving $44,000.

At UTS, their share, augmented by money from the Synodical of West Virginia, built a two-story apartment building, the West Virginia Building, located between the two existing buildings—Virginia Building and North Carolina Building. At CTS, with its share of the Birthday money, a new building, the Samuel N. Lapsley (see also 1931) Building was constructed. Since that time, other facilities have been erected, including in 1962 a Clothes Closet. At LPTS, the Furlough Home began in

1951 with contributions from both PCUS and PC(USA) women toward a home for missionaries. Because the seminary was, at that time, jointly supported by the two denominations, the furlough home was jointly founded. Contributions and memorial gifts were accepted between 1951 and 1953, but it was the Birthday Gift which provided the largest portion of the needed funds to purchase an old home in the Crescent Hill area. The home was purchased in May 1953, converted into five apartments, and occupied in September that year. In Austin, Texas, ATS used its share of the money to purchase land within walking distance of the seminary, the University of Texas, schools, shopping centers, a church, and a park. Four three-bedroom apartments were built with $46,459. The Synodicals of Texas, Louisiana, Arkansas, and Oklahoma contributed the additional $2,500, and Mission Ranch came into existence.

In the past few decades, travel has changed and missionaries make more frequent, shorter visits to the United States. There are, also, more short-term missionaries than long-term ones in service in missions abroad. Consequently, the need for the use of the furlough homes by missionaries has diminished.

In response to inquiries, the author received replies from the four seminaries with updated information about the homes. Dr. Louis Weeks of UTS wrote in a letter dated February 12, 1997, regarding Mission Court, "a group of five buildings on our campus which the Women of the Church owned until the 1970s. My understanding is that they ceded the buildings to the Seminary and that we promised to continue to use some of the apartments for missionaries on furlough and for international visitors to the United States. The apartments are currently in very good condition, and I am delighted that missionaries on furlough continue to use them, as well as international students who are here. The students find them attractive living quarters for their sojourn in the states." He added, "Thank you and other Presbyterian Women for your support. We deeply appreciate these gifts that you have made and the many other ways that you have helped Union Seminary."

Dr. Douglas Oldenburg, President of Columbia Theological Seminary, wrote in a letter dated January 31, 1997, regarding Mission Haven:

> The 1953 gift for Missionary Furlough Homes went to help establish and maintain "Mission Haven" on our campus, consisting of nine residential units for missionaries. The units are still occupied primarily by furloughed missionaries. When our contract with Mission Haven expires in 2002, three of the units will become the property of Columbia Seminary, leaving six units for furloughed missionaries.

He added, "Columbia Seminary is profoundly grateful for the support we have received from Presbyterian Women."

Dr. Davison Philips, former President of CTS, wrote that Columbia has also "been blessed by the personal, prayerful support by the Women of the Supporting Synods through the 'Columbia Friendship Circle.' They take advantage of the annual meeting of that group to visit Mission Haven, and deliver clothes and gifts to them."

Dr. Robert M. Shelton, Acting President and Academic Dean at Austin Theological Seminary, wrote in a letter dated February 12, 1997:

> With respect to your question about missionary furlough homes at Austin Seminary, we have four units which we use for missionaries on furlough and special guests who relate to mission work and globalization. . . . The money from the Women of the Church was given to the supporting synods of Austin Seminary, who owned the housing originally. Eventually, the property ("Mission Ranch") was transferred to Austin Seminary.

At the request of John Mulder, President of Louisville Presbyterian Theological Seminary, Dr. Grayson L. Tucker Jr., retired Dean of LPTS replied on February 5, 1997, to the author's inquiries:

> Now for a brief word about the . . . Furlough home project. Here at LPTS that money was spent to help purchase a house in the Crescent Hill area which could be converted to several apartments. The Lord was kind to us at about the time the Seminary relocated from 109 East Broadway to its new campus in the early 60s. Fire destroyed the house in Crescent Hill. Insurance and other monies built a new home on the new campus so its residents can be part of the Seminary community and frequently are in study there or one of the other educational institutions here in Louisville. The "new" structure has four apartments, either two or three bedrooms, and storage space near an attractive lounge. The Presbyterian Women of Louisville Presbytery have sponsored this work since its inception. Each church is invited to have a member on the advisory board and most of them do. The chair of the board is in contact with headquarters about overseas workers who may wish to use the facility. The women do inventory and cleaning after each change of occupancy. When an apartment has not been needed by some overseas missionary, it may be made available to one of the seminary's overseas students who sometimes come with family.

The First Fifty Years in Summary   43

Like ripples radiating out when a stone is thrown into water, this offering, as with so many others, keeps serving in special and sometimes surprising ways.

1954

Evangelistic Work among Appalachian Coal Camps

One-third of the 1954 Birthday Offering, almost $57,098, was given to Guerrant Presbytery (now part of Transylvania Presbytery) to establish churches and do evangelistic work among coal camp dwellers of Appalachia. Charles Sydnor, who came to the area right after graduation from seminary, said that "after many years of ministry in the rugged creek-and-hollow country of Kentucky's mountains, Guerrant Presbytery took a giant step into the dirty, teeming coal camps," thanks to the 1954 Birthday Gift (*The Birthday Book*). Among the many programs and projects this money accomplished was the purchase of land for the new community Presbyterian church house at Lothair and partial cost of building the new church at Leatherwood. Salaries of the mission workers were supplemented using a system whereby allotments were added to the base salary of each minister and lay worker according to the number of their children and the number of years they had served the church. Birthday funds also made possible advances in the teaching ministry of these missionaries and churches. Two mission churches received, between them, $2,000 to purchase a serviceable secondhand bus.

With the large influx of workers living in the camps, the mission work emerged from a rural-oriented period, thanks largely to a missionary couple, Bill and Isabel Brown, who recognized the needs of the many thousands of souls crammed into the drab coal camps. They organized and built some five new coal-camp churches. Bill, as Board Chairman of the Home Mission Committee, and Dr. Amick, Superintendent of Home Missions, recruited a gifted group of home mission pastors and women workers. Ahead of their time, Guerrant's pastors and workers learned to minister as fraternal workers, respecting the culture of the people among whom they ministered.

Goodland Presbyterian Children's Home, Hugo, Oklahoma *(For related projects, see also 1926, 1938, 1993; for updated information about Goodland, see 1976)*

Goodland Presbyterian Children's Home, Hugo, Oklahoma, received $59,000 of the Birthday Offering in 1954 for the construction of Bacon

Bacon Hall, Goodland Presbyterian Children's Home.

Hall, a building to house a dining room and kitchen, dormitory rooms, offices, and storage space. The home was founded in 1850 in a place the Indians called *Yakni Achukma*, or Good Land, because of its numerous springs, abundant timber, and fertile soil. Good Land School originated as a primary day school. Many families moved close by so their children

Goodland Christian Academy (Bacon Hall).

The First Fifty Years in Summary 45

could attend the school. Then the Civil War came, and a division in the church resulted. At the end of the war, each thought the other would pick up support of the mission. Indian Christians and their white friends in the area carried on the work as best they could. Finally, in 1894, the Good Land Mission became a special responsibility of the Presbyterian Church, U.S. General Assembly's Executive Committee of Home Mission. Also in 1894, the first dormitory was built for what eventually became the Good Land Indian Orphanage. In 1930, the rural school of the Goodland community was consolidated with the Goodland Orphanage School. In 1955, Bacon Hall was completed. It was named for Silas Bacon, a full-blooded Choctaw who served as superintendent of the school for twenty years. He himself was an orphan.

The Protestant Radio and TV Center, Atlanta, Georgia
One-third of the 1954 Birthday Offering ($59,000) in 1954 was used to build PRTVC's first permanent facility. In 1948, five major denominations, including the PCUS, established a production studio and employed personnel to turn out quality work. The center received a charter in January 1949. In 1966, PRTVC pioneered in the development of cassettes for use by ministers and others. Internationals often come to the center for training and find it convenient to stay at the nearby Villa International (built with Birthday money). One of the most important and familiar ministries of PRTVC has been the production of the Protestant Hour. At time of publication, the Presbyterian Church (U.S.A.) had withdrawn from participation in the program.

1955

Yodogawa Christian Hospital, Osaka, Japan
The entire 1955 Birthday Offering of $208,577 was given for the construction of the Yodogawa Christian Hospital, the first Presbyterian hospital in Japan. Before World War II, there was little need to build hospitals in Japan, which had the highest standard of living in Asia. However, during the war one-fifth of Japan's hospitals were destroyed, and the postwar government expressed interest in mission-sponsored hospitals. One of the most pressing needs was that of charity medical care. The Japan Mission decided to locate the hospital in Osaka, the country's second largest city, busiest Japanese seaport, and the center of Presbyterian Mission work. The mission only had funds for a twenty-bed unit. A sixty-bed facility was at that time the most feasible size to

Postcard from Yodogawa Christian Hospital.

operate, so the Birthday Offering was used to build a second unit. It was decided to name the hospital Yodogawa because that was the traditional name of Osaka—*Yodo*, the name of the local river, and *gawa*, the Japanese word for river, and because the hospital is located in the East Yodogawa District

By 1970, the hospital had 150 beds; in 1971 it had 3,400 admissions. Yodogawa was the first hospital in Japan to have women volunteers similar to "Pink Ladies." The hospital gained national recognition for its pioneering work in the treatment of jaundice in newborns. Other specialities at the hospital are cardiology, diabetes, orthopedics, pediatric surgery, neurosurgery, and renal diseases. The hospital has a staff of Christian Japanese doctors who are interested in the concept of treating the whole patient and the idea of total medical care. Through White Cross medical supplies, the Women of the Church continued their support of Yodogawa Hospital until this ministry became part of the Thank Offering Health Ministries of Presbyterian Women.

Kitty Peterson, retired missionary to Japan, described the growth and success of Yodogawa Christian Hospital. They have a large, new modern hospital, which has the same purpose and emphasis, on the same location. For those Presbyterian women who, like the author, remember Yodogawa as *their* first Birthday Offering, it is a cause for thanksgiving and praise.

The First Fifty Years in Summary 47

Postcard from the hospital.

1956

Ybor City Mission Expansion, Tampa, Florida *(See also 1938)*

By 1955, due to expansion of industry in the area, many of the Hispanic residents had moved from Ybor City to the western section of Tampa. There were no Protestant churches in the area, so the Westminster Presbytery, the Tampa Presbyterian Planning Council, and the Tampa Union of Presbyterian Women purchased five acres of land to be used as a new church site. By that time about 30 percent of the Ybor City congregation already lived in that area. In 1956, Ybor City Mission received $106,716 of the Birthday Offering to build a sanctuary and educational building for the new St. Johns Presbyterian Church. There was even enough money for some furnishings. The completed church was dedicated in September 1957. As a community church, the congregation set about developing a program with emphasis on youth and activities on every day of the week. The Ybor City Presbyterian Church was dissolved on February 9, 1962.

Area Laboratory Schools for Training Church School Leaders

According to Patricia Sprinkle in *The Birthday Book,* the 1956 Birthday Offering "expanded one of the most innovative programs Christian Education has ever known: the lab school teaching technique." In this way, church school leaders could watch experienced teachers teach children, discuss techniques observed, then take a turn at teaching, trying out what they had learned. In 1956, $75,000 of the Birthday Offering was designated to help support ten to twelve area lab schools each year for ten years. The money was used in three ways: 1) to set up the program and publicize it through all the synods, 2) to provide additional training for leaders who would teach in these area schools, and 3) to assist synods in paying transportation and small honoraria to these teachers and to assist in purchasing craft materials and textbooks for the schools.

1957

Student Homes in Mexico *(See also 1929)*

Because most of the rural schools in Mexico had only four grades at most, students who wished to continue their education were forced to go to centers that had secondary schools. The wife of a Mexican pastor recognized that many students at Zitacuaro (see also 1929) needed a Christian environment in which to live while they attended the government school. Many came from long distances, and she began to take girls into her home to live while they studied. She attracted the attention of the missionaries, and thus was begun the idea of Student Homes.

In 1957, the Mexican Mission asked for a part of the Birthday Offering for new girls' homes at Zitacuaro and Chilpancingo. They also asked for funds for rent and repairs on six existing homes and for scholarships for tuition at government schools and board at the homes. That year Mexico's half of the Birthday Offering was $100,000, and new homes were built at both schools. The directors of the homes were all Mexicans as the mission was embarking on a radically different course; it placed the money at the disposition of the Board of Student Homes in Zitacuaro. How pleased the Women of the Church were to learn that the Treasurer of the Student Homes in 1957 was Señorita Eufemia Manjarrez, who had been a Friendship Circle Student in 1942–1944! By 1959, there were nine student homes, four for boys and five for girls.

In 1972, Dr. Hervey Ross wrote that almost all the homes had been closed because the government had made primary and secondary schools available in almost all the smaller towns. The properties were turned over to the National Church of Mexico, but for many years they filled an important need.

Medical Work in Korea—Soonchun, Mokpo, Chunju, Kwangju

Medical work was a special avenue of Christian evangelism by Presbyterians in Korea. One-half of the 1957 Birthday Gift was given to Korea for special medical work with tuberculosis patients. At that time tuberculosis was the number one cause of death in Korea, and in 1956 the Korea Mission asked the Women of the Church to give part of their 1957 offering to be used for a vigorous ten-year attack on tuberculosis by means of mass x-ray diagnosis and treatment, plus education. Korea's share of the gift was divided among tuberculosis work in Soonchun, Mokpo, Chunju, and especially, Kwangju. A building for male leprosy patients suffering from tuberculosis, costing $5,000, was built at the Wilson Leprosy Colony in Soonchun. In Mokpo, a grant of $5,000 was used to increase the amount of public health assistance offered tuberculosis patients. At Chunju Medical Center, $12,000 helped provide blood and surgical equipment needed for chest surgery and a covered walkway between the surgical wing and the tuberculosis ward. The largest portion of the gift went to the 200-bed Graham Tuberculosis Hospital in Kwangju, where medical work was begun in 1905.

The hospital in Kwangju was built in 1912, destroyed by fire in 1933, and rebuilt the following year. During World War II the hospital was closed, but the Japanese used it to establish the first medical school in the area. After the war, the property was returned to the mission, and the medical school moved to another location. In 1951, the hospital reopened as a tuberculosis sanatorium under the direction of Presbyterian medical missionary, Dr. Herbert Codington. The rest of the gift was used in various ways, for drugs, blood transfusions (the money for this part of the gift ran out in 1964), and x-rays. Part of the gift, $40,000, was specifically designated for charity work over the ten-year period.

Today, the hospital at Kwangju is a General Hospital with a tuberculosis clinic. After Dr. Codington left in 1974, Presbyterian Dr. Ron Dietrick headed up the hospital until a Korean doctor became director and Dr. Dietrick retired. Missionary Arthur W. Kinsler wrote on April 16 from Seoul, Korea:

> As for the tuberculosis project it was a specialty of the Kwangju Christian Hospital. With the rise in income and health levels it is not so

much of a problem. The T.B. rest homes, one for those expected to recover & one for terminally ill in Soonchon, still do good treatment that the Soonchon clinic did then, but are not related to the PC(USA).

1958

Oklahoma Presbyterian College—Janie W. McGaughey Scholarship Fund *(See also 1926)*

The Women of the Church gave two Birthday Offerings to Oklahoma Presbyterian College in Durant, Oklahoma, for Native American girls. Because many of the students who wanted to come to OPC could not afford it, the Women of the Church gave OPC slightly more than $112,000 in 1958 for a scholarship endowment fund, the first such endowment the college had received. The endowment fund was named in honor of the newly retired Executive Secretary of the Board of Women's Work, Miss Janie McGaughey. In the early sixties pressure within the Synod of Oklahoma to close the school was mounting. Many thought that the original purpose, to provide Indian students with a quality education, was being carried out elsewhere as more schools admitted students of all races. Others felt that since the college functioned at that time mostly as a "student hostel-with-Bible-study," it was too expensive to operate. In 1966, the board of trustees voted to close the school. The facilities were sold and students transferred to other schools.

At that time, income from the Mary Semple Hotchkin Chair was transferred to Goodland Presbyterian Children's Home in Hugo, Oklahoma, and the Janie W. McGaughey Scholarship Fund was transferred to Presbyterian School of Christian Education in Richmond, Virginia. In the seventies the scholarship fund was yielding approximately $9,000 annually. At the time of publication, neither the author nor officials at PSCE and Goodland Home had been able to determine from Louisville or other sources where the funds are located, whether or not at some point the monies were pooled with other funds without knowledge of the institutions, and where the annual proceeds from interest now go. (See Appendix D for Board of Women's Work action.)

The Chinese Presbyterian Church, New Orleans, Louisiana

In 1946, the Chinese Mission had received a part of the Birthday Offering to build an educational building, which served also as a sanctuary for nearly ten years. In 1957, the Chinese Mission was organized into

The First Fifty Years in Summary 51

the Chinese Presbyterian Church with eighty charter members. The following year they completely outgrew the old building and applied for the 1958 Birthday Offering to be used for a permanent sanctuary. They received $65,000 of the offering that year for this purpose. The church carried on several special ministries including English classes for newcomers to the country and Chinese classes for children of Chinese parents. There was also a ministry among Oriental students at nearby universities, and $10,000 of the Birthday Offering was designated for use over a three-year period for further development of that work with Oriental students.

1959

Lay Training Center, Brasilia, Brazil

In 1959, the Presbyterian Church of Brazil celebrated its Centennial Anniversary Year. To commemorate the event, women of the Presbyterian Church, U.S. and the United Presbyterian Women, U.S.A., gave a joint Birthday and Thank Offering to establish a Lay Training Center in the new capital city of Brasilia. The Women of the Church contributed the 1959 Birthday Offering of $197,623, which included a memorial gift of $2,795 honoring Mrs. Leighton McCutchen, recently deceased Executive Secretary of Women's Work. United Presbyterian Church, U.S.A. women gave over $8,000 of the 1959 Thank Offering. The new facilities were opened in March 1964 with eighteen students from all over Brazil. In 1968, the name was changed to National Presbyterian Institute of Education. A three-year Bachelor of Christian Education degree was offered. Soon the curriculum was expanded to meet requirements for teachers. As with many Birthday objectives, the Institute developed and changed over the years to meet the needs of the people and the times.

1960

Classroom-Administration Building, Stillman College *(See also 1928, 1938, 1942, 1952, 1972, 1988)*

In 1960, the Women of the Church continued their strong support of Stillman College when they gave the entire Birthday Offering ($177,000) to construct a modern classroom-administration building, the Alexander Batchelor Building. Dr. Cordell Wynn, President of Stillman, wrote in a letter dated March 4, 1997:

The Alexander Batchelor Building continues in daily use, and I have my office in it. Batchelor contains the offices of the President, Vice-Presidents for Academic Affairs, Student Affairs, and Business, Registrar, Financial Aid Director, and many others. Most of our Business Education Department is also housed in Batchelor. The Stillman College Choir is housed in Batchelor until it moves to the new Humanities Center.

1961

Presbyterian Bible School, Hsinchu, Taiwan

In 1961, one-half of the Birthday Offering went to the Hsinchu Bible School in Hsinchu, Taiwan. The school was established by missionary Nettie Junkin in 1952 in the Chapel of the Taiwan Theological College in Taipei. It moved in 1955 to storefront buildings in Chupei, a few miles from Hsinchu, and then to Hsinchu in 1960. The 1961 Birthday Offering was used to launch an extensive building program for the school. Within a year after the gift was received, one faculty home was completed and two dormitories, classroom buildings, five faculty residences, and a kindergarten were under way. The school celebrated its tenth anniversary in buildings built with the 1961 Birthday Offering.

Decorative cut paper from Taiwan.

The purpose of the school was to provide enough training to equip lay leaders to assist in the work of their home churches. Full-time students took four-year courses with general religious training and specialization to become evangelists, Christian education workers, or church kindergarten teachers. A Bible correspondence course was also offered. Graduates of the school serve as both clergy and lay workers throughout Taiwan. According to Jessie Junkin McCall (retired missionary and sister-in-law of the founder of the school), the school is "accredited" now and educates students for careers outside the church as well as those ordinarily trained by a Bible college.

In 1987, when United Presbyterian Women and Women of the Church sponsored a study trip to China and Taiwan, the Women of the Church members of the group traveled one Sunday by train to Hsinchu, worshiped in a local church, visited the campus, and had lunch at the home of the Brad Longs, PC(USA) missionaries. The women were joined at lunch by local church women and leaders. It was a memorable experience for all who participated.

Christian Literature in Congo

In *The Birthday Book*, Patricia Sprinkle wrote that "when the announcement was made that half the 1961 Birthday Gift would go for Christian Literature in the Congo, some wondered if the Birthday Committee had made a mistake. Politically the Congo was experiencing the birth pangs of a new nation, and the American Presbyterian Congo Mission was having to evacuate." But, as in Mexico in 1943, the missionaries knew that this was a strategic gift; that printed matter could go where missionaries could not, stay when they had to leave, and be studied again and again. By 1960, due to the Belgian government's concern for literacy, the Congo had the best literacy rate in Africa; however, literature was almost nonexistent except for schoolbooks and Bibles. A PCUS missionary, Winifred Kellersberger Vass, studied journalism on furlough, thus preparing herself to train Congolese in the techniques of journalism.

The Congo's share of the offering, approximately $106,000, was used in four ways: 1) to purchase supplies and equipment for the Mission Press at Luebo, 2) to provide scholarships for four Congolese men to study journalism at the Ecumenical Training Center in Kite, Zambia, 3) to establish a Tshiluba-language Christian periodical, *Tuyaya Kunyi?* (Where Are We Going?), and 4) to expand a bookstore in downtown Luluabourg, a major city of the area. The editor of the periodical *Tuyaya Kunyi?* was one of the four men trained in Zambia. Another became a full-time translator for the American Bible Society, and a third was the head broadcaster and script writer for the Protestant radio station in Kananga.

For literature circulation to villages, the Birthday Offering provided a Volkswagen bus and a van to serve three circuits. As the vehicles wore out, new ones were purchased with trade-in and profits from sales at the bookstore. Who can say how much influence this gift has had in more than three decades since 1961?

1962

Presbyterian Guidance Program

In 1962, the Presbyterian Church, U.S. had a year of emphasis on the concept of Christian vocation, and as part of that emphasis, the Women of the Church gave their entire Birthday Offering, $168,479, to the Presbyterian Guidance Program, which began in the forties in the Synod of Virginia. *The Birthday Book* quotes from minutes of the Eighty-ninth General Assembly (1949):

> That in view of the growing need of a more practical type of help to pastors and Christian workers in the field of guidance and counseling on vocations, . . . the Assembly instruct the Board of Education . . . to set up a committee of interested individuals to study the practical phases of guidance and counseling being practiced throughout the Church, looking toward the possibility of supplying greater aid to Christian workers in this phase of the service of the Church to our people.

In 1951, a Department of Christian Education was set up in the Board of Christian Education. The Presbyterian Guidance Program was officially begun, and twelve centers were established in eleven synods. Most basic costs were carried by synods, presbyteries, and some local churches. The Birthday Offering was used to establish several additional centers, to upgrade facilities and purchase additional literature, and to assist personnel to continue their education in the counseling field. Birthday money was also used to meet criteria of the American Board of Counseling Services.

In 1971, the name of the program was changed from the Presbyterian Guidance Program to the Career and Personal Counseling Service in

The First Fifty Years in Summary 55

order to reflect the ecumenical nature of the program as it developed.

Today, some of the centers still exist and, among other things, help evaluate persons seeking admission to seminaries to help the person and the institution determine if the call to ministry is right for that person, considering aptitude and interest.

1963

Medical Work in Mexico *(See boldface entries below for gift disbursements)*

Three hospitals in Mexico received the first $75,000 of the 1963 Birthday Offering. The money was equally divided among hospitals in **Morelia, Ometepec,** and **Mexico City**. The Hospital of Light (**Sanatorio La Luz**) in Morelia is the oldest and largest of the three hospitals. Dr. L. J. Coppedge founded La Luz in 1921, and its work helped to alleviate the suspicion of Roman Catholics who thought Protestants brought a dangerous message. There were American directors until 1967 when La Luz became the first of the PCUS mission hospitals in Mexico to be operated completely under native direction. The hospital is now more than seventy-five years old.

In Ometepec, the Friendship Hospital (**Sanatorio de La Amistad**) was established in 1951 as a clinic and then as a thirty-bed hospital in 1958. When Dr. James R. Boyce and his wife, Marguerite, opened the station in 1951, they were given the usual treatment that Protestants were subjected to—no one could sell to, rent to, or have dealings with them. But as the missionaries provided much-needed, inexpensive medical care, a few of the people were won over. The 1963 Birthday Offering was used in several ways. Equipment was upgraded with $5,000. The remaining $20,000 was held in reserve to build a residence and classrooms for a school to train nurses' aides. The building was completed in 1970. In 1971, a Mexican doctor was named director of the hospital, and Sanatorio de La Amistad became the second mission hospital to be operated under native direction.

Originally, a third of the 1963 offering was to go to the **Hospital la Salud**, a small hospital in Mexico City sponsored by the National Presbyterian Church of Mexico. At the time of the offering, the hospital was located in a rented building but had to close its doors because it could not pay the rent or meet other expenses. In 1965, the Board of World Missions requested the Board of Women's Work to reserve the funds for future development programs at the other two hospitals in

Morelia and Ometepec. The money was held until 1972, when the Board of World Missions voted that the original sum of $25,000 plus accrued interest be equally redesignated to the hospitals at Morelia and Ometepec. In Morelia, the money was used to construct a nursing school facility; in Ometepec, the money was used to establish an endowment fund for the general work of the hospital.

Churches and Evangelistic Work in Brazil along BR-14
The Women of the Church gave $225,523 of the 1963 Birthday Offering for churches and evangelistic work along Brazil's new highway, a distance of 1,375 miles. In 1962, the Brazilian government blazed a trail through the wilderness north of the new capital of Brasilia all the way to the old port city of Belem in the mouth of the Amazon. The trail, a two-lane dirt road crossing thousands of miles of wild country, opened up a new frontier for Brazilian families looking for places to settle and land to farm. As pioneers traveled along the trail, often on foot or by mule, settlements sprang up.

All along the highway people faced hardships, struggling to build shelters and clear the land. There was, also, the threat of diseases such as dysentery, hepatitis, and malaria. The people also experienced isolation and loneliness. It was at this time that the Women of the Church decided to give part of the 1963 Birthday Offering to help the people along the highway. Some of the Birthday money was used to build churches. Sometimes it was used as a challenge fund to encourage the Brazilians to build their own churches. Sometimes it bought the land, and the congregation built the building. In all, fifteen different towns or villages received a part of the Birthday Offering to build schools, churches, or educational facilities. Some of the fund was also used to build medical clinics. The thrilling aspect of the work for many was that churches were built where churches had not been before. Tom Foley, a missionary at the time said, "To me, that offering did more good than any other. All you have to do is fly . . . up that highway and see all those churches in brand new towns."

In 1971, a full audit was made of all that the 1963 Birthday Offering had been able to accomplish. The list is long: fourteen trucks, jeeps, or motorcycles for transportation; fourteen churches or centers, with land; eight chapels; five manses for ministers or evangelists; four schools; two clinics with equipment; audio-visual equipment; literature; and agricultural workshops (*The Birthday Book*).

1964

Training Workers for Presbyterian Homes

In 1964, when half of the Birthday Offering of $256,233 was given to train workers for Presbyterian Homes, the Presbyterian Church, U.S. was sponsoring thirty-six homes for the aging and twenty homes or agencies for children. It had become evident that highly trained workers in the field of caring for children and the elderly were needed. The Birthday money was given for scholarships to be used by these workers for training and in-service events over a ten-year period. When the Birthday objective was announced, the Board of Church Extension made an announcement regarding scholarships from the offering that "Scholarships will be granted only to qualified persons who desire professional training in appropriate institutions and who are previously committed to working in one of our Presbyterian Homes." Within one week after the Birthday check was received, the board received and approved four applications from different homes across the Assembly.

A portion of the Birthday money was allotted for in-service training. During a two-year period, each children's home was eligible for two in-service events of at least four days each. Some of the money was set aside for workers in homes for the aging to be used to send administrators and other workers from these homes to seminars at the Menninger Foundation in Topeka, Kansas. Altogether, the money was used in many ways which benefitted all homes.

Evergreen Presbyterian Vocational School, Minden, Louisiana *(See also 1974)*

In 1964, the Evergreen Vocational School received half of the Birthday Offering, about $128,000, through the Board of Church Extension. Evergreen had made a name for itself in the field of vocational training for mentally retarded boys. The Synod of Louisiana, which owned and sponsored the school, requested the Birthday money to construct two dormitories and a domestic science building so that Evergreen could begin to admit girls as well. The school was begun by the Synod in 1959 as a "pilot school" in the field of education for "mentally handicapped children." The basic goal of the school was "to take retarded children and young adults who otherwise would be doomed to a life of inactivity and give them a useful place in society" (*The Birthday Book*). Actual vocational training was gotten through experience. At that time, the boys took care of the orchards and farm, practiced animal husbandry with the school's dairy herd, and did a variety of other kinds of work. Social life included sports and recreational activities. They participated in church and were taught habits of cleanliness and good grooming. On campus they participated in Bible study, prayers at meals, and daily chapel.

With the money from the Birthday Offering, the school purchased forty additional acres for the girls program, built a dormitory, completed a gymnasium, and applied all left-over money to a second girls dorm, which was completed in 1970. (For an update on the mission of Evergreen today, in 1997, see 1974.)

1965

Presbyterian Medical Center, Chunju, Korea

In 1965, the Women of the Church gave their largest Birthday Offering to date, and the major portion, $400,000, went to the Presbyterian Medical Center in Chunju, Korea, known in Korean as *Yesoo Pyongwon*, or Jesus Hospital. Medical work was begun in Chunju in 1897 by a woman, Dr. Mattie Ingold Tait, who opened a dispensary for women and children in a house she purchased. The facility grew, was burned, was rebuilt, then closed in 1940 due to World War II. Following the war, a medical-work survey was conducted by the Korea Mission, and the survey team recommended that the mission should establish one medical center that would emphasize the training of doctors, nurses, and lab technicians. On April 1, 1948, the gates of the center opened in Chunju with missionary Dr. Paul Crane in charge. The facility grew rather rapidly, and in 1961 a survey was made to obtain funds for expansion. Also in 1961, the Korea Mission gave approval for the hospital to request a Birthday Offering to be used for expansion.

The hospital also applied for a matching grant from the German Evangelical Central Agency (ECA) and appealed to the Medical Benevolence Foundation (MBF) (a validated ministry of the PCUS) for assistance with fund raising. A new site had to be purchased for the new center because the land owned by the mission was not sufficient for expansion. The final cost estimate for the land and buildings was $2 million. While waiting for an answer to the request to the German agency, the money from the Birthday Offering, MBF, and other sources was invested in Korea at a 20 percent interest rate! In 1969, word came that the grant from Germany had been approved. By that time, the invested money had grown to a level to qualify for a $1.3 million matching grant

The First Fifty Years in Summary

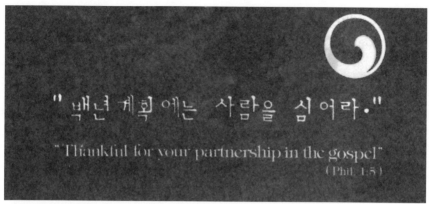

Korean inspirational material. Translation of the Korean words follow: "If you plant for a year, plant rice; if you plant for ten years, plant a tree; if you plant for hundreds of years, plant people."

from the ECA. Construction began, and in November, 1971, the Jesus Hospital was dedicated with Dr. Paul Crane representing the Board of World Missions.

The Presbyterian Medical Center is an independent institution with ties to the PC(USA) and the Presbyterian Church of Korea. In a communication dated April 16, 1997, from missionary Arthur W. Kinsler in Seoul, he wrote:

> It [Chunju Medical Center] is a large 300-bed hospital related to the PC(USA) without missionary staff and [to] the Presbyterian Church of Korea (Tonghap) our partner denomination here. They have many specialties such as a cancer center and mother-child specialty for the province, etc.

Taejon Presbyterian College, Taejon, Korea [Now Hannam University]

In 1965, the Women of the Church gave $100,000 of the Birthday Offering for a scholarship endowment to Taejon Presbyterian College, a coeducational four-year liberal arts college. The college was founded in 1956 to provide a quality college education for Christian students. At the time, establishing such a school in Taejon went against the trends in Korea because it was small, planned for 300 to 500 students, and it was located in Taejon, a city of 300,000. Koreans preferred very large universities and wanted to be educated in Seoul, the country's capital. However, many of the poorer students in the southern part of the country simply could not afford a Seoul education, so the mission planned the campus on the outskirts of Taejon.

In 1959, when the college received its permit to operate from the Korean government, the Korea Mission and the Board of World Missions of the PCUS adopted the following statement:

> The purpose of Taejon Presbyterian College shall be to make available to the Christian young men and women of Korea [a] college level education in which the Christian gospel is the central principle and in which full emphasis is laid on the academic and spiritual values of both the sciences and the arts, and to train capable leaders to serve the Korean nation, Church and society. (Board of World Missions)

In 1965, when the Birthday Gift was designated for scholarships at the college, the school was already granting scholarship inducements to help students, and the Birthday Gift freed the scholarship money that the college was using for other pressing needs. The Birthday Gift stipulated that part of the fund would provide partial scholarships for *all* women students.

In 1970, the board of directors of the college decided to merge with Soongsil College in Seoul, another Christian college, to form a Christian university. The name was to be Soong Jun University (a combination of the names of the two schools), and the university was to operate on both campuses.

According to missionary Arthur W. Kinsler of Seoul in a communication dated April 16, 1997, "Taejon College is now Hannam University with 10,000 students [and is] related to the PCK [Presbyterian Church of Korea] and PC(USA) [Presbyterian Church (U.S.A.)]." (See 1975 for Mr. Kinsler's comment about the present relationship of the PC(USA) and PCK.)

1966

Eastern Kentucky—Christian Service Ministry in Appalachia

In 1966, half the Birthday Offering, about $163,000, went to initiate the Christian Service Ministry in Appalachia as a way to participate in the human problems of that area and offer hope of solving some of them. The ministry was designed to help churches of Appalachia do a better job of ministry in their communities. The offering was received in May 1966, and by February 1967 the new ministry was already taking shape. Social workers were employed to work on the staff of three churches: First Presbyterian Church of Hazard, Haymond Church in Haymond, and Hull Memorial Church in Hazard. Other churches followed.

The Christian Service Ministry took different shape in different localities and situations, according to needs and circumstances. The Birthday Offering generated other money for the ministry. For example, the women in the United Presbyterian Church in the U.S.A. gave $25,000 to the ministry. Individuals added other contributions. The ministry lasted well beyond the five years projected at the time of inception.

Eastern Kentucky—Lees College, Jackson, Kentucky *(See also 1932)*

The 1932 Birthday Offering provided for an endowment fund to establish a home training department in two schools for girls in Eastern Kentucky. The two schools merged in the fifties, then in 1964, Guerrant Presbytery voted to close the school and make Lees College its legal successor. In 1996, the Women of the Church gave half the Birthday Offering, about $163,000, to Lees College to endow a Chair of Appalachian Sociology and help train social workers for Eastern Kentucky. Lees is a small college, and about eighty percent of the students come from Eastern Kentucky. The school was founded in 1883 when a Methodist circuit rider passed through on his way to establish a school in the Cumberland Mountains. His horse went lame in Jackson, so he decided to stay there. In 1891, ownership and control of the school passed to Central University in Richmond. The Presbyterian Church, U.S. assumed responsibility for Lees in 1907.

In requesting the 1966 offering, Lees wrote: "For many years . . . Lees College has served as means whereby our Church has expressed her concern for disadvantaged mountain youth." Lees College did receive half the offering that year to endow a Chair of Appalachian Sociology. A staff member of the Board of Church Extension pointed out that "the Church recognizes the uniqueness and worth of each individual and tries to motivate people to help themselves." Both the Christian Service Ministry and the Appalachian Sociology Program at Lees were aimed at that goal.

In July 1996, Lees College ceased to exist as a church-related college, and ownership was transferred to the University of Kentucky system. The author has not been able to determine what happened to the two endowment funds from Birthday Offerings, which were producing about $13,000 annual income in 1972 and would surely be worth more now.

1967

Kinjo Gakuin (Kinjo University), Nagoya, Japan *(See also 1935 and 1947)*

In 1967, Kinjo College added graduate departments in Japanese and English Literature and officially became Kinjo University, related to the United Church of Christ in Japan but governed by an independent board of directors. By 1968, Kinjo had graduated more than 31,000 students. Also in 1967, ties were again established with the Presbyterian Church, U.S. Japan Mission, and the first $100,000 of the Birthday Offering that year went to Kinjo University to assist in building a chapel and religious center. The First Presbyterian Church of Houston, Texas, gave to the project a like amount of money, and Ella Houston Hall, the chapel and religious center, was dedicated in 1971.

Shikoku Christian College, Zentsuji, Japan

In 1967, approximately $192,000 of the Birthday Offering was given to Shikoku Christian College to build a gymnasium and dormitories. The college was founded in 1950 by the Japan Mission of the Presbyterian Church, U.S. Twenty-two acres of flat land were bought in the heart of Zentsuji, a small city on Shikoku Island. Classes began with twenty students in buildings that originally housed the Japanese Imperial

Kinjo students.

Cavalry. Shikoku received accreditation from the Ministry of Education as a junior college in 1959 and as a senior college in 1961—and consequently began to draw more students. The mission gradually added new buildings. In 1967, Shikoku received the Birthday Offering as requested and added funds from a supporting agency. All the buildings at Shikoku had biblical names, and the new gymnasium was named "New Life" and the dorm "Zion Hall." According to retired missionary Lyle Peterson, Shikoku is thriving. It has grown considerably, both in number of students and facilities. It has not retained its once-distinctive Christian emphasis but continues important service to the people of that area.

1968

To Train Leaders to Proclaim God's Word Today's Way through TRAV, the Television, Radio, Audio-Visual Agency

In 1968, the Women of the Church Birthday Offering was given in support of a project in communications. That year the entire offering of $261,097 was given to TRAV, the television, radio, audio-visual agency of the Presbyterian Church, U.S. to provide funds for training Christian leaders in the effective use of mass media to communicate the Word of God (*The Birthday Book*). As a result of a 1956 two-year study of the Church's use of mass media, it was recommended that the General Assembly establish a new agency. The new agency, TRAV, created in 1958, merged work formerly done by the Division of Radio and Television of the Board of Church Extension and the Department of Audio-Visual Aids of the Board of Christian Education, adding several new duties. The agency struggled for a decade with an annual budget that was only a fraction of what had been recommended when it was created. So, in 1968, TRAV requested the entire Birthday Offering to provide funds for four types of training.

Bluford Hestir, retired staff person, described this training in conversation with the author. First, TRAV trained a few individuals to a high level of expertise, using scholarships from the Birthday money. Second, TRAV trained ministers for use of communications—audio-visual materials, TV, radio, and printing. Presbyteries, synods, and cities invited TRAV personnel to hold workshops within their bounds. These workshops lasted from a full day to several days. The ministers would listen to themselves on tape or watch themselves on videos and do self-evaluations, learning how they could improve communications. They also learned how to use effectively the time slots many of them were provided without cost on local radio stations.

The third type of training was when a team would be invited to offer intensive training in classes at seminaries. The staff developed training manuals with tapes built in. Sometimes they brought in consultants. TRAV also gave the seminaries equipment to be used in training the students. They provided other types of teaching material (written and taped) to enlarge the student's awareness of mass media and helped in analyzing performance. TRAV also held training sessions at summer conferences, including the first Montreat Communications Conference, paid for from the Birthday Offering money. The fourth training program was an overseas one through the training of missionaries. Birthday money was used for training events in this country and included int nationals who were residing in this country. TRAV also developed a media library with a mail-order division and placed books in the libraries at the four seminaries related to the PCUS.

In the early seventies, when the PCUS was going through a period of reorganization and funds from the offering were being depleted, the work lessened and TRAV became an office. During its life, TRAV held training events in almost every synod, four seminaries, and participated in other training events, which helped the Church enter a new era of communications.

1969

Good Shepherd Hospital, Tshikaji, Congo [Later Zaire]

In 1969, the Women of the Church gave most of their second largest ever Birthday Offering, nearly $400,000, toward the construction of Good Shepherd Hospital in Tshikaji, Zaire, located eight miles from downtown Kananga. The *Institut Medical Chretien de Kasai* (Province) was founded in 1954 by the American Presbyterian Congo Mission. It was originally located at Lubondai and included the first approved school for nurses in the province and the only formal dental instruction in all of Congo. Following intertribal fighting in the sixties, the Congo church and the mission concluded that a priority would be increased training of Congolese medical personnel with mission doctors assisting in this process. It was decided to locate the teaching hospital in an urban area. For the hospital, the government of the province offered forty acres of land and buildings, near Kananga, with permanent title to the land. Buildings on the property included two school buildings, a dining hall, ten faculty homes, and an administration building.

The First Fifty Years in Summary

Two difficulties faced the missionaries, Dr. and Mrs. William Rule, who were called upon to instigate the move. First, the buildings badly needed repair, and second, the buildings were occupied by Congolese soldiers who refused to move. Dr. Rule ingeniously worked out solutions, and within two weeks, the soldiers were gone. A bequest from a member of First Presbyterian Church in Winston-Salem made possible the most urgent repairs.

The 1969 Birthday Offering made up nearly half the total needed for the hospital, which was designed so that it could be built in six sections. Birthday money was used for the obstetrics, pediatrics, and surgical units. Thankfully, according to reports from former missionaries, at the time of publication Good Shepherd Hospital had survived the recent fighting that has taken place in that province and is still functioning. Government forces took all vehicles from the hospital except one, which they destroyed. Rebel forces are now in the area and so far have not been destructive to the hospital or the missionaries.

Reconciliation Ecumenical Conference Center, Figueira da Foz, Portugal

The first $35,000 of the 1969 Birthday Offering was given to build cabins for a new venture in Portugal—the Reconciliation Ecumenical Conference Center at Figueira da Foz, a coastal town 120 miles north of Lisbon. The Portuguese Evangelical Presbyterian Church first conceived of the idea in 1964. The leaders saw a need for reconciliation between different churches and different secular groups in Portugal, and they decided to establish an Ecumenical Lay Training Center where conferences, consultations, and work camps would bring together people of differing opinions for dialogue and worship. As a result of the center, ecumenical activity and understanding have progressed both within Protestant churches and between Protestants and Roman Catholics, the predominant religion in Portugal.

1970

Villa International, Atlanta, Georgia *(See also 1941, 1997)*

In 1965, the Board of Women's Work called together concerned Christians in Atlanta to make them aware of the loneliness, isolation, and lack of funds and friends that existed among international guests who visited the city, especially those who came to visit and study at the Center for Disease Control (CDC). During that year, many of the hundreds of

Top, Villa International hosts more than one thousand short-term guests yearly. Bottom, guests at Villa International work and study together, forming deep international friendships.

internationals were interviewed to find out their greatest needs. The primary need was for convenient and cheap housing. Out of this grew Villa International Atlanta (VIA; known simply as Villa International), an ecumenical project sponsored by five denominations of the Christian Church, including Presbyterians. The Women of the Church designated the 1970 Birthday Offering to the project, and that year the offering of $282,942 was used to construct a housing facility for VIA. Including accrued interest the final gift was $312,430. The Least Coin contributed $1,000 toward the project. In 1972, the Board of Women's Work redesignated money being held in an endowment fund from Collegiate Hall (see 1941) for furnishings for the project.

1971

Christian Family Service Centers in Congo, Korea, Taiwan

In 1971, women responded to the plight of families who were moving into rapidly growing urban cities around the world. To help people cope with their new situations and to minister to them as they developed ways of dealing with a new lifestyle, in the Congo, one-third of the 1971 Birthday Offering, $100,300, went to establish three Christian Family Service Centers. The first center was at Matete, a community within the capital city of Kinshasa. The center was planned to be a learning and resource center for eleven other communities that have Presbyterian churches that can be used for similar classes. Leaders in the churches were brought to Matete for training, participation in a baby clinic, and classes in literacy, homemaking, home nursing, Bible, health and hygiene, and marriage and family relations. Two other centers were established in Mbujimayi and Kananga with similar programs.

Seoul is the largest city in Korea, and the rapid influx of people from rural and outlying areas made for tremendous problems in the seventies. Housing was inadequate, jobs were scarce, and the rural people were ill-equipped to deal with a substandard urban lifestyle. Korea had no welfare program at that time to deal with these families. In an effort to minister to these families, one-third of the 1971 Birthday Offering, approximately $110,300, went to establish Christian Family Service Centers in Seoul. Some of the money was used to pay salaries for trained personnel to work in the slums. Other funds were set aside so that agencies and churches could apply for subsidies to help in special ministries to families. One program encouraged people to volunteer to help each other. Missionary Arthur W. Kinsler of Seoul wrote in a letter on April 16, 1997:

> As for the 1971 Christian Family Service Centers, Elder Chung Dong Tuk now retired who was the Executive Secretary of the PCK Society Department said he had no knowledge of this project which may mean it was done through NCC or some other organization. My guess is that this project helped the people moving into Seoul and may have been used through the Yonsei U. Urban Studies Office which used to be active in this kind of work.

At any rate, the money was consumed within five or six years to implement programs for which it was intended.

One-third of the 1971 Birthday Offering, $100,300, went to Taiwan to establish Christian Family Service Centers in Taipei and other cities. Because of the mountainous geography of the country, many tribal groups lived in isolation, and moves to urban centers seeking economic relief have resulted in confusion. In Taipei, the Birthday funds were used to establish a Family Counseling Center for research, training, and service, as well as other projects. As in Zaire and Seoul, the Birthday Offering has, once again, initiated a project for the benefit of a community of people.

1972

Chair of Business and Scholarships, Stillman College *(See also 1928, 1938, 1942 (1950), 1952, 1960, 1988)*

Stillman was once again the recipient of the Birthday Gift ($270,519) in 1972 to endow a Chair of Business and to provide additional funds for scholarship aid. Dr. Cordell Wynn, President of Stillman, wrote in a letter dated March 4, 1997, "Mrs. Mary Davis, chairwoman of the Department of Business Education, is our Women of the Church Professor of Business." He also mentions the importance of the scholarship aid. Today, the Business Department at Stillman is academically strong and prepares young men and women for careers in the business world.

American Bible Society *(See also 1949)*

The 1972 Birthday Gift of $50,000 to the American Bible Society was given specifically to print and distribute scriptures for "American Indians" and the more than one million migrant workers (at that time) in

Mrs. Mary Davis, chairwoman of the Department of Business Education at Stillman College.

the country. The American Bible Society estimated that 40,000 Cherokee Indians and 125,000 Navajo Indians lived within the United States. The 1972 offering provided New Testaments in their tongues. In addition, the offering provided Psalms in Choctaw for more than one hundred churches and Cherokee-English bilingual versions of the Gospel of John.

Scriptures for migrant workers met a different kind of need. Many of the workers can read English, but it must be simple, direct English. The migrant workers have few, if any, direct connections with the Church. With part of the offering, migrant workers who read English received *Good News for Modern Man* in everyday English and packets containing collections of colorfully illustrated Bible stories. For the majority who read only Spanish, a Spanish-English version of the New Testament was distributed.

PART II

The Years before Merger
(1973–1988)

CHAPTER THREE

The Women of the Church
(1973–1988)
*Office of Women—
Division of National Mission
Presbyterian Church, U.S.*

1973

Operation Unlimited: Amazon Breakthrough *(See also 1963)*
The 1973 Birthday Offering of $570,677 (See Appendix E for 1972 action of Board of Women Work, which added redesignated funds to the offering) was given to two projects. The first, Amazon Unlimited, was in many ways a supplement to the 1963 offering, which was designated for evangelistic work along Brazil's new highway, BR-14, a trail blazed through the wilderness in the early 1960s by the Brazilian government, beginning north of the new capital of Brasilia and reaching all the way up to the old port city of Belem. In 1973, the need was along another highway—the Trans-Amazon Highway, Brazil's east-west version of the Brasilia-Belem Highway. According to Charles R. Hughes Jr., Area Secretary for South America, writing in May 1973, the unpaved, two-lane dirt strip runs 3,500 miles and crosses four major rivers wider than the Mississippi. Linked up with another highway at the Peruvian border, it provided the first South American land crossing between the Atlantic and Pacific Oceans at the widest part of the continent!

Hughes wrote, "In one bold thrust, the road will open up to settlement and exploration an area half as big as the United States." The government "expects migration by more than a million persons when the work is completed."

Amazon Breakthrough program reaches the majority of the Brazilian population.

There is a recent precedent on which to base such predictions. It happened with the building of the BR-14 Highway. . . . When the road was completed in 1961, the population numbered 100,000 in the area along the road. Ten years later, in 1971, there were 2 million people. . . . And where the people are, there ought also to be the Gospel of Jesus Christ. . . . Through the Birthday Offering ten years ago, the Women of the Church made it possible for our missionaries and their fellow Brazilian workers to be among the first to establish churches along the BR-14 Highway. The effect of that pioneer effort, in terms of extension of the church and the influence of the church in the life of new communities through the establishment of schools and medical facilities, is one of the greatest chapters in the history of PCUS missionary work.

According to former missionary Bill Moseley, the preliminary plans for the Birthday money called for six veteran missionary couples to be located in towns or cities along or near the highway. A year later, the following had moved to their posts: Frank and Hope Arnold, Bert and Sandy Gartrell, Bill and Fern Jennings, Bob and Corinne Johnson, Paul and Merry Long, and Don and Laura Williams. Two Brazilian pastors had also taken up assignment there. The plans called for specialists in Christian education, agriculture, primary and secondary education, music, and preventive medicine as soon as available. The Brazilian Church bought land for the churches, chapels, and other programs, participating fully in the ministries.

The Years before Merger

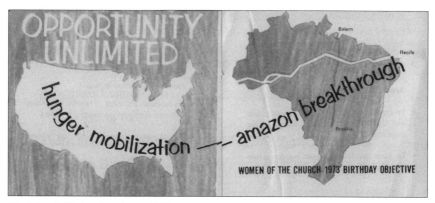

Birthday Offering brochure, 1973.

In a 1974 report mailed from Brazil by missionary Dr. Frank Arnold in May 1996, there is a summary of a 1974 Survey of the Presbyterian Mission in the Amazon Basin. According to the report:

> On April 5, 1974, Jule Spach, General Secretary of the Presbyterian Mission of Brazil [and Moderator in 1976 of the 116th General Assembly, PCUS], Olson Pemberton, Director of the 'Institute Biblico Eduardo Lane,' and Joe McLellan, pilot of Missionary Air Fellowship, left from Brasilia on a planned trip that was to go over a great majority of the Amazon Basin. . . . They covered a distance of 5,121 miles.

At that time, no detailed report had been prepared "to lay out the plans and involvement of the mission on the Trans-Amazon Highway." The purpose of the twenty-two page report was:

> 1) to provide historically accurate information on the Presbyterian Mission of Brazil's involvement in the Trans-Amazon and its specific situation up to the period of April, 1974; 2) to consolidate data as to cities, residences, transportation, personnel, etc. that are located on the Trans-Amazon Highway and in the area of the Amazon Basin; 3) to provide suggestions that have come out of the impressions that this team received as a result of their experiences during this trip.

In a brief background history of the mission of Brazil's involvement in the Trans-Amazon work, the report states that:

> Our Mission's permanent contact with the Amazon area . . . occurred during the decade of the 1960s. At that time there still existed the West

Brasil [Brazil] Mission whose geographical area covered the sector from Brasilia throughout the state of Goias to the Tocantine River at Estreito. The old North Brasil Mission picked up the responsibility for the work of the Church from Estreito and continued north to the city of Belem. With a very large gift from the Women of the Church of the Presbyterian Church, U.S. [approximately $240,000], churches were built and programs established in all the basic cities along the southern sector of the Belem-Brasilia Highway in the sector that was the responsibility of the West Brasil Mission. The sector to the north was still untouched territory, and the great majority of the funds applied here were to establish pioneer evangelism, educational programs, colonizational centers and agricultural work. . . .

In the late 1960s . . . came the great challenge to conquer the Amazon Forest. . . . Actual construction of the highway was only a small part of the total plan. Other highways were to fit into the total network of roads and communications systems. . . . The main task is the habitation and the colonization of this total area. . . . A strip of land along the Trans-Amazon Highway from five to ten miles wide on each side of the road, has been reserved for colonies. Each family receives a 250 acre parcel of land. . . . The colonists receive title to the land only if they live on and develop it for a period of five years. . . . [The government] has built frame houses along certain sections . . . approximately 500 meters apart on both sides of the road. . . . Industries such as a large sugar refinery [are] located at Abraham Lincoln. . . . Colonists in such sectors are required to plant a certain percentage of their land in sugar cane. The colonists must also leave a defined number of acres in woodland for ecological reasons. There is a plan of reforestation, and there is control over the cutting down of trees and the exploitation of the land that is under cultivation.

There follows a detailed report of ten centers visited by the team, including the cities in each, the schools, churches, personnel, buildings and equipment, funds allocated by the Women of the Church 1973 Birthday Offering, and plans for expansion. A list of the fund allocations from the Birthday Offering follows:

1. Estreito (located at the crossroads of the Trans-Amazon and BR-14 highways)
    $10,000 for the construction of a chapel

The Years before Merger

2. Marabá (organized as a city in 1913, located on a river, population has grown in four years from 24,000 to 35,000)
   $14,000 for the Marabá Center

3. Altamira (an old river town, experienced phenomenal growth)
   $26,000 for Mission residence
   $16,000 for Anapu Center (Agropolis)
   $19,000 for church in Brasil-Nova
   $10,000 for manse in Brasil-Nova
   $10,000 for church in Abraham Lincoln
   $10,000 for manse (Agropolis)

4. Santarém (located on junction of 2 rivers)
   $10,000 for Santarém Church
   $5,000 for Santarém Chapel
   $16,000 for Presidente Medical Center
   $15,000 for Itaituba manse
   $16,158 for Santarém manse
   Support for salary, transportation, manse and work from IPM

5. Boa Vista (pre-planned city, principally a military city)
   $12,000 for manse

6. Manaus (principal city of the Amazon Basin, grown to 400,000 population)
   $12,000 for chapel and to help purchase a river boat

7. Humaitá (at crossroads of Highway and Manaus-Porto Velho Road)
   $4,500 for aid in developing evangelistic center

8. Porto Velho (capital of the territory, hot and humid, lots of malaria)
   $8,000 to aid in completion of new church building
   Support for salary, transportation, manse and work from the Iglesia Presbyterian Brasil (IPB)

9. Rio Branco (western most point and center for Presbyterian work)
   $6,000 for a church
   Unspecified amount for land
   Support for salary, transportation, manse and work from the IPB

10. Vila Rondonia (the most frontier town of all)
    $10,000 for the development of chapels and churches

The Trans-Amazon Highway was eventually completed. Parts of it still are not paved and remain a challenge to travelers, but the basic concept proved successful. Dr. Frank Arnold wrote in his letter of May 4, 1996:

> Hope and I lived in and worked out of Altamira after the Longs left. We arrived with much of the plans, mentioned in the report, already under way and during the brief year and a half we worked there (I was called to the South to be Mission Secretary) a second church was organized in Altamira, with a Brazilian pastor, plus one of the points on the highway had a congregation organized into a church. Soon after the Report [see above] was made a missionary agronomist (Olin Coleman) and his wife moved to Altamira and started the "Milk Cow" project with settlers, which proved to be quite successful.

The basic policy of the Presbyterian Mission to turn over its work to the Presbyterian Church of Brazil (IPB) began around 1970, according to former missionary Jule Spach, and continued over a period of about ten years. He said in a telephone conversation in April 1997, that some parts of the mission, such as schools, were easier to transfer than others like evangelism, which were complicated in their structure and work. The IPB terminated their relationship with the UPUSA in 1975. In an article in the May 1975 issue of *Presbyterian Survey*, it states:

> Property owned by the Presbyterian Church in the U.S. (PCUS) will be transferred to the Presbyterian Church of Brazil (IPB) according to a proposed plan agreed to by both Churches and is not being demanded by the IPB's moderator. That information comes from Jule Spach, Presbyterian Mission in Brazil General Secretary, as clarification of a Religious News Service release which credited the IPB moderator with demanding transfer of the PCUS property.

> It is important to know that the PCUS took the initiative in a move to transfer PCUS property to the IPB, Spach explained. The action was taken through the Commission on Cooperation involving both Churches, because it is believed that it is time for the property to be transferred, he added. It has always been the PCUS goal to turn the church work to the IPB as soon as it is willing to accept it, he continued.

The article continues:

> "I inform you of all this, because I feel that the article (February, 1975, *Survey*) gives the impression that demands are being made by the Presbyterian Church of Brazil through Dr. Ribeiro (IPB moderator) that are in conflict with the wishes of the Presbyterian Church in the U.S. This is not the case, as I hope this letter explains to you," Spach wrote.

After reunion of the PCUS and PC(USA), the relationship between the IPB and the PCUS changed. There are no records after 1985, the year the mission was dissolved. The Trans-Amazon work was turned over totally to the National Church before that time. Like the schools and other ministries initiated by the Brazil Mission, evangelism, new church development, education, and other social services are carried on along this amazing highway by the Presbyterian Church of Brazil. Women of the Church can rejoice in the part they played in this continually unfolding drama in the heart of Brazil.

Hunger Mobilization

Presbyterians have been involved in the fight against hunger for so many years that it is somewhat difficult to think of when it was not a priority at every level of mission. The Women of the Church designated half of the 1973 Birthday Offering "to strike a blow against hunger and its root causes." The offering was used "to set in motion an Action Program against World Hunger through persons who know how to facilitate action against hunger in the local community, in the homeland and overseas" (*Presbyterian Women*, May 1973). The choice of Hunger Mobilization came in response to an action in 1969 of the General Assembly which stated that:

> *To meet the clear call of God which we see in the faces of millions of starving people, the 109th General Assembly of the Presbyterian Church in the United States declares that world hunger is so real and grave that this problem is a top priority concern for the Presbyterian Church in the United States and that all possible resources of the Presbyterian Church in the United States, for at least the next five years, must be focused on ways and means of dealing with the problem.*

In a letter from James A. Cogswell, Director of the Task Force on World Hunger, copied to Dr. Evelyn Green (Secretary of the Board of

Women's Work), dated September 12, 1972, he wrote:

> The Boards and Agencies of our church, in seeking to respond to this declaration of the General Assembly, formed the Task Force on World Hunger. During the first two years of the hunger priority, much attention was given to alerting and educating the church regarding this crisis. . . . [I]ncreasingly the response that was heard from the church was, "Tell us, what can we do?" The Task Force prepared a proposal . . . and presented it to the Board of Women's Work . . . for the 1973 Women's Birthday Offering.

Cogswell continued:

> Briefly, the Program has two prongs: First, to employ several "Hunger Action Specialists" to be located strategically across the church (probably in connection with several of the new regional synod offices) for a three-year experimental period. These Hunger Action Specialists have as their mandate to stimulate and facilitate action against hunger at the grassroots level by Presbyterian men, women, youth and church courts. . . . [These persons will] work with church courts, congregations and groups, helping them to find the handle by which they can get at root causes of hunger, in the name of Christ and as a witness to Him.
>
> The second prong is to fund carefully selected hunger action projects locally, nationally, and world-wide. In the Task Force we call these "model programs." These are programs that will serve as examples of what can be done when Christians really put their minds and their hands to the Task.

In the May 1973 issue of *Presbyterian Women*, Dr. Cogswell wrote about these models or projects:

> Growing out of the work of the enablers [are projects such as] . . . a nutrition clinic in Zaire or a breakfast program for children of poor families in the local community, the provision of land for a landless farm family on the frontier of Brazil, or assistance to a farm cooperative among the rural poor in the South.

In the promotional material in 1973, women were challenged to be creative and get involved on the local level in the fight against hunger.

One of the suggestions was to challenge families in the congregation to enter into a special "welfare-meal-a-week" project and from the family food budget make an additional gift to the 1973 Birthday objective, which was designed to help alleviate hunger. Devotional suggestions for Birthday "Parties" used the Emmaus story from Luke 24 with its themes of "road" and "bread" and ended with:

> Is it not true today that Christ is known to a hungry world in the breaking of bread—in all the simple acts and the complex strategies by which the people of Christ share bread with the world?

Indeed, is it not true today?

1974

New Ventures in Christian Services

In an introduction to the 1974 Birthday Offering, these words were written:

> *Somewhere tonight a mother and father will tuck their child into bed and talk quietly about the future. It won't be a happy discussion, full of dreams and plans. For them the future holds only uncertainty: their child is severely mentally retarded. Right now they can give the child love and care and security. But what will happen when they get older? Who will provide the Christian warmth and care for their child—this child who will never really grow up?*
>
> *Somewhere tonight a woman will look in the mirror and ask, "Who am I—and why am I here? But the question will only echo and die because there is no one who can really help her talk about it and discover the answers. Inside her are gifts and talents and ideas that have never been tapped. Until she explores them she will never reach her full potential, never move into full Christian discipleship.*
>
> *This year, through the Women of the Church Birthday Offering you can help with both these problems. You can begin new ventures in Christian mission.*

Evergreen Presbyterian Vocational School, Minden, Louisiana [Now Evergreen Presbyterian Ministries, Inc.] *(See also 1964)*

Evergreen is a story that constantly unfolds. It is a story of a boarding school in the rolling hills and pine trees of north Louisiana—not the usual

Evergreen provides job assistance training and placement.

kind of school, but one for retarded youth. Ralyn Parkhill, who was director of the school in 1974, said:

> It is a story of a crusade to free retarded youth from an age-old accumulation of misunderstanding, fear, ignorance and prejudice. It is a story of a campaign for the rights of retardates to be treated as human beings, God's children.... It is a story of a revolution which has developed new methods of training and procedures for equipping the mentally retarded to return to society as responsible and useful citizens. It is a story of countless men and women who have dedicated time and energies and resources to make this ministry possible. It is a story of [the youth] who have passed through her portals. But most of all, it is a story of Hope, Faith and Vision.

Evergreen received about $128,000 of the 1964 Birthday Offering to make it possible for the school to build facilities so that would it could accept girls. In 1974, Evergreen School received the major portion of the 1974 Birthday Offering, almost $300,000, to enable Evergreen to make extended care for retardates a part of the program that proposes a ministry to the aging mentally retarded with quality of care and concern for significant involvement in life and community. As Mr. Parkhill put it, "Evergreen does not exist apart from its program." The emphasis is on vocational training in a residential setting. Even though the training program is essentially stable,

> ... the total program is experimental and still in its formative stages. There is a constant seeking of new directions and methods, new programs that will complement and support the present program.

The Years before Merger

Evergreen provides family-like living for special-needs adults.

The school sees three needs for expanded services: 1) a maturation program for preadolescent group, 2) community residential care for those who are ready to leave the structured program at Evergreen but who continue to need some supervision in independent living away from the campus, and 3) an extended care program for those who will never return to society.

One plan for the Extended Care Program is to establish a foundation to receive trust funds for this purpose. Many parents have inquired about establishing trust funds so that their children will be guaranteed care for life. Evergreen already has in its program training as nurses' aides. These two programs can be correlated in a way that is beneficial to both—employment for the aides and care for those in Extended Care.

The Evergreen story is still unfolding. Women of the Church watched it grow and change from a "pilot school" of the Synod of Louisiana in 1959 with four young men to a vocational school for forty-nine boys and a goal of seventy-five in 1964, when the Birthday Gift made possible an expansion to include girls, to 1974, when, with 150 students and eighty staff, the Birthday Offering helped initiate the Extended Care Program. No longer is Evergreen a "vocational school" alone. Evergreen Presbyterian Ministries now serves more than 500 people of all ages (from the very young to the very old) with mental disabilities that range from mild to profound in three states—Louisiana, Texas, and Oklahoma—with plans to add the fourth state of the Synod of the Sun, Arkansas, to their ministries.

Under the leadership of Dr. Bernard Wagner, Evergreen has established seventy-two community homes in middle-class neighborhoods. Each home houses six or fewer residents. Under supervision they learn the tasks of housekeeping and cooking and how to function in society—some on a more limited basis than others, but all up to his or her fullest capability. There is a variety of other housing. One plan that has proved successful is the use of supervised apartments where the residents can live even more independently. Professional staff is on hand from one to twenty-four hours a day to a couple of hours a week. The degree of independence varies from individual to individual. For some, it is learning basic skills like learning to dress oneself and to feed oneself. For others, it means learning a skill and being employed.

Yes, the story at Evergreen is still unfolding. Evergreen's founders in 1959 had a vision of hope for the mentally disabled. Evergreen has come a long way since then, just as the public's understanding of mental disabilities has come a long way. The four young men with "mental retardation" and behavioral problems who, under the guidance of a Presbyterian pastor and skilled staff, took up residence in an abandoned school fourteen miles north of Minden, Louisiana, in 1959, wrote the first chapter. In this "pilot school" the young men raised crops, cleared ground, dug lakes and ponds, and built buildings. They functioned successfully in this setting and learned through positive experiences how to function in society. From this remarkable success, Evergreen's programs have expanded into the ministries of today (1974). No doubt there will be a new chapter tomorrow, but whatever the story, it will unfold with compassion and love, based on the belief that "all people should have the chance to reach their full potential." (See 1964 for a brief background of Evergreen)

Update: The "new chapter" in Evergreen's story is described in a letter from the President, Dr. Wagner:

> Over the years, the emphasis of Evergreen's ministry has changed dramatically. When these Birthday Offerings were made the typical model of services for individuals with mental retardation involved institutional settings. In subsequent years, the emphasis has moved away from institutional settings to placements in community. Evergreen has paralleled this movement. In 1994, we closed our institution outside Minden and moved all of our clients into community settings. This process began in earnest in the late 1980s and early 1990s.

Dr. Wagner enclosed an interesting article, "Voluntary Transformation From an Institutionally Based to a Community Based Service System." He also enclosed a "fact sheet" that provides helpful information.

The Years before Merger

Evergreen is a nonprofit agency (mission) of the Synod of the Sun and is governed by a nineteen-member board of directors elected by the synod. Since closing Evergreen as an institution and selling the property in 1994, seventy community homes, each serving six people, have been located throughout Louisiana and Texas. Forty additional homes are planned over the next five years. Supported living services are located in six communities in Louisiana. The yearly operating budget is $21 million; the main funding source is Medicaid.

Dr. Wagner wrote:

> It should be [noted] that the Birthday Offerings made to our Minden campus . . . continue to have value and continue to do good work. Certainly, the clients who lived at Evergreen in the sixties, seventies, and eighties benefitted greatly from the charity of Presbyterian women. Also, the value of the campus when it was sold in 1994, was enhanced by the improvements partially funded by Birthday Offerings. Proceeds from the sale of the campus were in turn used to start community-based services and programs. So, the generosity of your organization lives on today.

New Ventures in Christian Discipleship

The Birthday Committee in its report in 1974 wrote:

> Your committee shares the concern of many Presbyterian Church, U.S. people who inquire about the shape of the future. We believe that the full discipleship of women is a most important factor in the church of tomorrow. Because of this we recommend that $75,000 from the Birthday Offering be designated for this purpose:
>
> - To help women discover their potential as disciples of Jesus Christ.
> - To help them prepare for fuller participation in the world.
> - To help them relate to other Christian women around the world.

One of the women on the Selection Committee, Alice Magness of Virginia, wrote in the May 1974 issue of *Presbyterian Women* that a portion of the offering is

> . . . designated for the purpose of helping women realize their potential as disciples of Jesus Christ in the church and in the world today [through

'pilot experiences']. This will be done through seminars and retreats throughout the General Assembly. . . . We need to understand our places of responsibility as women in the whole church and in the world as we consider the meaning of 'full discipleship.' . . . The Board of Women's Work has for many years provided experiences such as these to women in places of leadership. The monies have come from the Board. That source of funding is no longer available to us, and the committee thought that . . . a part of the Offering for 1974 could be well used to finance these training experiences. Qualified women who participate in the first regional seminars will be responsible for sponsoring similar experiences in their presbyteries and local communities.

The "second pilot project," according to an article by Dottie Barnard (*Presbyterian Survey*, April 1974), "will give opportunity for about ten women to study, learn, and share with sisters in foreign countries. This is a small beginning with ever-widening influences."

Sara B. Moseley, at that time "Vice-Chairman," General Executive Board, had this to say about the proposed seminars for Women:

How can we measure the widened and deepened understanding of Presbyterian women who for 52 years have learned about and given to the variety of Birthday Objectives? . . . A continuing thread throughout has been the identification of a tangible, contemporary opportunity for Christian witness. . . . Now there is a need—very tangible, very urgent—among the women of our denomination for the awakening, the understanding, and the commitment to serve in broadly representative responsibilities. The church is limited in its recruitment and training. . . . Consider the possibility of some 15 seminars across the Assembly at which women, many who have not yet found their places of service, can study together the meaning of full Christian discipleship as it applies to themselves! . . . [T]hree assurances of the project: the theological study, the competent leaders, the on-going influence of the women who attend . . . will literally multiply the fruits of the original investment. . . . This seed money . . . will have both immediate and long term results, availing our church of a rich resource that now lies largely dormant.

A Birthday Gift by the women to themselves—a new concept that has paid rich dividends in the decades since.

1975

Focus on Asia: Preparing Christian Leaders in Korea and Japan

The 1975 Birthday Offering of $424,079 helped provide leadership training in theological and Christian education in Japan and Korea. Specifically, the offering contributed to the priorities of leadership development, evangelism and outreach, ministry to persons and problems, and strengthening the small church.

Seiwa School, Kochi, Japan [Formerly Miss Dowd's School] *(See also Introduction, 1922, 1947)*

After World War II, the First Church of Kochi had difficulty maintaining Seiwa School, so in 1948 the mission resumed control. In 1952, the mission purchased a tract of land on the edge of Kochi and began to build a new campus with a goal to "make Seiwa a thoroughly accredited and strongly Christian High School." In the years since the new school was built, Seiwa has increased in size and mission. Today the school is a respected, fully accredited junior and senior high school with an English and Secretarial College. In 1975, it was the only school in the prefecture, and one of the few in the country that accepted "handicapped students" on merit (*Presbyterian Survey*, April 1975).

One-fourth of the 1975 Birthday Offering (more than $100,000) went to Seiwa Girls School to expand facilities to provide Christian education. This was a sentimental favorite because a major part of the first Birthday Offering in 1922 went to Seiwa School, known as Miss Dowd's School. In 1996, the author of this history sought updated information about Seiwa Gakuen from Mrs. Catherine (Kitty) Peterson, retired missionary who served on the Board of Directors at Seiwa Gakuen for a number of years. Kitty graciously wrote to Mrs. Hiroe Ueno, a member of the faculty at Seiwa for almost thirty years, and this is Mrs. Ueno's reply in part:

> The 1975 "birthday offering" was given to Seiwa Junior Senior Girls' High School in October of 1975. Our records show that it was a most generous gift of 24,000,000 Yen. The school knew at the time that there would be soon a need to build a new campus and so deposited the money in the bank for the time being. With the interest from the account, the school set up 'The Southern Presbyterian Women of the Church Welfare Fund.' This program enabled two of our teachers to study abroad

The 1975 Birthday objective focused on Korea and Japan.

in the U.S., one student to study in Australia . . . and for seven years, the school was able to award scholarships . . . in recognition of merit.

In the 1980s the school began to search seriously for a new home. A new locale was found, and in 1985, the school moved to its present location in Nankoku, east of Kochi. By this time, the account from the birthday gift had grown to 28,180,000 Yen, and all of it was used to purchase the new land and buildings. The total for the new project was a staggering 2,000,000,000 Yen! So, you can see just how much we needed this generous gift. What a blessing!

Mrs. Ueno sent copies of school bulletins and brochures. The centerpiece of the beautiful new campus is an impressive chapel with stained glass and an imposing pipe organ. Featured in a promotional piece is a picture of Miss Dowd, the founder of Seiwa School.

Aerial view of Seiwa School.

What a change from a home for helpless young girls to a bustling, modern campus with the latest in facilities and equipment! Presbyterian Women can rejoice that their "love offerings" helped to keep alive Miss Dowd's dream. Surely it was not chance that determined that Miss Dowd's School would start the procession of Birthday Offerings.

Hanil Women's Seminary [Now University], Chunju, Korea *(See also 1947)*
One-half of the 1975 Birthday Offering, more than $200,000, was given to Hanil Women's Seminary (now Hanil University) in Chunju, Korea. Hanil's ties with the Women of the Church go back many years. According to G. Thompson Brown, at that time Field Secretary of the Korea Mission:

> The *name* of the institution comes from the names of two Women of our Church at home who did much in the cause of Women's Work. *Han* continues the memory of Ada Hamilton Clark, a missionary of our Church for many years in Chunju. *Il* perpetuates the memory of Miss Lois Neel of Charlotte, North Carolina, who gave funds for the Neel Bible School in Kwangju. (From proposal for the offering)

In 1960, two Bible Schools, the Neel Bible School in Kwangju and the Ada Hamilton Clark Bible School in Chunju, were merged and the name Hanil chosen.

The Birthday Offering was to be used for two purposes: One was to establish an endowment fund, the proceeds of which were to be used for student scholarships for women, field work by women students, faculty salaries, and library expansion. The purpose of the second portion of the gift was for making capital improvements at the seminary, such as a music building and kindergarten training center.

According to the proposal presented for the offering, in the early seventies the trustees of both Ho Nam and Hanil Seminaries voted to merge the two boards so that one board would operate the two schools with some opportunity for faculty exchange and cooperation in an educational program.

Arthur W. Kinsler, PC(USA) missionary wrote from Seoul in a communication dated April 16, 1997:

> The two Bible Schools which joined are now Hanil University which does not have as much emphasis on women as formerly and has added many other major subjects as well as now offering the M.Div. degree; it has 1,300 total students with 304 in theology.

Mr. Kinsler goes on to say that in 1995 and 1996, "the question of women's ordination won approval from the Presbyterian Church of Korea so we have a few women pastors and elders now with a lot more in the testing, choosing, calling pipeline."

Ho Nam Theological Seminary [Now University], Kwangju, Korea

One-fourth of the 1975 Birthday Offering, more than $100,000, went to the Ho Nam Theological Seminary in Kwangju to be used for capital improvements such as a chapel and student-activities building and for support of program. As a part of the proposal for the offering, John T. Underwood, faculty member, wrote:

> The seminary is located in South Cholla Province, known in Korea as the 'Honam Area.' Largely agricultural but turning to industry, rural at heart but challenged by urbanization, consistently under-valued by the rest of the country and not eagerly wooed by administration or politicians, the area must make its own future or do without. People flow out, and those who leave most readily seem the ones most able to break the cycle if they would only stay.
>
> The Seminary exists to take Honam Area Christian leaders and equip them to stay in the area as pastors. "With 130 graduates already, the Seminary draws more men every year. When the enrollment passed one hundred and the old and new dormitories together could hold no more, we diverted library space to dormitory use. In 1972 we began holding classes in the Assembly Room. In 1974, with 120 students and with the Assembly Room already in use, we put two of our four classrooms together to hold the larger classes. In 1975 we ought to have about 140. . . .
>
> The Ho Nam Seminary is a working school, organized with a program of student agricultural work to cut student costs and equip men for

rural service. Most of the students use our three-day weekends to commute to regular lay-preacher pastorates. . . . The faculty, too, does extra jobs, not only in the Seminary, but outside. . . . The campus is attractive but inadequate, and soon to be made smaller by a broad avenue slashed through it. Farm work is done both on and off campus. The new buildings are on a new, wooded campus secured from the Korea Mission of the Presbyterian Church, U.S. . . . We have no women students. By agreement, the women are referred to the Hanil Women's Seminary in Chunju.

In the proposal for the Birthday Offering for "Leadership Training in Theological and Christian Education" at Hanil and Ho Nam, Dr. G. Thompson Brown, Field Secretary, wrote that the money would be used for Continuing Education, the Department of Rural Church Development, the Field Work Department, Kindergarten and Day-Care Training, and the Music Department.

In a communication from Arthur W. Kinsler dated April 16, 1997, he wrote:

[Ho Nam] Seminary is now a Theological University with only church-related subjects. The old building is still being used, but they have a nice larger new one. Since 80% of Korea is now urban, this seminary trains rural and city pastors and has just begun to offer the M.Div. degree so it trains pastors for the SW area of South Korea for the PCK [Presbyterian Church of Korea] and has really upgraded its faculty. It has 480 undergraduate theology majors, 200 music majors, 280 M.Div. students, 30 Th.M. with 40 plus D.Min. in their program with Howard U. in the U.S.

Mr. Kinsler comments that:

. . . at present the relationship between PC(USA) and the PCK is of equal partners in mission. Some of our mission personnel perform services and the PCK institution rebates funds to the mission, and there are several missionaries in the third world supported by both denominations. The PCK has 470 full-time missionaries in 71 countries.

What a cause for rejoicing! Again, love gifts have borne fruit many times over, and women have seen strong, mature independent churches like the PCK emerge.

1976

Christian Service Ministry Unit in Appalachia—Transylvania Presbytery *(See also 1932, 1954, 1966)*

The promotional material for the 1976 Birthday Offering featured a rainbow signifying hope—hope to the people of Bangladesh, hope to Native-American youth in Oklahoma, and hope to the mountain people of Eastern Kentucky. This seemed fitting to the Birthday Committee in our bicentennial year.

The 1976 Birthday Offering was planned to give hope to some of the people of Appalachia. At the time the offering was given, the mountain area of Eastern Kentucky was a densely populated rural area with more than 600,000 people. It is a region of steep hills and narrow valleys, and coal mining was its principal source of employment. There were many jobless persons who could not leave the area either because of age, lack of education, family, or money. The housing problems were some of the most severe in the nation, with more than 60 percent in one area classified as substandard. The Women of the Church responded to these critical needs by designating one-fourth of the 1976 Birthday Offering, approximately $117,000, to Transylvania Presbytery in Kentucky for its unit of the Christian Service Ministry. In 1966, the Women of the Church had given one-half of their Birthday Offering (approximately $150,000) to initiate this ministry. Through this ministry, Christian social workers were employed to serve with pastors and lay persons to meet some of the tremendous social needs of the poor. Counseling with families, work with youths, establishment of day-care centers, legal aid for the poor, housing repair, and more happened as a result of that offering. However, the funds were running out, and new directions needed to be taken.

One vision for new directions was the use of Volunteers in Mission. A portion of the funds from the 1976 Birthday Offering assisted the Christian Service Ministry (CSM) in providing money for full-time, long-term (one and two years) social service volunteers. The duties of the volunteers included 1) counseling, referring, and assisting families with need; 2) locating and helping those who needed available services in order to survive adequately; 3) helping to set up small aid centers for emergency help—food, clothing, or referral; 4) playing the role of advocate for people facing public agencies (welfare, food stamps, school, courts); and 5) providing funds for and supervision of "double-duty" programs.

An example of the "double-duty" program grew out of a concern for the youth who needed part-time jobs and for the isolated elderly. The youth were "hired" to work directly with assigned elderly people (running errands, helping with house or yard chores, getting groceries, stopping by to check on the elderly), thus helping the elderly and, at the same time, providing the youth with money for school clothes, books, etc.

The second component of the CSM objective was the Home Repair Program. A portion of the funds from the Birthday Offering was used to organize home repair programs for the poor and elderly, using work camps made up of youth recruited from across the nation. Local leaders were hired for the summer in areas needing this service. These leaders worked with the volunteers and did such things as 1) locating those who needed housing repair and then made arrangements with them to do it; 2) setting up day-camp programs in isolated communities for children and youth; 3) accepting applications for work camps, screening the applications, scheduling the work, and providing orientation both before and after arrival; and 4) doing oversight of and supervising the work, then providing evaluation of the program.

Summer supervisors encouraged the volunteer work groups who came to bring with them supplies such as tools, paint brushes, and other things that could be used for house projects. The groups had to supply their own adequate adult leadership and, whenever possible, include in their groups persons with particular skills (plumbers, carpenters, electricians, roofers). This was another "double-duty" ministry—it provided needed service to people in the mountains; at the same time, it enabled youths from the Church at large to participate directly in the mission of the Church.

Jack E. Weller, in the April 1976 issue of *Presbyterian Survey*, wrote that "one of the rich benefits of CSM has been working together with other agencies *and* with other denominations doing similar ministries." The women in the United Presbyterian Church in the U.S.A. gave part of the Thank Offering one year, and many other individuals and churches began to send gifts to CSM. Weller said that the dynamic of CSM is simple: "People helping people in need by finding resources or creating them."

Some of the things done by "people helping people" included assisting with "Meals on Wheels," organizing and working with Boy Scout and Girl Scout troops, initiating day-care centers and playgrounds, turning an old coal camp theater into a youth/library/clothing center, and working with people who, as Weller described them, "fall between the cracks" of welfare programs. One of the cooperative programs involved Presbyterians, Roman Catholics, and Mennonites with a group called "Frontier Housing," which did home repair and even new housing for low-income families with the help of long-term volunteers. Jack Weller summed it up well when he wrote, "We like to think of the Christian Service Ministry as preaching the Word in deed."

The 1976 Birthday Offering began with the theme of the rainbow as a symbol of hope. It doesn't ever really end because what was begun with the Birthday Offering in 1932 to initiate home-training departments in two mountain schools (established by Presbyterians for girls who had no other opportunities for education) continued in an offering to impact work in coal camps in 1954, saw exciting avenues opened with CSM in 1966, and, with the 1976 offering, renewed the hope which all Birthday Offerings seek to inspire. The rainbow continues as a beautiful reminder of hope, which is engendered by "preaching the Word in deed."

Goodland Presbyterian Children's Home, Hugo, Oklahoma *(See also 1926, 1938, 1954, 1993)*

> Many years ago the American Indians found paradise. It wasn't located in the sky, but in Oklahoma. The Indians called it *Yakni Achukma* or Good Land because of the rich resources and numerous springs, abundant timber and fertile soil.

Thus began the article written by Ellen Weaver in the May 1976 issue of *Presbyterian Survey*. The article continues:

> A group of Indians, along with other Americans, is still living on the good land at Goodland Presbyterian Children's Home near Hugo, Oklahoma. Good things are happening there because residents are taking advantage of not only the abundant geographical resources but the human resources too. (See also 1954)

Goodland Presbyterian Children's Home has operated continuously since 1848. It began when a strong missionary woman, Mrs. Oliver Porter Stark, began teaching school in a two-room log cabin for the neighborhood children. Two years later, the mission built the Good Land Presbyterian Church. Established at the Yakni Achukma preaching station, the Good Land Mission and Day School provided preaching and teaching to the Choctaw-Chickasaw Nations. Beginning in 1930, the Goodland Indian Orphanage provided a boarding home, schooling, and church services with Presbyterian and federal assistance. Silas Bacon, himself an orphan and a full-blooded Choctaw, served as superintendent of the home for twenty years.

The portion of the 1954 Women of the Church Birthday Offering that went to Goodland was used to build a multi-purpose building for offices, dining room, kitchen, and additional dormitory space. The building was named Bacon Hall in honor of Silas Bacon.

In 1976, Bacon Hall was still in use, and Goodland was home to more than sixty children ranging in age from preschool through high school. According to Ms. Weaver's article in the *Presbyterian Survey*:

> It is a highly regarded children's home and family service agency designed to serve children from broken homes and homes financially unable to keep the family intact. . . . Although a majority of the young people are Indians, children from every background are welcome.

It was stated in 1976 that "Goodland's future is based on more than 120 years of expressing God's love to orphans and dependent and neglected children, particularly those of Indian background." One-fourth of the 1976 Birthday Offering (approximately $117,000) was designed to give hope to Native-American youth at the Goodland Presbyterian Children's Home in Hugo, Oklahoma, by providing funds to enlarge an agricultural development program using the home's 760 acres. The program included raising hogs, cows, catfish, and fruits and vegetables. Money was used to build a central farrowing shed for the sows, increase the size to a one-hundred-sow unit, accumulate a herd of cattle to be located south of the campus, develop a seven-acre lake north of the campus to be stocked with catfish, and use other acreage for cultivation of fruits and vegetables.

In answer to a request for an update on the ministry at Goodland, Executive Director David L. Dearinger wrote in a letter dated February 20, 1997:

> During the last couple of years, [Bacon Hall, built with the 1954 Birthday money,] has undergone extensive remodeling and is clearly the most multi-functional building on campus. In 1996 the large basement area was remodeled and now serves as a large classroom for the 28 students enrolled at Goodland Christian Academy. The school offers a self-paced Christian curriculum for its students.
>
> Bacon Hall's first floor area has been remodeled extensively over the past several years. This area once served as the kitchen and dining hall

The Years before Merger

Birthday Offering money helped build Goodland's agricultural program.

for the entire campus. The kitchen was modernized two years ago (for the first time since the building was constructed in 1955), and the large dining room was re-carpeted and completely refurbished. A central air and heating unit was installed for the first time ever in the building. An old storeroom, located just off the large dining hall, was refurbished and is now a women's bathroom. Bicentennial Funds, provided by Goodland's supporting churches through the Synod of the Sun, were used to complete this renovation work. The first floor kitchen and dining hall are used for all of Goodland's major activities. The area is also used by the Choctaw County Genealogical Society (which was started at Goodland and meets monthly here on campus) and by Goodland's own Boy Scout troop. Goodland Home has also hosted several large meetings/luncheons (including an Eastern Oklahoma Presbytery Women's meeting) as well as a recent summer gathering of Eastern Oklahoma Presbytery.

With a generous 1976 grant [1976 Women of the Church Birthday Offering] of $117,000, Goodland Home established a first-rate agriculture program. The home runs a 100-head herd of registered Brangus cattle. The Home's 390-acre cattle operation is supervised by a full-time farm manager. In addition to cutting hay each summer for winter use, the farm manager also supervises the clearing of additional pastureland. Boys in Goodland's care who are interested in agriculture have an opportunity to work with the farm manager on a variety of projects: feeding cows and calves; working calves; building fence; and clearing land. Boys participating in their school's Future Farmers of America (FFA) organization can raise their own livestock (calves, sheep, or hogs) here at the Home for competition in the county fair.

As we have seen, programs change with time. In information provided by Mr. Dearinger, the program today, in 1997, is described as follows:

> Goodland Presbyterian Children's Home provides supervised residential care for boys, ages 6–16 years. Boys who live at the Goodland Home attend church services each week in various Presbyterian churches around the area. The boys participate in weekly Bible study and worship services on the Goodland campus.
>
> ... [the] campus has four cottages, each with an eight-boy capacity. Cottage counselors (married couples) live with the children on a 24-hour basis. Through a variety of assigned household chores, the boys learn responsibility and how to contribute to the family structure. Under close supervision from cottage parents, the boys learn to cook, clean, and how to care for their own clothing. The boys are required to keep their rooms clean and are rewarded weekly according to the amount of effort shown in their chores. Goodland residents receive medical and dental care, a clothing allowance, and a personal allowance. Visitation is available for parents and guardians. ...
>
> Because of its unique location, Goodland Home provides a relaxed, rural lifestyle for its residents. ... Goodland Home promotes a diversified activity-based program. ... Students in first through eighth grades are educated at the Goodland Dependent School. When they reach ninth grade ... [they] attend nearby Hugo High School. ... Goodland Home has level systems in the cottages as discipline management tools. ... Corporal punishment is not a discipline alternative.

Goodland has come a long way from the two-room log cabin in which it began in 1850, but its primary mission is unchanged, and hope comes in many forms from many caring people.

The Years before Merger 99

Santa and the Goodland boys.

Note: A missing component in this record is the location and distribution of the Mary Semple Hotchkin Endowment, which was created in 1926 for an endowed Chair of Bible at the Oklahoma Presbyterian College (OPC) for Indian Girls and the proceeds designated for Goodland Presbyterian Home in 1966 when OPC closed. The income from this endowment was meant to be used for someone in Christian education at the home, but according to the present executive director, "I have served as executive director of Goodland Home since 1988 and, during this time, this facility has not utilized monies from the Hotchkin Endowment. I was unaware of this particular endowment until your letter arrived, but have had Presbytery officials checking for more information on the fund." Neither the director nor the author has been able to determine the location of the corpus of the fund or the distribution of the income. It is hoped that eventually this matter will be cleared up (see Appendix C).

Mary Semple Hotchkin, for whom the 1926 (transferred to Goodland in 1966) Endowment for Chair of Bible at Oklahoma Presbyterian College for Indian Girls was named, is buried at Goodland.

Bangladesh Christian Health Care Team Ministry Project

An article by Ellen Weaver in the March 1976 *Presbyterian Survey* brings to the mind and heart of the reader the kinds of choices the persons who work for relief agencies must face in the desperate country of Bangladesh.

> Polio has brought 20 Bengali children to their knees—so crippled they will never walk again. A relief agency in Bangladesh has $100 either to buy braces for the two children unable to walk or to vaccinate 75 other children to prevent their getting polio. What's the choice? The Presbyterian Church in the United States has made the choice to do both. . . . During the next four years the PCUS will be engaged in a Bangladesh Village Health Care and Agricultural Development program in which local Bengalis will be trained in various skills of health care and agriculture.

Preparation for this program began several years earlier. In 1973, Dr. Herbert Codington, veteran medical missionary in Korea, visited Bangladesh exploring needs and ways in which the PCUS could be involved. He felt the needs were more critical than in Korea, so studies were made and plans perfected. According to an article in the October 1974 *Presbyterian Survey*:

> Four missionaries of the Presbyterian Church in the U.S. (PCUS) have arrived in Dacca, Bangladesh, to begin the Church's first direct overseas involvement in that country. After six months of language study, Dr. Herbert Codington, a tuberculosis specialist, and Mrs. Codington, a registered nurse, will provide tuberculosis in-patient and out-patient services in a rural area to be assigned. The Codingtons have been missionaries to Korea the past 20 years.

> Another PCUS missionary couple, Mr. and Mrs. Sursavage, an agriculturist and registered nurse, will attend language school one year before taking up a regular assignment. The Sursavages were appointed to missionary service in Bangladesh by the PCUS General Executive Board in May.

> "The new work in Bangladesh is a real opportunity to proclaim Christ through a healing and service ministry," commented William Rice, Atlanta, Ga., GEB staff associate for Overseas Projects and Program Planning, in announcing the couples' arrival at Bangladesh's capital.

In the few years preceding the start of this ministry in 1976, natural disasters such as floods, droughts, and cyclones killed thousands of people.

Services in front of the Presbyterian Medical Clinic, Bangladesh.

Only five years earlier, a civil war had killed many thousands more. Promotional material for the 1976 Birthday Offering posed the question,

> Confronted with the overwhelming facts of Bangladesh—poverty, illiteracy, malnutrition, starvation, floods, famines, devastation by war and tidal waves—where do you begin to bring life and hope to lifeless and hopeless people?

The Women of the Church gave one-half of the 1976 Birthday Offering (about $230,000) as a symbol of hope to show that Christians care and to be partners in the Health Care and Agricultural Development Program. Financial support was channeled through Church World Service since it already had a staff and work under way when the PCUS entered the work.

In an article entitled "Pioneer Villages Offer Help," in the May 1975 issue of *Presbyterian Survey*, the Khulna Pioneer Village project is described as different because most of the refugees are Christian. In 1973, the churches in the Khulna district, working ecumenically, built 20,678 houses. U.S. AID contributed $1 million to Church World Service for the project. U.S. AID also gave more than $20 million to nongovernment agencies for development, including $8 million to Catholic Relief Services

Patients waiting for care at Tongi Clinic, Bangladesh.

and $100,000 to Seventh Day Adventists. Another pioneer village, Senhati, was just getting started.

The Codingtons and the Sursavages were assigned to the Health Care and Agriculture Development Ministry not only to alleviate suffering but also to enable Bengali people to carry on curative and preventive health care to people who live in rural villages and enable them to grow food to improve their diets and reduce the problem of malnutrition and starvation. The mission of the PCUS was to develop model, comprehensive community health care and agricultural programs that used resources available locally, including personnel, supplies, and equipment. The two couples worked through the National Christian Council. It was a slow and tedious process.

The specific aims of the project were to show that people who have no previous medical backgrounds or concept of modern farming methods can be trained locally to carry out basic medical care and experimental farming and gardening projects in rural villages. Sixty-five percent of the Bengali people operate small farms, with the average size three acres. The workers went out to visit neighboring villages to share the resources, to work out better water-management and food-preservation techniques, and to cooperate and coordinate these projects with government and other agencies.

How, you might ask, can this be done? The plan for the medical people was to set up a health center of twenty beds in a rural village of 100,000 people and employ native staff persons to carry on such a center and begin a paramedical training program for nurses' aides, laboratory assistants, and others. It was planned that the center would emphasize the control of tuberculosis and other communicable diseases, family planning, post and prenatal care, child health care, diet planning, and nutrition education.

The plan for the agricultural people was to set up an experimental and demonstration three-acre farm and begin training Bengali assistants to work directly with the Bengali farmers. It was planned that they would teach landowners how to increase crop production through irrigation, water control, better seed, sprays, fertilizers, and use of new crops. "Butch" Sursavage said, "The main emphasis will be that of investing in people and not in elaborate equipment or facilities."

Women needed to be taught vocational training, so a part of the program was to teach women how to weave, sew, and make handicrafts, baskets, and pottery. This way the women could work at home and not have to leave their children and, at the same time, supplement the family income.

Conversations with neighbor and fellow church member, Dr. Herbert Codington, added to the author's knowledge and understanding of the project. In notes dated January 1997, he wrote:

> The Birthday offering was used to establish the "Christian Health and Agricultural Project, Alhadipur" (CHAPA) which contributed greatly to the needs physical and spiritual in a rural area fifty miles west of Dacca. Those serving there: Mr. and Mrs. Nonweiler, Dr. and Mrs. Ted Kuhn,

Mr. and Mrs. Scott Smith, Mr. and Mrs. Stewart Bridgman. To my knowledge it is still serving—but in Bangladesh hands. Today our Church's mission has a new rural project twenty miles north of Dacca. The PC(USA) missionary couple there works in conjunction with the Anglican Mission, which has a long history of ministry in Bangladesh.

Dr. Codington continued, "I worked in medical care at Tongi 10 years—but am unclear how much [of the Birthday Offering] went for that project."

This remarkable man, who retired ten years ago at age sixty-five, still goes back to Bangladesh as a volunteer three times a year, staying for six weeks. While in Bangladesh, he works in a medical clinic, which he started when he retired, located in the slums of Dacca. Dr. Codington was able to start the clinic and keep it operating under the permit of a private Presbyterian group of Cape Cod, Massachusetts, "Friends of Bangladesh," which operates other services out of the same location. Today, there are 120 million people in Bangladesh in an area the size of North Carolina. When asked if he sees progress in the lives of people there, he says emphatically that while many problems still exist, such as overcrowded conditions and overpopulation, he is encouraged. Life is still hard for many of the people, but it is better than it was when he first went there twenty-three years ago. At that time, they saw few women on the streets because it is a Muslim country. Now, he says that the streets are full of young women going to jobs, mostly in the garment factories.

The Bangladesh Village Health Care and Agricultural Development project in 1976 was designed to teach, feed, and heal, as well as to express Christ-like compassion and love in word and deed. As Jack Weller said in reference to the Christian Service Ministry, which also received part of the 1976 offering, the development project in Bangladesh was also about "preaching the word in deed." The seeds were sown and, bit by bit, continue to produce. Presbyterian Women did well to invest in these three projects.

1977

Reaching Out to Those Striving

The theme of the 1977 Birthday objectives was ". . . reaching out to those striving." The objectives were designed to reach out to older people in our congregations and communities who were striving for opportunities; to reach out to people in jails and prisons who were striving for a new life; and to reach out to African people in emerging nations who were striving for a new day.

Center for Ministry with the Aging, Presbyterian School of Christian Education, Richmond, Virginia *(See also 1924, 1948, 1956)*

In 1973, 25 percent of the people in the United States were over the age of sixty, and by the year 2000 the number is expected to rise to 33 percent. One-third of the 1997 Birthday Offering (about $140,000) was designated for work with the aging in our homeland by establishing a Center for Ministry with the Aging. The goals were 1) provide new ways for a more effective ministry to the aging through research and experimentation; 2) provide materials for use in congregations, including color slides, cassette tapes, curriculum, and program materials; 3) provide educational events such as short-term courses, institutes, reading courses, and workshops; and 4) provide churches with an up-to-date directory of services by governmental, private, and church-related agencies.

With the help of the Birthday Offering, the Center on Aging at the Presbyterian School of Christian Education was built in 1978 and dedicated in April 1979. Dr. Albert E. Dimmock was installed as the first Director of the Center. In an article in the May 1977 *Presbyterian Women*, President Kenneth Orr of PSCE wrote:

> Through an extensive new program, this center will begin to highlight many ways a better ministry for older persons can be provided by churches. . . . The Center can help church leaders become more sensitive to some of the special needs of older persons. For many, loneliness is a major problem because of the death of spouses and friends as well as geographical separation from families. . . . Guidance can be given to church members about how to best provide for the needs of their elderly parents. And assistance can be given to those about to retire as to matters to be considered and planned for ahead of time.
>
> Most importantly, the Center can help congregations affirm a Christian theology that allows us to accept growing old as a normal process within the providence of God. . . . And it can help us to affirm the dignity and the joy of life at every age.

The Center on Aging is a Graduate Center for Educational Ministry. Six courses are offered in the curriculum of the Master of Arts program,

Birthday Offering program cover, 1977.

including Curriculum Development for Older Adults and Intergenerational Groups; Ministry with Older Adults; Aging and Ministry in America: History and Implication; Issues in Aging from Novels and Films; and Ethical Issues in Aging. Three continuing education seminars are also offered: Ethical Issues in Aging; Designing Model Ministries with Older Adults in the Church; and Pre-Retirement Training.

Dr. Henry C. Simmons, Director of the Center, wrote in a letter dated March 5, 1997:

> What has happened since then [Birthday Offering]? The Center on Aging is still serving an essential need in the church—assisting churches and congregational leaders to have a more effective ministry with their older members. The 1977 Birthday offering of the Women of the Church continues to bear good fruit.
>
> A few specifics: 1) Like my predecessor—and more than I used to—I am out in the church, working particularly at Presbytery level meetings and with local congregations; 2) Every year we get a handful of working pastors and educators who come and spend a week or more in intensive study and preparation for ministry with the elder of their congregations; 3) We currently have a complete collection of every book, article, and dissertation abstract published on the church and aging since the mid 1800s. This is a valuable research tool for students and scholars; 4) I continue to publish. I enclose a little book I did last year [*With God's Oldest Friends*] that will give you an idea of the people I am trying to reach; and 5) Budget cuts have taken their toll in the Center on Aging as everywhere. I am certain, though, that the endowment given by the Women of the Church has sheltered us from the most chilling financial winds!

In a brochure that Dr. Simmons provided, there is outlined the ministry of the center. The Center on Aging

> ... has a vision of the promise and challenge of aging, affirms the need for effective educational ministry, provides preparation for ministry with older adults, recognizes the large number of older adults in most congregations, offers research on aging, offers resources on aging, offers you enrichment for ministry with older adults, and affirms that aging is a blessing, that life is holy, and that growth in wisdom is God's gift.

Note: PSCE future—At the time of publication of this book, talks were under way for a "federation" of PSCE with its neighbor, Union Theological Seminary, Richmond, Virginia. According to a "Presbyterian News Brief" article (97148) dated April 11, 1997:

> A plan to join Union Theological Seminary in Virginia and the Presbyterian School of Christian Education in what its proponents call "an administrative and educational partnership" is expected to be voted on by the boards of the two institutions in concurrent meetings May 2.
>
> The plan proposes "federation" of the two schools under a single administration and board, with each retaining its own program of study. PSCE and UTS faculty would be members of a single "federated" faculty, with some responsibilities unique to each institution. Students would be part of a united student body, but with separate degree programs, governance, social events and worship, as well as alumni organizations. PSCE's board of trustees asked the UTS board to discuss the possibilities of joining the two schools administratively and organizationally in 1995 after several failed attempts to bring PSCE operating costs in line with annual giving.

Task Force on Criminal Justice *(See also 1988)*
One-third of the 1977 Birthday Offering (about $140,000) went to reach those involved in the criminal-justice system to provide direct services to inmates and their families, to provide identification of the root causes of crime, and to provide changes in the system at the legislative level. The Birthday Gift was used to begin a three-year program to explore ways for criminal-justice reform.

According to information from the promotional material for the offering:

> . . . the money was to be used to establish a financial reservoir from which seed money for pilot projects could be obtained by church and ecumenical groups to implement projects with particular attention given to projects relating to the unique problems of women.

Possible types of projects were outlined such as an

> . . . organization of volunteers to accept supervision of people who could be released from confinement while awaiting trial; organizations composed of volunteers to help probationers and work-releases, to

The Years before Merger

secure employment, and to furnish psychological testing and counseling; and an organization of volunteers modeled after Women in Action in Harris County Jail in Houston, Texas. . . . The essential idea is the promotion of model projects which will work for positive changes in criminal justice systems throughout the area ministered by the PCUS.

The Task Force on Criminal Justice and Prison Reform, established by the 115th General Assembly, had oversight of the grant and had the responsibility to review pilot proposals and determine the amount of the grant and then receive financial and program progress reports on a quarterly basis.

More specifically, the program had two main stages—first, development of a criminal-justice resource kit that explained the needs in the criminal-justice system, showed ways in which people had come together to meet these needs, and included some basic ideas of how to start working in the local community. Second was the funding of pilot projects in criminal-justice reform throughout the PCUS; these projects were to be initiated by church, community, and ecumenical groups and administered by the Criminal Justice Task Force of the General Assembly. A primary thrust of the projects was changing the criminal-justice system itself.

Countries of Southern Africa—Evangelistic Outreach

One-third of the 1977 Birthday Offering (about $140,000) went toward evangelistic outreach in newly independent nations in Southern Africa to provide funds for educating pastors and lay leaders, to provide literature for new church members, and to provide transportation for pastors to churches in remote areas. The offering was administered by the Division of International Mission under the direction of John Pritchard, area associate for Africa, Europe, and the Middle East.

The Birthday objective was designed to help the churches of Central and Southern Africa in their exciting work of evangelism and leadership training. The emphases of the funding were projects in evangelism in northern Mozambique, leadership development in Zaire through theological education, and witness through radio and literature in several African nations.

Mozambique, in 1997 a country of 8.5 million people, is a land that stretches along the southeastern coast of Africa. After almost five centuries of Portuguese colonial domination, Mozambique had been an independent nation for only two years in 1977, and colonial exploitation had left the country on the brink of economic bankruptcy. During

Portuguese rule, Protestants were not allowed to start churches or to evangelize in northern Mozambique. As individual Christians moved to the north, they began to organize small communities of faith, but these isolated congregations had no pastors and, because of colonial restrictions, they could not be helped by missions or churches in the south. With independence, the whole country became open to evangelistic efforts.

Although the opportunities for Christian witness in the northern part of the country were almost unlimited, the lack of financial resources made it difficult for Christians in southern Mozambique to share the gospel with their sisters and brothers in the north. Through the Christian Council of Mozambique, the 1977 Birthday Offering began a program of Christian outreach. At least two pastors were sent to the north to minister to the Christian communities already there and to reach out to the many persons who had not heard of the Good News of Jesus Christ. Some of the dollars helped acquire basic church facilities and housing, provided land rovers so pastors could travel to remote rural areas, and set up scholarships for the theological training of students from the north.

Another part of the offering began an endowment fund for theological education in Zaire and enabled the Presbyterian communities of Zaire to support the national theological seminary and to organize ministerial training programs at other educational levels. But not every church leader in Zaire could afford to spend several years in school, so in order to have pastors in the tens of thousands of villages and towns, a new method of training was developed—theological education by extension. In extension programs, teachers traveled from village to village on a regular basis, held classes for several days, then left behind self-study materials that could be studied until the teachers' next visits.

Part of the offering enabled churches in Africa to increase their witness and outreach through radio, audio-visuals, and literature. Though many people lived in isolated rural areas, radios were everywhere. Church councils and groups were already producing a wide variety of programs including Sunday worship services, religious music, short daily devotionals, and special Christmas and Easter broadcasts. Through the Birthday Offering, Women of the Church helped these ministries to continue and grow in African nations like Rwanda, Burundi, Swaziland, and Botswana.

The offering also provided new opportunities for evangelistic witness and Christian education through literature. PCUS missionary Mary Crawford had already revised and edited Bible commentaries in Tshiluba, one of the major languages in Zaire. With help from Birthday monies,

The Years before Merger 111

these much needed commentaries were printed. The monies also subsidized the printing and distribution of Bibles and short Scripture selections in other African languages such as Lingala, Swahili, Zulu, and Siswati.

The 1977 Birthday Offering made it possible for our Christian brothers and sisters in Africa to proclaim the Good News in places where the church was not yet visibly present, to those whose lives had not yet been touched by the joy and peace of Jesus Christ.

1978

Mexican-American Coordinating Council [Now Hispanic American Ministry Council], San Antonio, Texas

The theme of the 1978 Birthday Offering was "Then God's People Will Shine," taken from Matt. 13. "Through our Birthday Offering we can give, we can share, we can show concern. When we do, then all 'God's people will shine like the sun in the kingdom of their Father.'" The Offering in 1978 was divided equally between two differing needs in the U.S.A.—Mexican-American ministers and leaders in Texas and St. Columba Ministries in Norfolk, Virginia.

In Texas in 1978, there were 2.2 million Mexican Americans but only thirty-three active Hispanic-American Presbyterian churches with a total membership of about 3,200. One of the leaders among this group was Frank Diaz, an elder in the El Divino Salvador Church in Dallas. This elder had a vision for the future—more involvement of Hispanic-American Presbyterians in the life of the Presbyterian Church in the U.S. (PCUS). The Hispanic Americans wanted to be full partners in the church, not a minority group. In 1973, the Synod of Red River's Roundtable authorized the formation of an interim committee, chaired by Frank Diaz, to organize the Mexican-American Coordinating Council (MACC) as designed by the Interim Committee. Each presbytery in Texas was to name representation to MACC. With the formal organization of MACC, the council began to meet regularly, and the means for implementing the vision came into being. There were six ministers and seven lay persons on the council.

In January 1976, five major goals were adopted by MACC: 1) The recruitment of Mexican-American men and women into the gospel ministry; 2) the encouragement of Mexican-American pastors to participate in regular continuing education events; 3) leadership training throughout the congregations, especially those without pastors; 4) assistance given to involve the youth in the life of the churches, with participation in the annual youth conference at Mo-Ranch as one of the implementing strategies; and 5) development of lay pastors through training events to meet the needs of small congregations without pastors.

The 1978 Birthday Offering of approximately $250,000 was given to respond to the need for more Hispanic-American Presbyterian churches and to the need to provide professionally trained pastors and leaders. The money was deposited with the Texas Presbyterian Foundation, and funds from the offering were used at first to call a director of the Mexican-American Coordinating Council for three years and to subsidize leadership-training programs and conferences sponsored by the council. Part of the funds were used to recruit Hispanic-American Presbyterians, men and women, to attend seminaries to become fully trained and qualified pastors to bilingual churches. Selected lay leaders also qualified for theological training to enable them to lead small congregations.

In a letter dated March 5, 1997, from Angela Abrego, Associate Presbyter, Mission Presbytery, she wrote,

> The grant awarded to the Mexican American Coordinating Council (now Hispanic American Ministry Council) has indeed been a blessing to quite a number of persons and communities.

Amazingly, she states that:

> At the end of 1996 the total investment and cash [left in the account] were in the amount of $39,433.47. Since then we have awarded a couple of scholarships. We have one seminarian who will graduate in June and she has received the last of her scholarship funds. There is one seminarian who has finished his first two semesters, starting on his third, and we are praying for a new student to begin.
>
> The scholarships have been set up at $3,000.00 for a school year and $750.00 during the summer, should the student take courses then. For D.Min programs the amount has been set at $500.00 per session. Enclosed is a list of persons who have been recipients. . . . Some of these pastors are in Anglo congregations and some are in Executive positions.

She enclosed a list of thirty-six persons who graduated between 1978 and 1997—seventeen from Austin Presbyterian Theological Seminary, twelve

The Years before Merger 113

from McCormick Theological Seminary, one from Yale, one from Perkins School of Theology, one from San Francisco Theological Seminary, one from Union Theological Seminary (Virginia), one from PSCE, one continuing education grant to study in Mexico, one loan, and summer sessions.

The third name on the list is that of the Rev. Frank Diaz, the person who was so instrumental in organizing MACC. He graduated from Austin Presbyterian Theological Seminary in 1982 and is, at time of publication, Acting Director of the General Assembly Council. A recipient of two grants (M.Div. Austin Seminary 1982 and D.Min. San Francisco Seminary), Dr. Patty Lane works as an Associate in Program with Self-Development of People in Louisville.

Abrego concludes:

> The grant from the Birthday Offering has been a gift of immeasurable value to the Hispanic Community in the Synod of the Sun. It has been a gift which not only served to provide an education for all these people but, through them, has touched and been a light for all those to whom they have ministered and continue to minister to. What has been done has been a marvelous thing for which we continue to be grateful.

What an incredible track record for one Birthday Offering! Good stewardship and wise management have stretched dollars and strengthened the Presbyterian Church (U.S.A.) in ways that will go on into the future as more people are reached with the Good News of the Gospel.

St. Columba Ministries [Now St. Columba Ecumenical Ministries, Inc.]

In 1978, nearly 6,000 people, many below the poverty level, were living in the run-down Robin Hood Apartments in Norfolk, Virginia. The two-story barracks-like buildings each housed four apartments. Some of the fathers of families living there were at sea for months on end. Mothers were left with small children, handling all of the bills and the responsibilities of raising their family. The crime rate was terribly high, and the women stayed inside their apartments, frightened of their neighborhood. Within this privately owned complex, right behind the rental office, St. Columba Presbyterian Church established the St. Columba Ministries.

In the early 1970s, it was decided to put the efforts of the St. Columba congregation into major community outreach. In cooperation with the Mission Group on Persons in Special Need of the Synod of the Virginias, and the Special Ministries Committee of Norfolk Presbytery, the congregation launched the Family Center Ministry at St. Columba.

In 1978, St. Columba Church was pastored by a clergy couple living on one salary. The church had only twenty-five members, and many of these members did triple duty serving as teachers, recreation leaders, baby-sitters, janitors, repair people, and countless other tasks, though they worked elsewhere at full-time jobs.

The Women of the Church gave one-half of the 1978 Birthday Offering (approximately $205,700) to support this ministry. The money was designated to provide a combined day-care center and kindergarten that reaches out to both children and parents. It provided for the employment of a person to work with juveniles, those who had already committed offenses, and those who seemed to be headed in that direction. The offering also provided funds for recreational programs for those in the four-to-twelve age bracket. Through the careful stewardship of the funds, the Women of the Church Offering was able to provide funds for the ministry into 1982 when the final Birthday dollars were disbursed. Alice Taylor, the current Director of the St. Columba Ministries, began her employment in 1978 as the Child and Teen Worker.

In 1978, bad news also came to the St. Columba Church. The city of Norfolk announced that they were purchasing the Robin Hood Apartments and would level them to make way for an industrial complex. Nevertheless, the new wing for the Child Development was built, and the Child and Teen Worker hired. The process of closing St. Columba came in 1982 with the decision to dissolve the congregation. The vote was taken by the congregation in December 1982 and ratified by Presbytery in April 1983. The church property was sold and the new wing was disassembled and moved to the campus of Old Dominion University for Norfolk Presbytery's University Presbyterian Ministry. The money from the sale of property was set aside by Presbytery as the Community Ministries Fund. The St. Columba Ministries moved its offices to Azalea Garden Road.

The history of St. Columba has not yet ended. Presbytery acted to allow the St. Columba Ministries to become an independent agency in the Tidewater area. On January 1, 1987, St. Columba Ecumenical Ministries, Inc., took over the operation and program that Presbyterians in Norfolk Presbytery had long supported.

The ministries of St. Columba today have grown beyond imagination and, with the support of community and cooperation of denominations, are truly remarkable. For example, one hundred families per month receive a four-day supply of food, almost 4,500 hours of volunteer service are donated, and more than $55,000 in in-kind gifts, including $40,000 in food, are made.

St. Columba proudly claims a Presbyterian heritage. Presbyterian women in our churches can proudly claim that they once played a small part in the ministry.

1979

Mission through Education

The theme of the 1979 Birthday Offering was Mission through Education. Jesus told his disciples, "You are the light of the world" (Matt. 5:14). The Apostle Paul wrote to the Corinthians, God shines forth in the "light of the knowledge" revealed through Jesus Christ (2 Cor. 4:6). "The light shines in the darkness," the gospel of John proclaimed, "and the darkness has not overcome it" (John 1:5). In 1979, at Birthday Celebrations across the denomination, Women of the Church affirmed that Presbyterians wanted to let the "light of the knowledge" of Jesus Christ shine forth in wider circles—from a lamp in the home to a city on a hill, even as the light of the world—through the objectives chosen for the 1979 Birthday Offering, Mission through Education.

Christian Higher Education Ministries

The Women of the Church gave approximately two-thirds of the 1979 Birthday Offering (over $200,000) to Christian Higher Education Ministries to be administered by the General Assembly's Task Force on Higher Education. A great portion of the offering went to the $250,000 Challenge Grant Fund (see below). The theme was "Changes and Challenges—New directions in mission for Christian Higher Education." The educational/promotional article in the May 1979 issue of *Presbyterian Women* began as follows:

> Communication; Challenge; Commitment: These three words are no strangers to Presbyterian women. Indeed, they are hallmarks of great accomplishments as church women over the years have sought to strengthen and support a variety of important fields of mission throughout the world. . . . The challenge is to find new and exciting ways to carry out the mission of higher education—and the commitment is to the stewardship of knowledge as it is entrusted to us by God.

The 1979 offering focused on Mission through Education.

Presbyterian women have an "opportunity to help the church re-think, regain, and re-articulate this commitment."

It was envisioned that the 1979 Birthday Offering would strengthen Christian Higher Education as a field of mission for the whole Church—local churches, campus ministries, and church colleges—all working together in a renewed partnership. The funds were designated to *communicate* the crisis in Christian Higher Education to the Church through seminars and workshops at all levels; *challenge* the Church to explore new forms of ministry by establishing a $250,000 "Special Challenge Grant Fund" to be used to initiate new projects and to encourage mutual programs in which local churches and colleges would work together; and *commit* the Church to its stewardship and partnership in Christian Higher Education as its field of mission.

The Presbyterian Church, U.S., authorized by the 117th General Assembly in 1977, placed a three-year emphasis, through 1981, on the Church's mission through higher education. Major changes in society had drastically altered the conditions in the church-related colleges, and the Assembly felt it was time to call the Church back to its heritage in Christian Higher Education. A special task force was organized with representation from across the denomination. Some of their task was to look at ways for campus ministry to take place on the campuses of state universities in light of the large number of Presbyterians attending these institutions. Another important task was to study ways local congregations could become more involved in these ministries. The third task was in exploring ways church-related colleges fit into this mission.

In 1979, the Women of the Church became partners with the denomination by helping to open Christian Higher Education as a field of mission for the whole church.

Ecumenical Institute, Bossey, Switzerland

Through the 1979 Birthday Offering of the Women of the Church, our church reached out in partnership with our global Christian family. One-third of the Birthday Offering (approximately $115,000) went to Bossey Ecumenical Institute, to be administered by its board of directors to provide short-term educational opportunities for theological students, missionaries, and pastors and to provide seminars for groups of church lay leaders to put their concerns into an international perspective.

The Institute is located on a campus in a little Swiss village nestled amid rural farmland above Geneva. Since right after World War II in 1946, Bossey has been a place where Christians have met each other across all boundaries and divisions and have been opened to fresh perspectives about the church and the world. It is a Christian community whose primary work is developing teachers and leaders for the future. Several hundred persons from more than fifty countries come each year to study the Bible together, to appreciate and understand one another's cultures and Christian experiences, and to explore together what the Gospel says about the issues of our time. Bossey is a miniature version of the whole global Christian community struggling to discover what faithfulness to Jesus Christ means in our time.

More than 80 percent of the students who come to Bossey are from the Third World—Africa, Latin America, Asia, and the Pacific. In promotional material for the offering, it stated,

> If the destiny of the church is in its future leadership, Bossey is one of the most important institutions at work these days to fulfill the mission of the church as understood by the Presbyterian Church in the United States.

A student at Columbia Theological Seminary, Lib McGregor Simmons, described her experiences at a two-week summer course at Bossey in the May 1979 issue of *Presbyterian Women.*

> For two weeks in the summer of 1978, I immersed myself in a sea of experiences at the Ecumenical Institute. . . . The particular course in which I was involved was one for students, "Christian Vigilance and Solidarity on Six Continents." . . . Sixty participants—students who are active churchfolk on their own continents and in their own denominations—students who are straining to understand what the church universal might do and say to the burning, divisive issues of the day [were brought together for the summer course].

Lib continued, at Bossey

> . . . study is active engagement with one another as each participant passionately speaks of her or his own cultural experience . . . so I learn as I argue, discuss, and even shed a few tears with real people. . . . Bossey is also worship. Every morning dawned with gathering of the community in song and prayer. [Back home on campus] I cherish the rekindling of the richness and diversity that worship can embody when various cultural experiences are valued and employed. I will never forget the

moving sound of the Doxology with each worshipper praising God . . . by intoning the familiar words in one's native language . . . I will treasure the redemptive experience of passing the peace to someone with whom there had been a continuing conflict as we struggled to understand each other . . . I have begun to see that the church of Jesus Christ is much more than the Presbyterian Church in the United States.

The Associate Presbyter for Mission in the Presbytery of Western North Carolina and, until her ordination, a fellow church member, Bobbi White, recently shared something of her experiences at a five-month graduate-school course during the fiftieth anniversary year at Bossey. There were sixty Christians from thirty-five countries all over the globe, mostly pastors and seminarians, but some laity. The mix was about two-thirds men and one-third women. The group studied, worshiped, and lived together. For some of the participants, it was a new experience to see women read the Bible and pray in public worship. There were more Presbyterians than any other denomination from Rwanda, South Africa, Brazil, Jamaica, Taiwan, and the United States. For Bobbi, part of the excitement and value of the experience was the mix of the faculty—Roman Catholic, Orthodox, Lutheran, and Reformed.

Also part of the excitement for Bobbi was to listen as women in the third world expressed their faith and shared how they contributed to the church in those areas where they live. She recalled Myramyr from Burma, who teaches in a seminary, and how she returned home empowered as a woman and with a new vision of the many and varied ways God is working in the world today. She summed it up by saying that the purpose of Bossey is "Ecumenical formation—to learn from each other Christian traditions and to broaden our understanding of how God is acting in the world." In a letter dated May 20, 1997, the newly elected Director General (and first woman director) of the Ecumenical Institute at Bossey, Heidi Hadsell, wrote:

> I am aware of the 1979 Birthday Offering that went to Bossey. People close to Bossey still mention it with some frequency . . .
>
> Bossey continues to be an open place of encounter and creative education across national and denominational lines. Both the fall graduate school and the winter, spring, summer seminars continue with energy and creativity. . . . Bossey, it seems, is ever more important today in a world marred by increased parochialism and nationalism. It will also

continue to be important as the World Council of churches evolves. . . .
Three Presbyterian students from the USA will be at Bossey this fall.

Dr. Hadsell has served for nine years as Dean of the Faculty and Vice-President of Academic Affairs at McCormick Theological Seminary in Chicago.

1980

Youth in Service—The Tithe of Life

The enthusiastic response of the youthful Isaiah when called upon by the Lord for service was, "Here I am, Lord, send me" (Isa. 6:18). In an explanation of the 1980 Birthday Offering objective, William Ross Forbes, Staff Associate for Youth Ministry, said that:

> . . . there are hundreds of young men and women throughout the Presbyterian Church, U.S. who have an equally enthusiastic desire to serve their church in a significant manner. . . . What avenues of service are available for them? . . . What if this individual wants to work in his or her church?

In the brochure developed for the 1980 objective, a scenario is presented.

> Imagine, if you will, that you are in your early twenties; you are about to graduate from college, or perhaps you graduated several years ago. You are an individual who has been closely related to the church for your entire life. Your childhood memories of the church are good ones. During your college years you have become aware that the church will always be an important part of your life in the future. You are enthusiastic, feel pretty good about who you are as a person, and your outlook on life is positive. What you are really interested in doing is some meaningful work with young people.

The 1980 Women of the Church Birthday Offering provided a unique avenue for just such a service. Through "Youth in Service—The Tithe of Life," the Women of the Church answered the call of these young adults described above by providing means for an internship program to enable young adults to be involved in youth ministries in churches with small memberships. Their primary responsibility was to develop a significant

The Years before Merger 121

Youth in Service provides internship programs for young adults.

program for the youth in the churches they served and to develop lay leadership to continue this ministry in the future.

Through the 1980 Birthday Offering of more than $500,000, young adults of the PCUS were given an opportunity to offer two years in service by assisting congregations in developing their youth ministry programs (youth from sixth through twelfth grades) and at the same time to benefit personally from firsthand experience what it means to serve the church. It was, in effect, a training program for young adults that enabled them to become engaged in youth-ministry leadership and to make a visible and meaningful commitment of their life in service to their church. As noted, people selected were asked to tithe two years of their life. They took part in a six-week intensive training in summer, then were placed in churches. The young people were encouraged to use their creativity in developing new ministries for youth. At the same time, participating presbyteries and congregations agreed to provide an effective support system that would help the young interns grow in faith and develop organizational communication skills. The plan was for fifty young adults to be involved. They worked in ten presbyteries for the first year, then another ten in the next year.

For young adults in the PCUS, the 1980 Birthday Offering provided opportunities to say, "Here I am, Lord, send me." For the Women of the Church, it was a sound investment in future church leadership.

1981

God's World, One in Christ—PCUS Seminaries *(See boldface entries below for gift disbursements)*

As was the custom, the objective for the 1981 Birthday Offering presented to the women began with a scriptural and theological basis.

> "I gave them the same glory you gave me, so that they may be one, just as you and I are one. I in them and you in me, so that they may be completely one, in order that the world may know that you sent me and that you love them as you love me." (John 17:22–23)

The presentation continued:

> There is a hard reality in the idea that the world is to be one in Christ. Two thousand years ago slavery was an accepted policy, women had few rights, and the Roman rulers were cruel beyond description; yet Jesus was born into that world and for that world died. The Holy Spirit, continuing the ministry of Jesus Christ, deals with our world just as it is—war-prone, hungry, and selfish for oil—in order to bring to it the peace of God. . . . It is the responsibility of our seminaries to train their graduates in such a way that they become more deeply aware of, and more responsible for, evangelism in the United States and throughout the world.

A project to stimulate global awareness and involvement in the four Presbyterian, U.S. theological seminaries received the entire 1981 Women of the Church Birthday Offering. The offering of more than $500,000 was divided equally among the four seminaries: Austin Presbyterian Theological Seminary, Austin, Texas; Columbia Theological Seminary, Decatur, Georgia; Louisville Presbyterian Theological Seminary, Louisville, Kentucky; and Union Theological Seminary, Richmond, Virginia. The offering was given to encourage faculty and students as they prepared the church for its ministry throughout the world.

The title of the joint proposal dated September 19, 1979, was "That the World Might be WON and Become ONE." The stated purpose was "to strengthen and expand the national and world mission ministries of the four seminaries of our Presbyterian Church in the United States." The objectives were listed:

> To help the four theological seminaries expand their efforts to instill a missionary spirit in our ministerial candidates, to broaden the perspectives of seminary professors, to develop an awareness of the spiritual resources and needs of people in overseas countries, and to relate the evangelism emphasis of the gospel to the needs of the world.

The time proposed to accomplish the objectives was five years. During this five-year period, the seminaries had time to develop sources of funds to carry on those activities that had proved helpful and successful for the continued mission-minded development of students and faculty.

Each of the seminaries outlined their plans for accomplishing the objectives. At **Union**, the plan included Evangelism and Mission Study Events (including continuing education courses), student exchange, teacher exchange, and travel-study seminars. At **Columbia**, the plan was to be accomplished by exchange of students in seminaries in third world countries, by faculty exchanges between Columbia and seminaries in other countries, and by inviting visiting lecturers from other countries to come to Columbia. At **Louisville**, the plan was to invite a missionary or professor in a theological seminary from India, Africa, or South America to be a visiting professor, to send out professors to other countries to raise their consciousness about the world mission of the church, to work in cooperation with the Division of International Mission to send students to other countries for mission work and study, and, under the supervision of one of the professors, take small groups of students to a foreign theological center.

At **Austin**, the shape of the plan was impacted by the geographical fact that the Republic of Mexico is a close neighbor, and the seminary planned to establish cooperation between Austin Seminary and the Presbyterian Seminary in Mexico City. Plans included exchange of faculty and students, visits by selected students and faculty to the Mexico border area where mission and evangelism projects were under way, similar cooperation with at least one other country in the Third World, a call on the resources of the Asian communities that were developing rapidly in the Synod of Red River (now Synod of the Sun), and expansion of the world mission collection in the seminary library.

The proposal was signed by the four presidents: Jack M. Maxwell of Austin, J. Davison Philips of Columbia, C. Ellis Nelson of Louisville, and Fred R. Stair Jr. of Union in Richmond.

In response to inquiries about if and how the 1981 Birthday Offering had affected an awareness of and involvement in world mission, letters were received from all four of the seminaries. From Austin Seminary a most impressive six-page report was received. Unfortunately, space limitations do not allow for its inclusion in this history. Dr. Robert M. Shelton, Acting President and Academic Dean, wrote on February 12, 1997:

> I well remember the generous gift of the Women of the Church to our seminary in 1981. . . . The money was a tremendous resource for us, and we tried to plan and use it wisely. It was used for everything from library acquisitions to special lectures to faculty development to student travel. I am enclosing a final report which was produced by one of our professors summarizing how the money was spent during that decade.

The report states that the Women of the Church money enabled the seminary to rejuvenate the Settles Lectures (he mentions seven of the lecturers) and made it possible to establish and to provide partial funding for a Synod of the Sun Mission Conference. The seminary began a missionary-in-residence program, updated curriculum to include a required course on mission and evangelism, and included a special track on mission and evangelism in a revised Doctor of Ministry program. Professors from overseas were part of the program and courses for credit were conducted in relation to travel in Israel and Central America. There were many more components of the program including conferences, Spanish language instruction, racial/ethnic concerns, visitors to campus, and international students. "The Birthday Offering allowed the seminary to expand the number of international students receiving scholarships," and the list includes eighteen names from Kenya, India, Germany, Korea, Austria, Cameroon, and Thailand.

The report concludes:

> It is not possible to gauge the overall impact of the WOC/BO [Women of the Church Birthday Offering] upon the faculty and students of Austin Seminary and others within the reach of these persons and of the literature produced by them. It is safe to say, however, that most, if not all, have a new and more positive consciousness of the importance of mission and evangelism in the life of the church. . . . This is in sharp contrast to preceding decades. . . . It seems clear that the Women of the Church discovered a way in which they could influence the life and thought of the seminaries in the denomination. Austin Seminary wishes to express its

The Years before Merger

profound gratitude to the women's organization for their provision of resources which made it possible for the institution to address afresh and creatively this long neglected area of mission and evangelism.

In a report from Columbia Seminary prepared by Dr. Davison Philips, former President of the Seminary, it states that the funds from the 1981 Birthday Offering were used in the following ways: 1) implementation and expansion of supervised ministry experiences of every student in the Master of Divinity program through alternative context placements for the winter term; 2) faculty used sabbatical or personal leave to attend seminars in Jamaica, Central America, Korea, and Japan, and a supervised alternative context experience for many students was established with the West Indies Theological Seminary in Jamaica; 3) sharing of students with others on their return from these experiences; 4) faculty, administration, and board members began to formulate a number of ways to reach a goal of "globalizing theological education"; 5) faculty was expanded to call Professors of Evangelism and World Christianity, and students and faculty "have been exchanged between Columbia and the Seminary in Nanjing, China; 6) placements in some of the most depressed areas of the United States; and 7) a stream of visiting faculty and students from around the world. The Birthday Offering was "seed money" to get programs started and came at a crucial time in developing the programs.

Dr. Douglas W. Oldenburg, President of Columbia Seminary, wrote in a letter dated January 31, 1997:

> As you can see from his [Dr. Philips's] report, the Birthday Offering Gift has had lasting and significant effects at Columbia. The International Program at Columbia has become a hallmark of our seminary and nationally esteemed. It has had a profound impact on both students and faculty. . . . Columbia Seminary is profoundly grateful for the support we have received from Presbyterian Women.

Grayson L. Tucker Jr., now retired, who was Dean of Louisville Seminary at the time of the Birthday Offering in 1981, replied for President John Mulder:

> The immediate accomplishment [of the gift] was an increase in the flow of students from overseas, the bringing onto our campus of several church leaders for a January term or a semester of teaching, and making possible a trip I made in 1983 for about three and a half

weeks with John Pritchard (coordinator for Africa) as leader to visit Ghana, Zaire, and Kenya. There were about 20 clergy from the PCUS on that journey. Several years after our return I coordinated a visit from Beatrice Affum, the principal of a school we visited in Ghana, among the churches of the pastors who made the trip. Thus began a similar practice of bringing people to Louisville on a regular, every-other-year basis. One of these was Abiel Matitsoane Moseme of Lesotho who received a D.Min. degree at Louisville and is now president of the Seminary in Lesotho. LPTS has developed a "sister seminary" relationship with that seminary. Another D.Min. student from Taiwan, Han-Luan Chih, became Professor of Homiletics at Yushan Theological College and is now its President. He served as Moderator of the Presbyterian Church of Taiwan.

These are illustrative of the impact of the offering. These also illustrate the ongoing impact of a seminary culture altered to take much more seriously the international nature of our mission.

He goes on to mention the later establishment of an Endowed Chair in International Mission and Evangelism. Resources have been found

> . . . to bring six or so new overseas students to our campus each year. . . . John [the President] came to Louisville . . . with a deep conviction about the internationalization of theological education. The change in culture here helped strengthen that conviction which, in turn, further deepened the culture change.

Dr. Louis Weeks of Union Theological Seminary in Richmond wrote February 12, 1997:

> I understand that the money from the Women of the Church was expended here to begin a program of partnership with the Presbyterian Church and subsequently with the Evangelical Presbyterian Church in Ghana. We have had more than ten years of significant trips to Ghana by groups of students and faculty of Union Seminary. In addition, the seed money enabled us to begin to invite Ghanian pastors to come to Union Seminary for an educational experience. My understanding is that more than twenty have come so far, and we receive two each year. Currently Dr. Daniel Antwi is here, the principal of Trinity Theological in Lagon (ACCRA) Ghana. He is teaching on "Hospitality According to the Bible

The Years before Merger 127

and the African Experience." His course is exceedingly fine, and we had a good group to the house just last week for supper talking to him about the church there. . . . Thank you and other Presbyterian Women for your support. We deeply appreciate these gifts you have made and the many other ways that you have helped Union Seminary.

Presbyterian women can rejoice in the role they played sixteen years ago in making it possible for four Presbyterian theological seminaries "to address afresh and creatively this long neglected area of mission and evangelism."

1982

Ministry with Families in Need

The theme for the 1982 Birthday Offering was Ministry with Families in Need. The Scripture passage used was from Acts 2:39—"For the promise is to you and to your children and to all that are far off everyone whom the Lord our God calls to himself." The offering was used to enable families to combine their human resources in caring for each other as they worked together. These projects offered the opportunity for the church to become partners with these families as the Women of the Church sought to be the people God intended them to be.

Edmarc Hospice for Children, Inc.

Edmarc is a private, nonprofit organization which offers supportive care to terminally ill children and their families in Tidewater, Virginia. Edmarc's approach is based on the hospice concept of care that seeks to meet the physical, emotional, social, and spiritual needs of the patient and family through an interdisciplinary team approach. One-half of the 1982 Birthday Offering (approximately $300,000) was designated for this ministry whose purpose is "to provide supportive services to families of terminally ill children, to strengthen the family, and to witness to God's healing powers" (Edmarc brochure).

Edmarc started as an idea and a dream of a small steering committee at Suffolk Presbyterian Church in 1978. It became an organization providing a unique ministry to a special group of children and their families. The inspiration which guides Edmarc is reflected in its name—*Ed* for the Rev. Edward Page, pastor of Suffolk Presbyterian Church when the steering committee was formed, and *Marc* for Marcus Hogge, a child in

Edmarc Hospice brochure.

the congregation who was a victim of a terminal neurological illness. Ed Page provided the leadership and direction that guided Edmarc's early development. He died in April 1979 of a recurrent brain tumor. Young Marcus Hogge was the emotional impetus for the program and focused attention on the need for services for children like himself. Marcus died in February 1980 at home with his family.

Hospices exist in almost every city and community across our denomination. Edmarc is somewhat unique because it provides for the needs of children and their families through a coordinated home-care program. A specially trained nurse is assigned to each family that decides, with their doctor's advice, to take their child home. The nurse coordinates all the services needed by the family and is available to them day or night for any reason. Working with the family and the child, she or he develops an individualized care plan and arranges for the personnel and services to carry out this plan. Services may include physical therapy, counseling services, medical support, and recreational therapy. The aim of home care is to help the child live life to the fullest with maximum comfort and support.

Volunteers who have been trained to give the kind of spiritual, physical, and emotional support needed supplement the professional support. The family's own pastor and congregation are included in forming a support team. Much of the support needed is in such areas as child care, housework, and transportation. Close contact is maintained with the child's physician at all times.

The Years before Merger

Despite the best of supportive care, the pain of death for parents, siblings, and others cannot be avoided. The home-care nurse helps the family deal with the child's impending death. This may include describing what the final moments will be like when the child dies and helping with necessary funeral arrangements. Care does not, however, stop there. The support system continues to help the family after the child dies.

According to Julie S. Sligh, Executive Director of Edmarc, in a letter dated April 25, 1997, Edmarc Hospice for Children, Inc., has served 467 families, more than 2,100 people, since the Birthday Offering was received in 1982. Edmarc now provides services in seven cities and two counties. The agency employs or contracts with more than fifty people to provide highly skilled and compassionate care to families of children who have life-threatening illnesses or conditions. More than one hundred families are under Edmarc's hospice care or receiving Edmarc's comprehensive bereavement support services on any given day.

Ms. Sligh, describing Edmarc services today, said:

> Edmarc Hospice for Children has a two-fold ministry. One aspect of care is the professional, technical care that is necessary to keep a very sick child at home in his or her own bedroom, for as long and as much as possible. Edmarc has highly qualified pediatric nurses to do everything from bed baths to blood transfusions. The other aspect is the family support system where a multitude of services are provided to the siblings, parents, grandparents and, sometimes, to the extended family.

One of the services of Edmarc is a bereavement program of Edmarc Hospice for Children called "Project M.A.G.I.C.," an acronym for My Active Grieving Instills Courage. The goals are to support families through a time when they may feel vulnerable and isolated, to educate families on the grief process, and to help prevent the complications of grief. The services include visits, phone calls, notes, a memorial service, retreats that allow time for parents to deal with specific issues of their grief, educational materials, bereavement news letter, parent (or moms and dads separately) and sibling support groups, and Camp M.A.G.I.C., a camping weekend for the entire family in a safe and supportive environment.

Just as the number of children and families served by Edmarc has grown, so have the resources and support. Covered health-care services are reimbursed by insurance. Edmarc is a United Way agency and receives support through Combined Campaigns. It is an ecumenical agency in that it receives support from a number of churches of various denominations.

Project M.A.G.I.C. receives support from Ronald McDonald Children's Services and grants from sources such as Tidewater's Children's Foundation. Edmarc has formed partnership with Children's Hospital of the King's Daughters (CHKD) in a cooperative effort to facilitate bereaved parents groups. Civic groups such as Kiwanis and Norfolk Jaycees are involved in support and activities. It is evidence of what happens when churches and communities get involved in a serious way.

Ms. Sligh wrote, "Edmarc has been an instrument of peace at a time of terrible crisis for families. There is no doubt that God's hand is on this work." Presbyterian Women can rejoice that they had a part in the early stages of this ministry through the 1982 Women of the Church Birthday Offering in helping it "to get off the ground."

Pembroke Area Presbyterian Ministry (Project Green Thumb)—Pembroke, North Carolina

One-half of the 1982 Women of the Church Birthday Offering ($300,000) was given to the Pembroke Area Presbyterian Ministry for Project Green Thumb, a nutritional development program for the Lumbee Indians of Pembroke, North Carolina. The Pembroke Presbyterian Ministry requested the offering "to provide low income persons, ninety-two percent of whom are Native Americans, simple, more self-reliant tools to cope with the rising cost of food and the necessity to improve their diet. . . . The people are malnourished, illiterate, and impoverished. Their land is deficient."

The project was comprised of two major components: a Nutrition Education Program and a Food Supply Program. The Nutrition Education Program included the creation of nutrition information resources tailored to the needs of the Pembroke community; the development of a Farmers' Market, which would provide a location to purchase fresh food, to sell excess food for supplementary income, and a place for sharing nutrition information; and the formation of Home Demonstration Clubs to train low-income persons to prepare food nutritionally and to share those skills with others in their neighborhoods.

The Food Supply Program focused on helping people grow food on small parcels of land and preserving their food for use during the winter months. The plan was for four community gardens to be equipped with basic tools for gardening, fertilizer, and seed for the first year. The land was divided among the enrolled participants. It was planned that a mobile cannery, which could handle up to 2,000 jars a day, be purchased and operated by the program to provide a safe and economical means of preserving the produce the participants themselves had raised or purchased through the Farmers' Market. Each person who used the cannery, according to the program, would be asked to contribute some of their produce to a community food closet to provide food for the needy.

The Lumbee Indians of eastern North Carolina were a peaceful tribe situated in a region of early colonization and among a fairly populous rural area of early settlers. Since they did not wage war against the United States, they had no treaty with the federal government and were denied status as an Indian tribe, ineligible for government aid. In the early years, the land was productive, but as time went on, the land was depleted. Robeson County, where Pembroke is located, is the largest in the state in land area but, in 1982, was the poorest. Out of a population of 30,000, a third of the families had incomes too low to provide adequate food for their families. More than 37 percent of the adult Lumbees were functionally illiterate. The combination of low income and illiteracy made "Project Green Thumb" a twofold challenge.

The Director of the Pembroke Community Workshop wrote in the proposal for the funding:

> This work will be carried out with heavy reliance on participant responsibility, and a small staff to train and assist volunteers. Two interns will be recruited each year to direct the ongoing operation of the project. This will provide community ministry experience for recent college graduates and seminary interns.

In early March in a telephone conversation with Robert Miller, Executive Presbyter of the Presbytery of Coastal Carolina, he said he has no knowledge of this ministry in the Pembroke area at this time. The work was obviously phased out. A letter of inquiry was sent to the Rev. John Robinson, former Director of the Pembroke Community Workshop, but no response was received. The author did learn that statistics from the 1990 census showed that unemployment in Robeson County was 7.5 percent, a marked difference eight years after the 1982 project.

1983

White Cross Shipping Fund

"Seeing the injured person he had compassion and went over and bandaged the wounds" (Luke 10:33–34). To enable Presbyterians to witness through a ministry that shows their interest in and love for people of all nationalities and races and to witness to the power of God's love, the Women's Coordinating Committee of the Synod of the Southeast (Georgia and South Carolina) proposed the 1983 Birthday Offering.

In 1922, Hallie Paxson Winsborough visited mission fields in the Orient. That visit inspired the first Birthday Offering to "Miss Dowd's School" in Japan. Less known is the fact that Mrs. Winsborough was touched by the desperate need for medical supplies at the hospitals she visited. Upon her return to the United States, she challenged the women to come to the aid of their overseas partners and suggested that local groups make some of the items needed by the hospitals. Thus, in 1923, the White Cross program was born to supply materials to hospitals and clinics abroad. Ever since the first packages were sent, medical mission has benefitted from White Cross gifts.

On the sixtieth anniversary of the initiation of the White Cross program, the Women of the Church decided to designate the 1983 Birthday Offering for an endowment fund to undergird the work of Presbyterian medical missions and to insure the continuation of delivering medical supplies overseas. The cost of freight had greatly increased through the years, and the amount of money given to overseas hospitals by U.S. AID for reimbursable freight had been drastically cut. Furthermore, changes were constantly taking place in the work of overseas hospitals. Both the Presbyterian Church, U.S. (PCUS) and the United Presbyterian Church, U.S.A. (UPUSA) were encouraging preventive work rather than curative work. The countries to which gifts were sent were changing, and the specific items requested by hospitals and clinics changed almost every year. It was decided that money from the 1983 Birthday Offering (more than $550,000) would be invested by the Presbyterian Foundation and the interest used to pay freight costs. The funds would be administered by the Director of the Office of World Service/World Hunger and the Staff Associate for Church World Service, Division of Corporate and Social Mission.

White Cross was a voluntary service project through which health-care supplies were made or purchased for use in international mission hospitals and clinics. In the early days, many of the supplies either could not be purchased in the overseas country or were prohibitively expensive to purchase. Requests for supplies were tabulated in Atlanta and divided among the synods and presbyteries. Each Women of the Church group in presbyteries received a "quota" and divided these requests equitably among the local women's groups. The White Cross program was originally directed to three overseas mission sites—China, Korea, and the Belgian Congo (now Zaire).

Many hours of service were given to this area of mission by women in the churches. Groups of local women either made or purchased gauze squares, bandages, baby clothes, surgical gowns, pajamas, towels, sheets, and uniforms. For many years, rolling bandages from strips of donated, used sheets was a tradition in the churches. Baby layettes and other items were proudly displayed at annual meetings. For the women, each item was a gift of love and compassion. For the receiving hospitals, in the words of two of the missionaries in Zaire, "White Cross is our salvation," and "White Cross is the difference of beds with sheets or no sheets" (Nancy and Walter Hall, Zaire). Dan Sheperd [sic], Director of the Good Shepherd Hospital, which in 1981 was using 300 four-inch by four-inch bandages daily, said that White Cross "keeps us going" (Margaret Montgomery, White Cross, Atlanta). Similar endorsements and letters of appreciation were received from missionaries in Korea, South Africa, Lesotho, and Haiti.

In 1983, White Cross supplies assisted eleven hospitals and some forty clinics in four countries around the world. These included medical centers in Zaire, Lesotho, Haiti, and Korea. White Cross Sewing supplies went to an additional five hospitals in Korea. These supplies made it possible for the hospitals to maintain a high quality of service at low cost for the patients of low-economic status.

An example of the kind of ministry White Cross had in 1983 is that of providing specified supplies to the Kasai rural clinics in Zaire. The Kasai Rural Clinics Program is a medical ministry of the Presbyterian Church of Zaire in small villages. The rural clinics asked for linens for the sixty-five dispensaries in the Rural Clinics Program, such as towels and curtains; sheets with a hole in the center to be used for small wounds and instrument table covers; uniforms—both men's white medical jackets and women's scrub dresses; and dressings and bandages of all kinds.

In 1981, the Presbyterian Church, U.S. was moving toward reunion with the United Presbyterian Church, U.S.A., and there were quite a few "union" presbyteries. A new program was begun in 1981 for women in these union presbyteries—the White Cross Sewing program. Instead of receiving a list of requests from the PCUS White Cross program *and* a request for sewing and supplies from the UPUSA, one combined request was received by the presbytery chairperson and then distributed to the local groups. In addition to hospitals and clinics overseas, this program included national projects such as children's homes and urban centers.

As costs of freight increased, the amount of money required from the women for shipment also increased. The Women of the Church contributions for shipping costs in 1981 was more than $50,000. This was money that could have been used to buy additional supplies. The Birthday Offering in 1993 made available a permanent fund, the interest of which insures that the supplies are transported by ocean freight from the Brethren Service Center, New Windsor, Maryland, where they are packed to designated hospitals and clinics in response to official requests.

In 1983, the annual cost of ocean freight exceeded $100,000. The fifty cents per pound sent by the women simply was not enough. It was anticipated that the 1983 Birthday Offering, together with continued U.S. AID reimbursement, plus a small amount per pound, would be adequate to cover shipping costs.

In 1988, after more than three years of planning and working together, the National Executive Committee of United Presbyterian Women and the Women of the Church Committee of Women of the Church completed plans for a new organization, Presbyterian Women—a merger of the two organizations. A part of the new organizational plan was Creative Ministries, the program that directs the offerings. It was decided and affirmed that the traditional Birthday Offerings of Women of the Church in the Spring, the Thank Offering of United Presbyterian Women in the Fall, and the White Cross/Sewing projects of both would be continued. Today, the White Cross program and Summer Sewing are carried on as part of the annual Thank Offering (including Health Ministries).

According to Jean Cutler, Associate for Mission Participation, who staffs the Creative Ministries Committee, the "White Cross Endowment Fund" continues to be a much needed and valuable resource in providing for the ongoing ministry of delivering medical supplies overseas.

1984

Third World Church Leadership Center, Seoul, Korea

The message of Paul to the church in Philippi might be the message of the churches in the United States to the Presbyterian Church in Korea: "Thankful for your partnership in the Gospel" (Phil. 1:5). Thus was stated the theme of the 1984 Women of the Church Birthday Offering—partnership in the Gospel. The entire 1984 Birthday Offering (more than $525,000) was designated for the Third World Church Leadership Center in celebration of partnership with the Korean Presbyterian Church.

Dr. Cyrus H. Moon, Director of the Third World Leadership Center, wrote in the May 1984 issue of *Presbyterian Women*:

> As the church in the Third World increases in strength and begins to rely less upon Western sources for support, there will be an increasing necessity for Third World persons to exercise leadership. If the church in the Third World is to continue to grow and be able to bear witness to Jesus Christ in the particular Third World context, it is essential that the Third World develop its own future church leaders.

In response to the growing need for trained leaders in the Third World, the Third World Church Leadership Center was founded a few years earlier by the Presbyterian Theological Seminary in Seoul, Korea, as a place to train church leaders from developing countries and serve as a place for American missionaries to receive orientation to the Third World.

No sooner had the Birthday objective for 1984 been announced than questions began to arise: What do we mean by Third World? Where did the term come from? Why is this distinction necessary? Isn't the term outmoded and, in a sense, demeaning? Jean Guy Miller, staff in the Office of Women in Atlanta, wrote in the May 1984 issue of *Presbyterian Women:*

> About the time of World War II there began a practice of referring to political, economic and military circles in this way. Capitalistic countries of the West (Europe and the U.S.A.) were considered to be *First World*. Communist countries of Russia and its satellites were called *Second World*. All nonaligned, nonindustrialized countries, which the First and Second Worlds called "underdeveloped," were termed *Third World*. These were countries of Asia, Africa and South America, primarily nonwhite people.
>
> From the beginning lines were not clear. . . . Where would countries like Japan, Australia, and South Africa belong? Nevertheless, Third World has become a way of referring to nonwhite peoples and nations who have been colonized, oppressed, "used" by the first and second white worlds.

She concludes:

> It has been evident for many years that building centers for leader development and education in the Third World is preferable to sending students to the Western countries, where the culture and affluent living

are a deterrent to their returning to serve at home. . . . We are enthusiastic about this new center, whose goal will further full partnership in mission.

Soon W. Moak, President of Korean-American Presbyterian Women and a colleague on the final Women of the Church Committee (1986–1988) before her death, wrote in the May 1984 issue of *Presbyterian Women*:

> Shortly after a diplomatic treaty was signed between the United States and Korea in 1882, Presbyterian missionaries came to Korea with the gospel of Jesus Christ. This year we are celebrating the one-hundredth anniversary of partnership with the Korean Presbyterian Church, with the theme, "Behold, I am doing new things." . . . During the past hundred years of Christianity, the church in Korea has been rapidly expanding. . . . We are grateful for the hundred years of partnership between the [Women of the Church of the PCUS] and the Korean Presbyterian Church. Now, new problems and changes require new visions of partnership.

There is a Korean proverb, "A small beginning can make a great ending." When missionaries went to Korea, it was a small beginning. Now the Presbyterian Church of Korea has a larger membership than one of its parents, the former Presbyterian Church, U.S., and is ready to assume leadership in its whole area of Asia. That is the reason it started the Third World Leadership Center. A small beginning had been made, but the center needed a building and money for program and scholarships. That is where the Women of the Church and the Birthday Offering came in to help "the small beginning make a great ending."

The Presbyterian Theological Seminary in Seoul was built to accommodate 300 students. In 1984, it was serving 1,800 students in its various programs. The proposal from the seminary for the Birthday Offering was $150,000 for a share of the cost of a building on a lot that had already been purchased next to the seminary and to provide $360,000 toward program and scholarships, for a total of $510,000. The Korean Presbyterian Church agreed to contribute almost as much. All administrative expenses, building maintenance, and faculty salaries were paid for by the seminary. The Women of the Church, in this way, became partners in training leaders from Samoa, India, Ghana, Indonesia, Thailand, Uganda, Pakistan, Australia, the United States, and other countries. All the students are representative of various denominations and national churches and come to the seminary on the recommendation of ecumenical agencies.

The Years before Merger

In the long term, it was hoped that the center would become a place for theological reflection and ecumenical dialogue that will focus on the problems and opportunities unique to the churches and people of the Third World.

In a facsimile communication from the Rev. Arthur Kinsler, the PC(USA) Financial Representative in Korea, dated January 31, 1997, he replied to questions:

> *Current number of students?* 11; *What countries are they from?* India, Indonesia, Sierra Leone, Ghana, Kenya, Sudan, Nigeria; *Approximate number of faculty who are teaching Third World Students either full or part time?* 1 mission co-worker full time with program (more than teaching), 10 faculty teaching part time; *What degrees are the students pursuing?* Th.M. in Missions, Christian Education, Old Testament, Methods of Counseling; *Special successes of the program:* Increased exposure to missions of Korean Church which now sends out many missionaries; *Areas of difficulty:* Need more students, need to raise more money in Korea.

Soon Moak said, "New problems and changes require new vision." In this vision for the future and new model of partnership in the Gospel, "mutuality has become not only one of faith but of mission."

1985

Gift of a Lifetime: Enabling the Ministry of Older People *(See also 1977)*

"Each one, as a good manager of God's different gifts, must use for the good of others the special gift . . . received from God" (1 Pet. 4:10, NIV). The principle of the tithe recognizes God as the creator and sustainer of life and the giver of all life holds. By giving the first portion of all we receive, we commit all of life in response to God's gracious love toward us. Jesus taught that much is expected of those to whom much has been given (Luke 12:48).

People live longer today than in the past, and retirement brings opportunity to use the knowledge, skills, and judgment that come with added years (Introduction to the 1985 Women of the Church Birthday Offering). Like many other organizations, the Church two decades ago was caught off guard by rapid increases in the number of older people. It

was predicted in 1985 that in just a few years, retired Presbyterians would number more than 700,000. Older adults are a significant and growing part of the Church.

The Birthday Offering in 1977 was given to help establish the Center for Aging at the Presbyterian School of Christian Education in Richmond, Virginia. In 1985, the women again gave an offering for older adults. The Presbyterian Office on Aging, Division of National Mission of the General Assembly Mission Board, made the proposal. The entire offering of more than $530,000 made possible a ministry to older adults using the experience and skills of volunteers in early retirement years. These volunteers were trained and spent up to two years in full-time service with congregations and governing bodies helping churches develop effective ministry with older adults.

"What's around the bend?" For those freed of the demands of working and child-rearing, the later years are a time for turning life in new directions. Those who picture retirement as a time of leisure and play often find that this life does not have enough meaning and purpose. They find life "around the bend" richer and fuller when they seek new uses for experience and skill. Effective ministry with older adults requires understanding of their life experiences and the ability to respond to their pastoral skills. Leadership is needed to help develop such ministries.

The Gift of a Lifetime program was planned to cover a period of five years, 1985–1990. During those years, the Office on Aging annually recruited and trained five Presbyterians in their mid-sixties to help develop older adult ministries throughout the church. During the summer, volunteers were given training that included Biblical and theological bases for this ministry, college-level courses in the psychology and sociology of aging, outreach and evangelism, and program and polity of the Presbyterian Church. The volunteers spent up to two years in full-time service working with congregations and presbyteries under the supervision of the local pastor or presbytery executive. The project was under the oversight of the Director of Aging, assisted by two regional coordinators, themselves volunteer retirees.

The Years before Merger 139

The Tithe of Life program enables the ministry of older people.

Funding for the program was sufficient for two two-year cycles. The budget for the project provided for twenty-five participants to receive stipends of $2,400 per year. The rest of the money was used for training expenses and administrative costs (salary for director and secretary, travel, and supplies).

In taking up the challenge of ministry to older adults, Women of the Church affirmed two basic principles of our faith. Regardless of age, each individual is precious in the sight of God and entitled to the caring ministry of the Church. Regardless of age, each of Christ's followers is called to minister to others and care for them in Christ's name.

1986

The Serving Church

In Gal. 5:13 (RSV), we are admonished to *"Through love be servants of one another."* In response to this call, the theme for the 1986 Birthday Offering was "the Serving Church," and the offering went to two objectives—the Border Ministry, a partnership mission of the National Presbyterian Church of Mexico and the Presbyterian Church (U.S.A.) and the libraries of the theological seminaries of the Reformed Church of France.

Border Ministry, Mexico-U.S.A.

A large cross with an accompanying inscription in Spanish and English—*The Serving Church, Serviglesia L'eglise Servante*—was the logo for the 1986 offering, displayed on bulletins, place mats, offering envelopes, etc. The cross of Jesus Christ bridging the border of Mexico and the United States is symbolic of the Border Ministries, the recipient of a major portion of the 1986 offering. One of the projects, *Puentes de Cristo,* which means *Bridges of Christ,* symbolizes the projects. The model of the *serviglesia,* the serving church, is key to this ministry. The church is both a worshipping and a serving community—providing health care, child care, counseling, legal aid, nutrition programs, establishment of co-ops, as well as spiritual needs.

The 2,000-mile border between Mexico and the United States marks sharp contrast of wealth and extreme poverty. It has become a crossroads for people of Central America and Mexico. By 1986, population had tripled over the past fifteen years. Thousands of adults cross the border daily. Health-care, housing, education, and child-care needs are only some of the signs of suffering in this region.

The Birthday Offering was a response to a proposal from the Border Ministry to join in partnership with them in an effort to meet some of these needs. The unique aspect of the proposal is that it was developed by both the National Presbyterian Church of Mexico and the Presbyterian Church (U.S.A.). The Joint Commission for International Mission responsible for mission between Mexico and the United States created the Border Committee with specific responsibility for oversight of Border Ministries and expansion of Presbyterian witness along the border using the *serviglesia* model. These *serviglesias* encompass a strong evangelistic, worship, and service emphasis.

Five separate projects along the border received portions of the offering to be used over a three-year period. *Puentes de Cristo* (Bridges of Christ), mentioned above, received $105,000; Project *Amistad* (Friendship) received $45,000; Project *Verdad* (Truth) in the El Paso/Juarez region received $94,800; *Pueblos Hermanos* (Brother or Sister Cities) received $145,000; and *Frontera de Cristo* (Christ's Frontier) received $97,500.

In the Project *Verdad* region, there were in 1986 eight worshipping communities where there was only one in 1970. These *serviglesias* have child care, feeding centers, cooperatives, clinics, nutrition programs, and community-organizing projects, as well as offering direct relief services. Four kindergartens function in Juarez. Teachers give a year of social service to these kindergartens prior to graduation from the university. A pilot co-op in one of the poorer sections of Juarez was set up with sewing machines and was marketing products at the time of the proposal. Project *Verdad* also worked to help community groups obtain electricity, apply for drinking water, improve roads, and obtain other public services. They have

The 1986 offering supported a number of Mexico/U.S.A. Border Ministries.

promoted inoculation services and other community services. The Birthday Offering made possible co-op development in other *serviglesias* in addition to building a worship site for a new congregation (see also 1996).

Puentes de Cristo is another joint project of the National Presbyterian Church of Mexico and the Presbyterian Church (U.S.A.), specifically Mission Presbytery (in the Synod of the Sun). It has strengthened three existing congregations and developed three new *serviglesias*. There are programs to feed the hungry, provide health care, and improve housing conditions, as well as programs in Christian education. Evangelistic work has grown rapidly in Colonia, Lopez Portillo, where the Birthday Offering made possible a new *serviglesia* by providing land and a building where health and nutrition services are provided. *Puentes* works closely with the Salvation Army Orphanage in Reynosa, Mexico, coordinates emergency food supplies and disaster funds, and assists in feeding the "street children" of Reynosa.

Project *Amistad*, which operates in the area of Del Rio-Acuna and Eagle Pass-Piedras Negras; *Pueblos Hermanos*, which operates in a geographic area where Mexico and the United States meet, San Diego-Tijuana; and Christ's Frontier, which operates in Agua Prieta, Mexico, across the border from Douglas, Arizona, are the three other border project areas funded by the 1986 Birthday Offering—all in establishing new churches while at the same time providing needed services.

Jerry Stacy sent a copy of a 1996 report—Program History of Presbyterian Border Ministry—via Angela Abrego. It is a detailed, well-organized eight-page report and would be an excellent resource for those who are interested in more detailed information about this ministry. In 1986, the Joint Mission Commission (JMC) approved the creation of the Presbyterian Border Ministry Corporation. Established under Texas law, it was charged with promoting financial support for the work of the border. The corporation charter and bylaws make it accountable to the JMC. In 1989, a consultation was called by the JMC, and the full scope of the ministry was studied, and after careful analysis, changes were made. In 1990, the Border Committee of the JMC reviewed and received long-range plans as a program guide for all projects.

The report included a strategic plan that included a mission statement with goals: To do evangelism and develop new churches, to engage in ministries of compassion, to engage in mission education, and to be a collaborative ministry; Theological Affirmations; an Overview; Needs, Vision, and Plan in including Church Development, Community Health, Community Education, Economic and Community Development,

Creation of Support Structures to Enable Effective Ministry, and Providing Opportunities for Mutuality in mission; and Funding Summary.

As Stacy says in the report:

> People of this hemisphere are learning to live as neighbors. The Bible reminds us that what we sow will be reaped by our children's children. As Presbyterians sow seeds of cooperation and reconciliation along our border with Mexico today, our grandchildren will reap the fruits of trust and understanding with all of Latin America.

Women who are Presbyterians can rejoice that these neighbors have taught us much about *serviglesia* and that we have had a small part in bridging the border that separates us.

Theological Libraries, France

Part of the 1986 offering went to help build new libraries in the theological seminaries of the Reformed Church of France. The proposal from the Reformed Church of France begins:

> Our conviction is that in a thoroughly secularized country such as France, where Catholicism is divided between traditionalist resistance and evangelical advances, Protestant churches must bear specific witness to the Gospel, for the sake of our people. Our task today is to give our churches the means to fulfil that mission: the training of women and men able to "account for the hope that is in them" (1 Pet. 3:15) has become the priority for our churches.

The Reformed Church of France is one of the oldest Reformed churches. In that land that gave birth to Presbyterianism, Protestant churches account for barely 1.5 percent of the whole population. President Monsarrat of the National Council wrote in his endorsement of the proposal that the eighteenth-century persecutions were so violent that they "broke down our churches." Many Huguenots fled abroad; many died because of their faith. The libraries of the two theological seminaries (in Paris and Montpellier) guard the memory of this story "of suffering and resistance, one of the most moving contributions to world Presbyterianism." Except for some historical clusters of Protestants, the churches are scattered throughout the country into small, isolated groups. Theology is crucial to the heart of the church, and the seminaries train lay people as well as clergy. The witness of laity as well as clergy extends worldwide.

The Reformed Church of France is well-known for its outreach in social concern, especially among immigrant refugees. It is also active in mission in African countries and the Pacific. There are many students from the Third World represented among international students in the two seminaries.

A gift of $50,000 was made from the 1986 Birthday Offering for these libraries. The total budget, $800,000, enabled the seminaries to build new buildings at both locations on land they already own. The offering from the women is a small but symbolic gift, for in this way, Women of the Church have manifested their link with the Church in the land that gave birth to Presbyterianism—a Church seeking to be a faithful, witnessing, serving Church.

1987

Communities of Hope and Caring

The New Testament teachings about love for one another and reminders that when one part of the body suffers, all suffer, were a part of the promotion for the 1986 Birthday Offering. "What does the Lord require of you but to do justice, and to love kindness, and to walk humbly with your God?" (Mic. 6:8). The 1987 Women of the Church Birthday Offering established community centers in Khayelitsha, near Cape Town, and provided a shelter for ministry to families of burn victims at a burn center in Mississippi—both "Communities of Hope and Caring."

Khayelitsha Community Centers, South Africa

The first $350,000 (plus any amount over the next $150,000, which amounted to $90,000) of the 1987 Birthday Offering was designated for community centers at Khayelitsha to provide a Christian ministry in the midst of a place of controversy, strife, and oppression caused by apartheid. Khayelitsha is a fast-growing residential area for black Africans. In 1987, people were being moved there from Crossroads and other areas into a crowded and desolate city. A church group was organized and began meeting in a garage, resulting in crowds that soon caused the building to overflow. The center built with the offering is a general-purpose building, a place of worship, job training, education, day care, and health clinics. The building can be subdivided to accommodate various activities or opened up for corporate worship of up to 350 people.

The Presbyterian Church of South Africa submitted the proposal for the offering and listed objectives for the community center: 1) skills training during the construction; 2) facility for the proclamation of the Gospel and for worship; 3) community service through activities with preschoolers, children, teenagers, and adults—to include clinics, a day-care center, and educational facilities; 4) point of multi-racial contact; and 5) center for lay leadership development. The purpose of establishing a Presbyterian presence in this particular place was to serve as a witness that the Church, the people of God, cares for the needs of suffering people who live bruised and battered lives.

In late 1985, African Christians issued a statement known as the *Kairos* document which says in part:

> *At the very heart of the gospel of Jesus Christ and at the very center of all true prophecy is a message of hope. Nothing could be more relevant and more necessary at this moment of crisis in South Africa than a Christian message of hope. We believe that God is at work in our world turning hopeless and evil situations to good so that his "Kingdom may come" and his "Will be done on earth as it is in Heaven." We believe that goodness and justice and love will triumph in the end and that tyranny and oppression cannot last forever. True peace and true reconciliation . . . are assured.*

Much has changed in the political structure in South Africa since 1987, but the Birthday Offering in that year was a means by which the Women of the Church could send to their hurting sisters and brothers in South Africa a message of reconciliation and hope.

Shelter for Families of Burn Victims, Greenville, Mississippi

In April 1984, Women of the Church of St. Andrew Presbytery became involved in a ministry of compassion to families of burn victims at the Mississippi Fire Fighters Memorial Burn Center in Greenville, Mississippi. This center receives patients from a nine-state area. A portion of the 1987 Birthday Offering, $150,000, was designated for this ministry, The women of St. Andrew Presbytery have provided a model for women in mission in any community. They dreamed and planned for a shelter for families who came to be near family members who were severely burned, often in fires that had destroyed the family's home and possessions. Doctors affirmed that presence of family is important to the recovery of burn victims.

Since the shelter was more than one group could do alone, these local Presbyterians worked with other churches and community organizations. Women in the Presbytery became involved. With the Birthday Offering, Women of the Church assembly-wide also got involved. The offering of $150,000 provided the majority of the funds needed to construct the building ($213,532 altogether, including furnishings, parking, and walkways). The Women of the Church [now Presbyterian Women], with ecumenical and community partners, offers hospitality through the shelter for families who are experiencing the trauma of anxiety and distress.

These women took seriously the teaching that when one of the body suffers, all suffer. They, along with other Women of the Church, gave of themselves in love and compassion, bearing the message of "hope and caring."

1988

New Songs of Life—Hope for Women and Children

The last of the Women of the Church Birthday Offerings ended as they began, in celebration and in concern for women and children. The two theme Bible verses were "Sing to the Lord a new song" (Isa. 42:10) and "Behold I am doing a new thing" (Isa. 43:19). It was a cause for celebration because in July 1988, Women of the Church and United Presbyterian Women would be joined together in one organization—Presbyterian Women. The culmination of more than five years of cooperation and work resulted in a new and exciting venture, and the women were eager to sing "the new song."

Stillman College *(See also 1928, 1938, 1942, 1952, 1960, 1972)*

Nineteen eighty-eight marked the last gift to Stillman College from Women of the Church since the objective is chosen the previous year (in this case, 1987). Beginning in 1989, the Birthday Gifts became gifts from Presbyterian Women. The 1988 gift of $200,000 was earmarked for scholarships. This was an appropriate choice because Women of the Church had helped to bring about coeducation at the college and because for 110 years Stillman had included the identification, recruitment, education, and financial support of young people who are economically disadvantaged. This particular gift was also a "song of celebration" for faithful women. Throughout its history, Women of the Church had shown interest in and support of Stillman College. This proposal in 1988 had a

Birthday Offering brochure, 1988.

different focus as it suggested the objective pay tribute to the past contributions of Women of the Church through the education of future leaders. Women of the Church were, through this gift, holding up two particular issues that the denomination had determined of critical importance: education of minorities for lives of leadership and service and the utilization of the gifts of women in church and society.

Dr. Cordell Wynn, President of Stillman College, wrote in a letter dated March 4, 1997, of the importance of the scholarship assistance: "Scholarship support is our number one need to keep open the doors of access and opportunity in higher education. More than 90% of our students qualify for financial aid based on need!" Dr. Wynn then mentioned several scholarship recipients: Tameka Gibson, 1995, from Boligee, Alabama, one of the poorest communities in the Southeast. She now has a permanent position with Regions Bank. "Several students from the Caribbean have received significant scholarship support and are making important contributions." Carleen Payne, 1992, completed a master's degree in international studies at New York University. She is now pursuing a doctorate at Auburn University. Bonnie Edwards, May 1996, is a paralegal in New York City and is taking courses at Brooklyn College. "These are all fine young women of whom you can be proud—both for their academic performance and for their character and potential."

Presbyterians are proud of Stillman College. It is symbolic that the support of Stillman by Women of the Church began in 1921, even before the first Birthday Gift and ended in 1988 with their final gift as Women of the Church.

In 1988, women had the opportunity to celebrate sixty-six years of Birthday Offering Gifts by Women of the Church. As always, the gifts were expressions of reconciliation, hope, and love.

Ministries with Women in Prison, Atlanta, Georgia *(See also 1977)*

A portion of the 1988 Birthday Offering, $100,000, was given to provide help and hope for women newly released from prison. An offering in 1977 was given to the denomination's Task Force on Criminal Justice. The 1988 objective seemed to be a fitting "follow-up." Ministries with Women in Prison, Inc., (MWP) is an established program in Atlanta, Georgia, which witnesses to the Good News of Jesus Christ to both women in prison and those who have been released and are trying to reshape and refocus their lives. MWP is a nonprofit organization.

The money from the offering was allocated to establish a women's center for women newly released from prison, a place that would provide supportive services necessary for women ex-offenders to reenter society

The Years before Merger   149

and take charge of their own lives. Because it is difficult for women to make the transition from being an inmate in a structured environment to being a citizen in the secular world, MWP stays in touch with released women so that they will not lose the momentum in their spiritual journeys begun behind bars.

When women are released from prison, they often feel isolated and have few "religious" contacts; consequently, they may easily slip back into the world they knew before incarceration. Through prayer groups and Bible studies, women are given affirmation that they are children of God, with God-given gifts and talents. They are encouraged to join a church and advised which ones will provide a friendly environment so that they can make a new set of friends.

These women have a critical need of a center that provides them with services otherwise unavailable to them. They also need a place of "sanctuary" from a society that does not readily accept them. The proposal is to provide a large two-story, four-bedroom house where staff can supervise a program of counseling, job training, and support. Recruitment of volunteers to serve as sponsors of parolees and to help with other services is part of the plan. The center can offer a viable lifestyle by providing supportive services (educational, spiritual, emotional) necessary for the women to reenter society successfully. The center will be a place to build self-esteem and self-confidence, showing the women that

The house purchased by the 1988 Ministries to Women in Prison program.

they are valued human beings. Provisions are made for therapy for drug/alcohol addition. Education in parenting and family planning will be available, as well as job information and referrals.

God's grace is evidenced through ministries such as this one. As Women of the Church closed the door on sixty-six years of offerings in one tradition, it was fitting that part of their offering in 1988 would help to "release the captives" and open doors for those who needed it so badly, joining together to sing "new songs of life."

Volunteer Emergency Foster Care, Richmond, Virginia

> Volunteer Emergency Families for Children (VEFC) is a private, non-profit organization, established in 1979, and dedicated to helping children and youth have their varied needs met within their own community. VEFC recruits, trains, and maintains a unique statewide network of highly motivated and committed volunteers who provide quality short-term shelter care and effective mentoring services to children and youth of Virginia. (VEFC's brochure)

In short, VEFC is a "children-in-crisis" ministry. VEFC was founded in Virginia on the philosophy that children's needs are best met in a caring, well-functioning family that is undergirded and motivated by a compelling faith and purpose.

What do the volunteers do? They are trained to help abused, neglected, victimized, and homeless children. Host families provide the unconditional acceptance and love that witness to God's grace and love. The program provides intensive training for the host families and establishes networks with volunteer families, churches, court, and social service agencies. VEFC families nurture the child for twenty-one days or less; the average is ten days.

VEFC's short-term shelter-care services include Respite Care Services (parental incarceration or hospitalization, situational or family stress, suspected abuse or neglect, special-needs children, and family-child conflict); Children and Youth in DDS Custody (homeless, runaway, abandoned, respite from foster care, entering emergency protective custody, transition between placement, preadoptive placement, and entering foster care); and Youth Before the Juvenile Court or Court Services. VEFC also offers Alternatives to Detention and Tutoring-Mentoring programs. VEFC has launched a nationwide ministry and is active now in North Carolina.

Women of the Church designated $200,000 of the 1988 Birthday Offering to VEFC and joined in another song of praise for ministries like this.

VEFC provides shelters, mentors, and alternatives to detention programs in Virginia.

PART III

The Years since Merger
(1989–1997)

CHAPTER FOUR

Presbyterian Women
(1989–1997)

*Women's Ministries—
National Ministries Division
Presbyterian Church (U.S.A.)*

1989

The "First" Birthday Offering of Presbyterian Women *(See also 1988)*

The largest previous offering had been the 1982 offering of $596,226, and women were excited about the prospect of new participants and new opportunities for mission. The amount of money contributed was never the main driving force of Birthday Offerings; the objectives and how Presbyterian women could be partners in filling the needs expressed in those objectives was the main thrust. The offerings were, and are, a means of educating women about mission at home and abroad, a means of broadening awareness and participation, and one means of sending messages of reconciliation and hope in Christ's name throughout the world.

In recognition of the heritage of Presbyterian Women, and continuing the tradition of the Birthday Offering, "We lift up and celebrate the birthday of Presbyterian Women." Thus began the introduction on the program covers for the 1989 celebrations with the theme, "Hearts and Hands, Lifting God's Children." The Creative Ministries Offering Committee of Presbyterian Women announced three projects with a goal of $950,000. The goal was not realized, but an impressive $811,000 was contributed to this "first" Presbyterian Women Birthday Offering for the three objectives—Child Advocacy, Manos de Cristo [Hands of Christ], Austin, Texas, and Concerns Arising Over Prostitution (CROP) in the Philippines. According to established practice, projects were funded proportionately according to the requests made, the goal assigned for each, and actual offerings.

Child Advocacy

The Presbyterian Church has a strong involvement in child advocacy, and by 1989, a growing number of women's groups and local congregations were becoming involved in the ministries of day care and public advocacy. The 1988 Churchwide Gathering of Presbyterian Women (the first jointly planned Churchwide Gathering) lifted this concern. The largest portion of the 1989 offering, almost $350,000, was given to Child Advocacy, USA for three complementary programs involving service, awareness education of constituency, and advocacy. The programs were designed 1) to assist in providing direct service to children through seed money grants for the creation and expansion of high quality day-care centers and outreach programs, to expand ministries to children of women in jails, and to establish ecumenical experimental family day-care homes—one of these to be located at the Presbyterian headquarters in Louisville—that would offer training in child-care development, curriculum, health and safety, etc., and publish materials to assist other centers; 2) to undertake awareness education of constituency—i.e. to mobilize the constituency to advocate for children by publishing and sending information to congregations to address child poverty, child care, child help, youth self-sufficiency, and teen pregnancy prevention; and 3) to make the Presbyterian Church an effective public policy advocate for children in the United States by creating an advocacy network prepared to respond to local, state, and federal policy with the National Council of Churches and local coalitions.

These programs were to be developed through the cooperation of the Women's Ministry Unit and the Social Justice and Peacemaking Unit of the General Assembly, and the funds were payable to the Social Justice and Peacemaking Unit. The awareness education program was to be carried on in cooperation with other churches through the National Council of Churches and cooperation with the Children's Defense Fund. Presbyterian Women fully funded the project for 1990 through 1994. Print and video resources were developed, including a video adopted by Friendship Press for 1994–1995.

Image from *Horizons* magazine.

According to a *Child Advocacy Project Update*, the Child Advocacy Project Committee's (CAP) first task was stated:

> ... to solicit ideas from Presbyterians and ecumenical child advocates from across the country.... To accomplish this, a call for participants to a conference was made to the sixteen synods. Over 130 people representing every synod gathered in Tampa, Florida for reflection, education and discussion and are the core of an emerging child advocacy network....
>
> The CAP developed a comprehensive five year plan. Vital to the work of the project is coordination of efforts with others, both ecumenically and in the secular area. The Children's Defense Fund, the Child Advocacy Office of the National Council of Churches, the Ecumenical Child Care Network and others have worked closely to support this project.

In a one-year follow-up report (1990), it was stated that:

> ... the Presbyterian Child Advocacy has over 400 members and will soon affiliate with PHEWA.... A grants program has been developed for child care centers to get accredited and for seed money grants for quality child care. A twice yearly newsletter updates advocates on church and public issues related to children.

In the restructure of the church in the early nineties, the Women's Ministry Unit was dissolved, but the concern women have for children is ongoing.

Manos de Cristo [Hands of Christ], Austin, Texas

Manos de Cristo is a Servi-Iglesia ministry serving east Austin, Texas. The proposal for the 1989 offering stated:

> Austin is 180 miles from the Mexican border, but the problems affecting the poor and needy is as close as the people who migrate to this part of the country. Mexican migration has created many problems for those churches that are located in the neighborhoods where the immigrants and refugees choose to live ... the poorest parts of town.

To meet the many and varied needs of these people, the ministry of Manos de Cristo was established. The ministry was designed "to bring together Mexicans and Anglos who are ready to offer, in the name of Christ, a helping hand to homeless transients and thousands of Mexican and Central American refugees and immigrants who are concentrated in the Central/East Austin Corridor in Texas."

The Creative Ministries Offering Committee of Presbyterian Women allocated $328,350 of the 1989 offering for Manos de Cristo for the following:

> 1) to meet the physical ailments that poverty brings into the life of people; 2) to encourage people to seek a spiritual life by offering opportunities to join in Bible study, prayer groups and worship where the ministry is located; and 3) to revitalize Hispanic ministry and to open the door for fellow Anglo-Presbyterians to join in ministry in the inner city. In the area where the ministry is carried on, every conceivable ailment that afflicts the poor is found: hunger, discrimination, unemployment, illegal drugs, alcoholism, illiteracy, poor housing, poor health, murder, robbery, and more. Work is planned in the areas of education, hunger, health, legal aid, housing and community development and spiritual life development.

The proposal continues:

> In Texas, for over one hundred years, [Presbyterian] Hispanic congregations and Anglo congregations have traveled on two separate roads. . . . In recent years, however, the Border ministries [see 1986] have indisputably shown that both Anglo and Hispanics can work together to present Christ's love in a meaningful and helpful way. Hundreds of people, working together, have built bridges not only between borders, but between Christian cultures.

It was planned that Manos de Cristo would be locally controlled by a governing board made up of as many as twenty-five cluster Presbyterian churches. The project was hosted by El Buen Pastor Presbyterian Church, where the idea for Manos de Cristo originated. The concept was *serviglesia*, the Serving Church. The church members, as well as volunteers from the other fourteen Presbyterian churches in Austin, were involved in numerous ways. The proposed program covered a period of five years.

The one-year follow-up report stated that there is evidence that work started quickly and progressed well. The report shows that benefits included education—including after-school tutoring, help with funding for preschool day care, and amnesty education; basic needs such as provision of food and clothing by means of a food pantry and clothes closet; a dental clinic in the planning and construction stage; and a listening ear for caring and referrals to other community services.

The Years since Merger

The two-year follow-up report showed good news:

> The three-chair dental clinic was completed after eighteen months and the first person seen on July 9, 1990. This provides the only dental services in Austin to low-income people not on Medicaid or welfare. During the first year of dental services we treated about 700 patients in over 1400 visits. Forty-five dentists and fifteen hygienists volunteered their services. . . . Our greatest challenge is to keep the waiting list manageable.

But that is not all.

> A weekly legal clinic was started with volunteer attorneys from the sponsoring churches to give advice and make referrals. . . . Emphasis has also been placed on the pastoral care goal. . . . A sewing group has just begun, that will teach a marketable skill, provide Bible study and fellowship.

The Trull Foundation contributed $24,000 to Manos de Cristo over a three-year period, and other Austin churches contributed $22,000.

In answer to an inquiry regarding Manos de Cristo today, the executive director, David Batlle replied on March 7, 1997:

> A Presbyterian ministry, Manos de Cristo remains the only combined effort by Presbyterian churches here in Austin. In 1990, Manos de Cristo opened the dental clinic thanks to a generous grant from Presbyterian Women [the Birthday Offering].
>
> The dental project simply would not have been possible without this grant, and the impact it has had in the community is still felt very strongly today.

He continues to tell of Manos de Cristo's progress in the last seven years:

> The dental clinic has seen almost 20,000 patient visits . . . 5,350 in 1996; In 1996, Manos de Cristo expanded its original service area [for the dental clinic] to include all of Austin as well as the Del Valle School District outside Austin; A dental education program teaches basic prevention and hygiene to thousands of children per year in twelve surrounding schools; English as a Second Language (ESL) classes are held daily (volunteers teach a standardized curriculum) with immigrants' rights classes integrated into the lessons once a month; after school tutoring; clothes closet; food pantry; pastoral care done on site at the dental clinic; citizenship classes once a week; and computerized I & R (Immigration and Refugee) database, which is continuously

updated thanks to United Way and a part-time intern from Austin Presbyterian Theological Seminary.

Mr. Batlle concludes, "Allow me to thank . . . Presbyterian Women for what you have done here in East Austin . . . it has had enduring impact with no signs of diminishing. God bless you."

Concerns Rising Over Prostitution (CROP) Drop-In Center, Manila, Philippines)

> The Christian communities in the Philippines have been struggling with the growing problem of sexual exploitation in the country. Prostitution, which has existed since colonial times, became a major industry under the Marcos regime, and it is now [1989] estimated that there are 200,000 to 300,000 prostitutes in the Philippines. This was due to rapidly increasing poverty in the country, lack of appropriate paid work for young women in poorer provinces, and the development of sex tourism.
> (From the proposal for the Birthday Offering)

In 1986, Ellinwood Church sponsored a day-long seminar on prostitution, addressing the growing problem of sexual exploitation in the Philippines. The seminar exposed the mass prostitution and the double standard of morality, which condemned the prostitutes while condoning their sexual and economic oppressors. One activity that was proposed as a solution was the establishment of a crisis center in Manila's tourism belt. A Christian group sponsored by the churches established a "Drop-In Center" to provide counseling and medical and legal advice to prostitutes. Women of the Philippines who were working to lift up their sexually exploited sisters submitted a proposal to Presbyterian Women for the 1989 Birthday Offering. Their proposal included short-term and long-term goals. The Creative Ministries Offering Committee of Presbyterian Women decided to allocate approximately $96,575 to support the objectives.

The short-term goal was to encourage prostitutes to use the Drop-In Center (CROP) for learning and organizing purposes to enable them to participate in resolving their problems. Young women were employed to go onto the streets of Manila, at some risk from pimps, to invite girls and women prostitutes to the center, where they received health and legal advice, vocational training, and job referrals. CROP operated as a center to drop in for snacks, meeting other workers, rest, and seek informal advice. In extreme emergencies, overnight accommodations were available, but the center did not act as a rehabilitation agency for individual women but

The Years since Merger 161

as a means of referral to other agencies that offered that kind of service.

The medium to long-term goal was "to support local efforts in the worst-affected provinces, and advocacy work" to eliminate the root causes of poverty.

The long-term goal was "to help establish at least one model income-generating cooperative project for young women and girls in one of the affected areas, in coordination with local agencies. Once established such a project would become independent under local management." As contacts develop, the plan is as follows:

> . . . to provide regular courses in legal and employment rights, health, nutrition (including child nutrition), and drug abuse prevention. Spiritual development seminars will be provided . . . It is hoped that . . . [there will be] an increased awareness of common problems and the possibility of common solutions.

Two other components of long-terms goals included research in which the CROP would investigate tourism establishments in Manila to increase knowledge of issues confronting workers in the hospitality industry and to identify other areas needing help. The other part of long-term goals involved advocacy. CROP is a member of the Alliance Against Institutionalized Dehumanization (AAID), an alliance of cause-oriented, civic, church, and women's organizations, including both female and male prostitutes, that are concerned with the issue of prostitution. The aims of AAID are:

> . . . to influence the government in determining advocate [sic] for the welfare of those forced to work as prostitutes, and asks the government to address unequal regional development and distribution of wealth, and the social problems caused by the militarization of U.S. foreign policy to the Philippines and the implications of the American bases.

A member of the staff of the National Council of Churches in the Philippines served as project coordinator. The grant covered a three-year period. No follow-up reports were available to the author.

1990

Most Urgent Needs in the World

Three projects that "seek to meet the most urgent needs in the world today" were chosen to receive the Presbyterian Women's 1990 Birthday Offering: Africa's Children; the Menaul School, a secondary school for

Birthday Offering brochure, 1990.

Hispanics; and a Center for the Prevention of Sexual and Domestic Violence in Seattle. The goal was $950,000; the actual offering was $957,449, the largest offering to date. As always, the offering was an extension of, and separate from, Presbyterian Women's mission pledge support.

Africa's Children—Ministering to Africa's Future

What happens to a people once a war ends? What happens next in the life of a starving child once the child is given a meal? What becomes of those people after the immediate needs in times of famine or war are met? What kind of life awaits Africa's children, Africa's Christians, Africa's churches, and Africa's nations after the emergencies? The proposal for the offering was made by the Partnership in Mission Office of the Global Mission Unit in what they termed the "tangible next step beyond Christian relief and charity to empower our companion churches in Africa . . . through basic Christian ministries involving Christian training, faith, discipleship, and self-help development." The Creative Ministries Offering Committee of Presbyterian Women designated $290,000 for "Africa's Children."

Overall, this project was planned to minister to the future needs of two of Africa's most troubled regions—Ethiopia/Sudan and Malawi/Mozambique—where millions have been uprooted and relocated because of civil strife, and where women and children have suffered disproportionately to men. Youths are returning to the church in droves looking for hope. It is envisioned that the project will empower churches in Africa 1) to address crucial issues through basic Christian ministries, 2) to train young people for church and community leadership, and 3) to concentrate resources on specific African initiatives that take young people out of a "survival mode" and set them on a road to Christian discipleship, responsibility, and leadership.

According to Bruce Gannaway of the Partnership in Mission Office, "The impact of our efforts will be quickly felt and assistance effectively utilized." It was planned that the funds would be used to maximize African involvement and self-help within an African context. The plans included youth-program and infrastructural support ($25,000), pastoral care and training ($15,000), facilities renovation and construction ($100,000), literacy assistance ($10,000), self-help production ($25,000), training incentives for young women ($50,000), and emergency youth funds ($25,000).

The proposal was for a four-year period. The Global Mission Unit's Partnership Office had the responsibility for managing and evaluating the project. In a follow-up report in 1992, it showed that $113,000 of the offering had been disbursed. These funds were used to support women's church-based cooperatives in northern Sudan, development assistance to Mozambican refugee families living in Malawi, and other projects. The report continues, "The last year has seen major upheavals in all four countries targeted by the project."

The introduction to an article in the September/October 1994 issue of *Horizons* magazine relates another use of the 1990 offering:

> One of every four adults is HIV positive in the country of Malawi in Central Africa . . . this small nation of 9 million people will have 250,000 to 350,000 orphans by the year 2000. . . . A child survival Program has been started by the Blantyre Synod . . . as a result of monies received from the 1990 Birthday Offering.

Ruth and Doug Welch, mission coworkers in Malawi who work with Blantyre Synod of the Presbyterian Church of Central Africa wrote:

> The entire continent of Africa will have ten million orphans by the end of the century. . . . Traditionally, the doors of the African extended family are open to all members. . . . Today, the extended family is overburdened. . . . Blantyre Synod envisioned a Child Survival Program rooted in local communities . . . to encourage the communities to look at the problems they faced and come up with their own solutions.

> Hope comes to us as we see the Central Africa Presbyterian Church and the Presbyterian Church (U.S.A.) directing resources to this need. Hope lives as we see volunteers, themselves living in poverty, reaching out to make a difference in their communities through their faith in Christ.

Of the 1990 Presbyterian Women's Birthday Offering, $100,000 was allocated to the Blantyre Synod Child Survival Program.

In a recent update, records show that Centers of Hope in Sudan provide displaced women, children, and men with their only educational opportunity; centers for worship have been set up in squatter camps of Khartoum and Kosti in Sudan; Gotcheb Clinic in Ethiopia reaches women and children; a Child Survival Program is under way in Malawi; and a Women's Department in the Presbyterian Church of Mozambique is functioning.

Menaul School, Rendon Hall, Classroom and Laboratory Project, Albuquerque, New Mexico

Menaul School was founded in 1881 and is the only Hispanic secondary school receiving denomination-wide support. Menaul School

The Years since Merger 165

Rendon Hall, Menaul School, Albuquerque, New Mexico.

is a Christian, coeducational school open to qualified students regardless of their circumstances. Students—Hispanic, Native American, and others—come from diverse backgrounds, from farms, reservations, and "latch-key homes." The proposal for a share of the 1990 Birthday Offering ($190,000) was for a renovation project as a part of the school's plans to expand facilities and course offerings in science and mathematics to accommodate a growing student population and prepare students for tomorrow's jobs in science, technology, and engineering.

In the proposal to the Creative Ministries Offering Committee of Presbyterian Women for the offering, the school's director of development wrote:

> Without updated instructional facilities Menaul School cannot provide its largely Hispanic students (56% of the student body) the preparation they need . . . to compete with ethnic majority students graduating from private academies and some public schools. . . . The Rendon Hall renovation would enable the school to provide facilities to support an enhanced curriculum and a larger student body. . . . Menaul has a solid record of good stewardship through maximizing its available resources. Rendon Hall, now 35 years old, is one such resource. . . .

In a one-year follow-up report, the president of the school wrote:

> The newly renovated building is just being used for the first time during the fall of 1991. The school's students will benefit from new science labs and math classrooms and a new home for Modern and Classical

Classroom at Menaul School.

Language Dept . . . The Rendon Hall Renovation Project has been part of an overall effort to upgrade Menaul School's program. . . . This effort has provided new physical science, life science and chemistry laboratories and classrooms, as well as renovated facilities [Rendon Hall] for the mathematics, fine art, and modern and classical languages classes.

A Faith Response to Abused Women and Children, Seattle, Washington *(See also 1997)*

A grant of $301,000 was made from the 1990 Birthday Offering of Presbyterian Women to transfer into video format the education and training programs used by the Center for the Prevention of Sexual and Domestic Violence in Seattle, Washington, and to distribute them to the widest possible national audience. The epidemic of domestic violence in the United States has created an urgent need to alleviate the suffering of victims in churches and communities. No one is spared. Families of all denominations, all racial groups, and all classes suffer tremendously. In response to these cries, the Center in Seattle was established in 1977. Since that time they have provided resources to the religious community not only to alleviate suffering but also to keep it from recurring.

The Center for Sexual and Domestic Violence is a national, ecumenical, educational ministry. Through its educational program it presents the church ways to alleviate violence and to change attitudes that perpetuate it. The videos produced by the center, together with accompanying written materials, are available to clergy, laity, and local churches, as well as to secular professionals to increase their sensitivity to their religious clients. Another purpose of the project is to prepare the clergy and laity of the church to address the pain of families suffering in silence and isolation. Equally as important, the project has the potential to help the church bring hope and healing to those crying out for help and understanding.

In a one-year follow-up report, the center stated, "We have conducted market research and are in the process of completing production of the first two videos, which will be available in January, 1992. We will then begin working on the videos on child abuse."

Three videos had been produced by the time of the two-year follow-up report: *Not in My Church*, *Not in My Congregation* (for Jewish use), *Once You Cross the Line*, and *Hear Their Cries*. These three videos were the first three in the series, *Keeping the Faith*. Two of the videos, *Not in My Church* and *Once You Cross the Line* represent material related to issues of clergy professional ethics and sexual misconduct. *Hear Their Cries* is an educational video dealing with religious responses to child abuse.

One of the videos, *Not in My Church*, won several awards in 1992, including First Place Gold Camera Award in the U.S. Industrial Film and Video Festival; Gold Special Jury Award at Worldfest Houston, Houston International Film Festival; and a Bronze Plaque Award at the Columbus International Film and Video Festival. Another video, *Hear Their Cries*, won a Gold Plaque Award at the Chicago International Film Festival.

Presbyterian Women once again have served as partners in a "faith response" to hurting people as together they share Christ's love.

1991

Children at Risk, Intermountain Children's Home, Helena, Montana

The Intermountain Children's Home (ICH) is the only Presbyterian-related children's home in the Rocky Mountains area that provides residential care for severely abused and emotionally disturbed children, age five to fifteen. Since 1909, the home has helped children who have needed a home. In 1991, the program offered by ICH was unduplicated in the northwestern United States. More than 95 percent of the children served by ICH are wards of the court. Without this home they would be left in dangerous and life-threatening situations. ICH is a private, nonprofit organization and is a mission of the Presbyteries of Yellowstone and Glacier.

In 1991, ICH had the capacity to serve only one of every five to ten referrals for long-term residential and rehabilitation, with no space for a therapeutic day program. A grant of $265,000 was made from the 1991 Birthday Offering of Presbyterian Women to underwrite the cost of constructing five classrooms in a new, multipurpose, educational, and therapy building as a part of a $1.2 million capital campaign. The five new classrooms allowed the home to double the number of children in residential and day treatment, and made possible the only day treatment program within a hundred mile radius. A new multipurpose room made possible winter indoor recreation for the children.

According to the January/February 1991 issue of *Horizons* magazine:

> The day program at Intermountain Children's Home is currently for children living in the community but struggling with severe educational/emotional problems. The individualized education and counseling this program provides go a long way in preventing more costly residential treatment in the future and help prevent further deterioration of family units.

The 1991 offering helped to build an educational facility at Intermountain Children's Home.

Specific services offered by ICH include 1) school for grades kindergarten through eight, 2) special education classes twelve months of the year, 3) intensive psychological treatment for children who are seriously emotionally disturbed, and 4) specialists in working with emotionally "unattached" children. The average length of stay of the children is two years, and the average age is nine. Seventy-five percent of the children have had previous psychiatric hospitalization. Forty percent of the children are female, sixty percent male, and twenty-five percent are Native American.

According to the latest report from the home, construction of the new building is complete and children no longer attend their special education classes in the basements of cottages but are learning and succeeding in new classrooms aboveground.

Presbyterian Women became, with this offering, partners in mission to children at risk—children who are orphaned, rejected, abandoned, severely abused, and emotionally disturbed.

Mother and Toddler Group, Belfast, Ireland

Part of the 1991 Presbyterian Women Birthday Offering, $300,000, was designated for an ecumenical project in an area of violence and high unemployment in Belfast, Northern Ireland—the Townsend Street Presbyterian Church Mother and Toddler Group. The Townsend Street Presbyterian Church has been in existence for more than 160 years and has a long history of involvement in social welfare. The proposal stated that "support was sought for a comprehensive socio-educational development, initially Mothers and Toddlers [sic]. This is a genuine cross-community venture involving both Protestants and Roman Catholics."

The Northern Ireland troubles started in 1969 in the immediate vicinity of the Townsend Street Presbyterian Church. At the time of the proposal in 1990, it was one of the most peaceful locations along the length of the dividing wall between the Protestant and Catholic communities. Despite the conflicts, cordial relationships had developed between the Townsend Street Presbyterian Church and its neighborhood Roman Catholic community, especially with St. Peter's Parish and the Townsend Enterprise Park. Joint membership of the Enterprise Park encouraged cooperative working and sharing. As a result, an open relationship evolved.

The Townsend Social Outreach Centre is an independent charitable trust sponsored by the Townsend Street Presbyterian Church. Townsend Enterprise Park, which was established in 1985, is an independent job-creation agency supported by the government, and it has received

Challenge brochure, 1991.

significant capital support from the International Fund for Ireland. In 1990, 300 persons were employed on site. The park has been highly successful with continuous pressure for expansion. The board of directors of the park has equal representation of Protestants and Catholics. Both Townsend Outreach Centre and Enterprise Park work together to encourage social welfare in the immediate area, including education and training as well as job creation. Townsend Social Outreach Centre also cooperates with Cathedral Community Services, a Roman Catholic social welfare group who are the nearest neighbors to the Presbyterian Church on the Roman Catholic side of the divide. Plans call for the Mother and Toddler Group to be a cross-community venture linked to an organization involved in temporary job creation, the Grosvenor Environmental Society.

The geography of the area is important. Townsend Outreach Centre and Townsend Enterprise Park are immediate neighbors. Their boundary wall forms the dividing line between the Protestant and Catholic communities. Both are located in close proximity to the inner city and in the heart of heavily populated public-housing developments. Protestants and Catholics can have access to the joint premises without having to pass through "hostile territory." The plan is for the Mother and Toddler Group to be the first located on the "peace-line" to pull down the dividing wall between the two communities, both physically and psychologically.

To the outsider, the problems in the area seem almost beyond solving. According to the proposal, there are serious paramilitary problems, which spill over into political activity. Of the sixty-seven sectarian murders that occurred in 1989 (the year before the proposal), some occurred in the immediate vicinity of the center. Petty crime and extortion are endemic, along with vandalism. Unemployment is 20 percent overall, with much higher rates in pockets close to Townsend Street. Violence within families is commonplace. Child abuse is rampant; child sexual abuse is at least double the national average. Alcohol addiction and general alcohol abuse is widespread. There are many drinking clubs with paramilitary involvement. Education attainment is poor; children do not have a proper start in life, and their parents provide poor role models. Some 25 percent of families in the area are single parents, either unmarried mothers or the father in prison due to involvement in paramilitary terrorist activities. These mothers need support and opportunities to return to the labor market.

The purpose of the project is to overcome the "welfare mentality" in favor of independence and self-reliance. The planned project will make it possible for individuals to acquire additional skills through training in literacy, mathematical, and social skills. Another goal is to help the mothers develop self-confidence and enhance self-esteem by education and group activities that will be part of the Mother and Toddler Group. The plan is for the group to meet in the mornings, with separate programs for mothers and toddlers. The toddlers will have supervised communal play and have access to a "toy library" where toys may be borrowed on a short-term basis. The educational process will be initiated with constructive play, story telling, sand play, and early socialization.

A portion of the monies allocated to the project was spent to help renovate a large but unused school building of the Townsend Street Presbyterian School into an up-to-date Education and Training Center. The project covered a five-year period. Other needs met from the offering were salaries, utilities, and staff development.

The two-year follow-up report showed that a permanent director had been employed and twenty mothers and toddlers were in attendance. Some of the mothers had passed through the program and were involved in helping and managing the project. It was reported that there were many manifestations of greater involvement of the community and participation by mothers in the project. Plans were being made to move into the "purpose built" center in October. The next goal was to establish an after-school club for homework and to build up the Youth Club, in the hopes that peace between Catholics and Protestants might begin with children. The Vice-Moderator of Issues/Presbyterian Women attended the dedication service for the new building in October 1993.

Presbyterian Women can be thankful that they have had some small part in tearing down dividing walls in an area that has suffered for at least three decades.

Nanjing Theological Seminary Expansion/Renovation, China—Solidarity with Chinese Theological Students

In the early part of this century, the facility that is now Nanjing Seminary was a Presbyterian Women's Bible College. Over the years, it was transformed into a theological seminary that valued its Presbyterian origin. Founded in 1952, the Nanjing Seminary was a union of twelve theological seminaries in east China. By 1960, it had graduated more than 500 students, most of whom are, today, key leaders of the Church in different parts of China. In 1961, it was joined by Yanjing Union Theological Seminary, itself a union that had combined thirteen theological schools in north China in 1953. Nanjing then became the only Protestant seminary in "New China" until it was closed during the Cultural Revolution.

As soon as it was politically possible for the churches to begin operating openly in China, the Church moved to reopen Nanjing Seminary in February 1981. At the time of the proposal (1990), the seminary offered the following programs: 1) four-year courses for senior middle school graduates (156 students); 2) a graduate program for theological and university graduates (22 students); 3) one-year training for lay church workers from rural areas (64 students); and 4) a three-year correspondence Bible course with 1,000 students. The Extension Department compiles and publishes a quarterly syllabus, or teach-yourself material, for rural and lay church workers, with a distribution of about 30,000. Since 1981 there have been twelve new Bible schools and seminaries opened in China. Nanjing Seminary serves as the basic training center for these schools.

Today, Nanjing Seminary is China's premier theological seminary. The seminary tries to integrate Biblical teaching with theological research and spiritual nurture. Through participation in the life of the Church and in social involvement, students are committed to the Three-Self Principle (self-administration, self-support, and self-propagation) and practice

Nanjing Seminary, China.

"love country, love church." A wide variety of extracurricular activities are encouraged to enhance balanced growth and community life.

Overwhelming numbers of students are competing to attend an already overtaxed facility; at the same time, the physical plant is in urgent need of repair and expansion. The school was devastated during the Cultural Revolution: the library was dismantled, classrooms given to other purposes, and general deterioration occurred in all facilities. When the seminary reopened, there was space for forty students; more than 700 applied! The demand is even greater today and facilities are terribly overcrowded.

The China Christian Council and Nanjing Seminary made a request for a portion of the 1991 Birthday Offering in support of a renovation project for the seminary that touches many facets of the Christian community in China. The Creative Ministries Offering Committee, on behalf of Presbyterian Women, chose to designate $143,816 of the 1991 offering to show solidarity with today's young Chinese Christians and, at the same time, to honor the memory of the Presbyterian women who began the institution. It is interesting to note that previous Birthday Offerings helped to establish and maintain Bible schools, the forerunners of the seminary.

It was the privilege of the author to visit the Nanjing Seminary on three different occasions, once in 1987 on a Global Experience with

Presbyterian Women, the latest in 1994, and to observe first-hand the positive changes and growth of the campus.

One frequent quote heard in China is, "Before we had shepherds looking for sheep; now we have sheep looking for shepherds." Presbyterian Women became partners, through this offering, in training the young "shepherds" so badly needed in China today. These young leaders will receive the baton passed on from the elderly pastors now in leadership and, in turn, lead the church into the future.

1992

Boggs Rural Life Center Redevelopment, Burke County, Georgia

> At the turn of the century, along the red clay roads of the Deep South, the great promises of Reconstruction had been abandoned and African men and women, former slaves and their children, struggled to subsist and preserve their culture. Churches established missions in the "Black Belt" South to provide literacy training, methods of sustainable agriculture and training in the trades. The missions became the center of religious and cultural life.

Thus began the introduction to the proposal for a portion of the 1992 Birthday Offering by a group in Burke County, Georgia, located in the "Black Belt" of the rural South.

Boggs Academy, founded in 1906 by the Presbyterian Church, was one of the most successful and enduring of the church missions and was

Services celebrate the first anniversary of Boggs Rural Life Center.

started as a source for basic education. It evolved into a fine college preparatory school for rural black children. The school closed in 1984, but the needs that inspired its founding remained. In the unincorporated areas of the rural counties surrounding Boggs, the poverty rate in 1992 exceeded 40 percent. Former slaves and their descendants who remained in the South had depended on land for their survival. Recent land loss devastated farm families and caused disruption of rural life.

On June 5, 1991, African-Americans from Burke County, including three generations of Boggs graduates, joined the Presbyterian Church (USA) in a covenant to return Boggs to its original purposes: fighting rural poverty and its damaging effects on family life, literacy training, development of a sustainable rural economy, empowerment of the disenfranchised, celebration of African-American culture, and training of rural church leadership. The deed to the sixty-acre campus and 1,200 acres of farm and timberland was transferred to the Boggs Rural Life Center, the nonprofit entity to oversee the institution's redevelopment. The plan was for Boggs to be an interracial institution with its programs open to all and its leadership predominantly African-American.

The total cost of the redevelopment was projected at $1,500,348, with renovation of buildings estimated at over $1 million, infrastructure at $165,000, furniture and equipment at $245,928, and supervisor's salary at $35,000. The Birthday Offering from Presbyterian Women was $375,000, the major portion of the 1992 offering. Predevelopment costs were covered by grants totaling $205,000 from the Georgia-based Sapelo Island Research Foundation. The U.S. Department of Health and Human Services made a grant of $300,000, the Needmor fund gave $150,000, the Sapelo Island Research Foundation gave $340,000, the Burke County Improvement Association gave $25,000, and others contributed the rest.

At last report, both church and business retreats are being held at the center; literacy training is ongoing; special attention is given to the problems of young black males; and future plans include cooperation with Fort Valley State College to assist area farmers.

Presbyterian Women, through the Birthday Offering, were significant participants in a new center for family support and rural development involving innovative programs to combat drugs, teenage pregnancy, family violence, and poverty in rural Mississippi.

San Francisco Network Ministries—Low Income Family Housing

In 1989 in the San Francisco Bay area, 20,416 family units (62,676 parents and children) had an episode of homelessness; in 1990, 23,944 family units had an episode of homelessness. In a ten-year period from 1980–1990, an additional new 119,651 low-income housing units were needed in the San Francisco Bay area, but only 23,833 were constructed. This is the situation that led the San Francisco Network Ministries (which is related to San Francisco Presbytery through two of its committees—Congregational & Mission Development and Christian Discipleship in the World) to apply for a portion of the 1992 Presbyterian Women Birthday Offering. The Creative Ministries Offering Committee designated $500,000 of the offering to help construct a multi-unit, service-enriched dwelling for families of the working poor located in San Francisco's Tenderloin District.

The objectives of the project were 1) to develop twenty to twenty-five one-, two-, and three-bedroom apartments at monthly rents of $425 to $650; 2) to make the ground floor commercial space, providing job training and jobs for the tenants and neighborhood residents, while contributing to the economic development of a multiracial poverty area; 3) to provide a community room to be used for tenants' meetings, potlucks, celebrations, etc., as well as for classes, workshops, tutoring in budgeting, parenting skills, conflict resolution, resume preparation, sewing, nutrition, basic literacy and more; and 4) to provide education of congregations and individuals by involving them in developing and ongoing programs.

In a one-year follow-up report from the director, a glimmer of hope comes through. The director reports, "Building is just now under construction, but members of the Board and staff working on this [project] have been blessed with miracle after miracle, of which the Birthday Fund was the first and greatest." It was also reported that other principle funds had been received from the city of San Francisco ($2.4 million), from Federal Tax Credits ($3.1 million), from the Presbytery of San Francisco Bi-Centennial Fund ($130,000), and from the Roberts Foundation ($50,000).

The building is a five-story, thirty-eight-unit residence for families of working poor and some seniors. The onsite programming is planned to aid in building stable, healthy families and supporting residents in breaking the cycle of poverty. The city of San Francisco considers the "life center" a model project. In a later report it was learned that the city had decided to clear a vacant lot across the street for use as a park.

In 1996, a letter was received from the executive director:

> This is an update on the 555 Ellis Street Family Apartments which you so generously funded. Some very good things are happening and we want you to be able to rejoice with us. First, we have received one of

The Years since Merger 177

twenty-one Honorable Mention Awards from the Maxwell Awards of Excellence Program for the Production of Low Income Housing. There were 197 applications. We were thrilled with this award.

Second, we will be included in a forthcoming book entitled *Rebuilding America: Design Excellence in Affordable Family Housing*. . . . A generous gift from a married couple who had previously given a gift for the construction of the building, has now enabled us to finish the roof garden. On August 3rd, residents gathered for a potluck brunch and a chance to choose which planter boxes they wished to use for their own cultivation. . . . This rooftop garden provides opportunity for our residents to grow some of their own vegetables . . . and to interact with one another in yet another way.

Programs in place for the residents now include help with homework for children, a summertime reading program, special tutoring for a few who have deficiencies in reading, special tutoring in upper division math, training in computer skills, art classes for children and youth and a high-level computer-assisted design program for some young people who have shown particular aptitude for that.

Women's Ordination for Ministry in Egypt and the Nile Valley (WOMEN)

The third objective to receive a portion of the 1992 Birthday Offering ($72,500) was the National Women's Association of the Synod of the Nile in Egypt to provide scholarships and education leading to the ordination of women.

The Evangelical (i.e. Presbyterian) Church of Egypt is the largest church of the 1.5 percent Protestant minority in a country where 90 percent of the population is Muslim, about 7 percent Coptic Orthodox, and 1.5 percent Catholic. The seeds of the Christian faith were planted in Egypt by the Apostle Mark in the first century, and the Church has had a continuing presence since that time despite various invasions and episodes of persecution throughout its history. The Evangelical Church began as an indigenous Christian renewal movement through mission work and was established as a distinct entity in 1863. From its earliest beginnings, the Evangelical Church, through the vision of its leaders and missionaries, placed a significant emphasis on the role of women in the life of the church. Female education was first instituted in Egypt by the Church's schools and other training centers.

As a result of the Church's full acknowledgment of the importance of the role of women, the National Women's Union of the Evangelical

Church of Egypt was established in 1954, with the purpose of networking, organizing, coordinating, unifying, and strengthening church women and their activities in the more than 200 congregations of the church.

Women have an important leadership role through various aspects of the life and witness of the church, such as voting at session meetings, carrying out social ministries in the community, leading Bible studies and preaching at women's meetings, youth conferences, leadership development events, counseling, and sometimes participating in evening Sunday worship. For a society that preserves traditional values, that is significant progress. However, only two women have been ordained as elders, and this has caused considerable controversy in the synod while at the same time raising consciousness on the issue.

Advocacy work is needed for full implementation of the action of the one-hundredth General Synod (1990) calling for representation of women on Church sessions and Church councils. In applying for funds from the Birthday Offering, the National Women's Association stated their goal and plans. The women plan to enter *intentionally* into a phase of planning and preparation of the Church and of women for the eventual ordination of women leaders for ministry. The project (WOMEN) is designed for training, which involved: 1) identification and recruitment of women leaders; 2) preparation of women's studies courses and theological seminary training of women candidates; 3) special seminars for women in leadership roles; 4) special opportunities for women in diverse ministries (chaplaincies, counseling, campus ministry, church education, etc.); 5) continuing education opportunities; and 6) participation in international conferences for women in ministry.

In a follow-up report, it is learned that the project began in January 1992 and three "inceptual/educational" training sessions and conferences were held—in Minia, Upper Egypt, in February 1992; in Alexandria in July 1993; and in Fayoum in September 1993. Women from all over Egypt and the Middle East attended. A meeting was held in April 1993 with leaders of the Presbyterian Church in order to pave the way for women's ordination. An intensive program on theological and social studies was planned for mid-November 1993, with four women from each of the eight presbyteries in the Synod of the Nile as participants.

The director of the project, Fawzia F. Ayad, wrote in the follow-up report: "Due to deeply rooted values and traditions, we are facing obstacles. In spite of that, challenging steps are being taken to prepare women for ordination. In the meantime, we are working on overcoming the obstacles."

At a meeting in 1991, forty Egyptian women, meeting to consider their status in the Church, concluded by having their picture taken behind a sign in Arabic which read, "Who will roll away the stone for us? For indeed it is very great."

Presbyterian Women in 1992 joined in partnership with their Christian sisters in Egypt to begin the process of "rolling away the stone."

1993

Gifts of Education

The theme of the 1993 Birthday Offering was "Gifts of Education"—education for inner-city youth in New York City, for young Pakistani women, and for Native American church leaders. The offering of $800,000 was divided among the objectives.

Operation Exodus—Inner City (OEIC) Youth, New York City

Operation Exodus—Inner City works with disadvantaged Hispanic children from upper Manhattan and the South Bronx. This area suffers from New York's highest crime rates, highest poverty levels, and lowest educational levels. On a daily basis these children face violence, drug abuse, and physical and emotional abuse. Furthermore, fewer than one in three students entering public high school will actually graduate. Many children will choose what are seemingly more accessible alternatives than education and jobs—joining street gangs, selling and using illegal drugs, and adopting crime-filled lives.

OEIC is strongly committed to freeing these inner-city children from poverty, oppression, and hopeless futures through education at every level—academic, social, and spiritual. OEIC works in cooperation with private schools across the country, placing children in schools and environments where their needs can be met. Children in grades seven through twelve are placed in Christian day or boarding schools outside New York City. Students attending day schools live with families from local churches. Children in nursery school through grade six attend private schools in New York City. Children also attend summer academic programs, summer camps, Vacation Bible School, and a Saturday tutoring program (during the school year). The children are required to attend church and Sunday school weekly, as well as other church-sponsored youth events.

OEIC works closely with the families of the children (usually single mothers with more than one child who are totally dependent on public assistance for the livelihoods of themselves and their children). OEIC holds mandatory parenting workshops, which include such topics as helping children study, self-esteem, and family budgeting. Counseling referrals are provided, where needed, for both children and parents. So far, OEIC has seen eight parents get off welfare and into jobs as a result of OEIC programs.

The results of OEIC, and the successes of its children, have been spectacular. OEIC has never had a child drop out of school and has placed students in colleges. OEIC is accountable to its board, which meets quarterly. It is also accountable to three local, PCUSA Hispanic churches, which are an integral part of the program.

When the proposal for the Birthday Offering was presented in late 1992, Operation Exodus was serving 115 children in thirty-four schools in New York City and across the nation. The idea was tried on an experimental basis in 1991–1992 at one Christian day school and on local church families. Students attending the school and living in stable home environments matured tremendously—academically, socially, personally, and spiritually. OEIC would like to expand this vision to include up to twenty new day schools and local churches across the country. The Creative Ministries Offering Committee designated $150,000 of the 1993 Presbyterian Women Birthday Offering to assist OEIC in expanding this ministry. Again, Presbyterian Women, through prayers and gifts, have helped to make a difference in the lives of children.

Young Pakistani Women (Two Schools)—Sangla Hill Girls School Hostel, A New Commitment to an Old Project

In 1903, the Women's Foreign Missionary Society of the United Presbyterian Church of North America established the Christian Girls Hostel, Middle and High School in the rural village of Sangla Hill. This school has offered educational opportunities to needy rural girls since that time. In 1993, ninety years later, a proposal was made for the Presbyterian Women Birthday Offering. The main target group to receive benefit from the offering was the same group that was benefitted in 1903—poor, rural, minority females.

Only 7 percent of girls participate in primary schools in rural areas of Pakistan. The estimated average annual income for rural minority families in Pakistan is $385; the average number of children per family is six; and the population growth is more than 3 percent, one of the highest in the world.

In 1993, 150 girls were housed in obsolete facilities with inadequate water supply and an unhealthful sanitation system. Half of the original

The Years since Merger

New residence hall for Christian Girls Hostel and High School, Kinnaird College, Pakistan.

buildings were in totally unusable condition, and the other buildings, though occupied, were becoming too dangerous to be occupied. According to engineers, the buildings should not be used for more than twelve months from that date. The proposal for the Birthday Offering was for money for totally new residential facilities for up to 200 girls (two double-story hostel blocks), and one floor of a new high school, plus immediate emergency provision of water supply and toilet block. In the next phase of the project, a hostel for primary boys, a second floor on the high school, and housing for administration and support staff will be built. In the final phase, there will be another hostel block for girls, the final floor of the high school, and a large hall for chapel and assemblies.

The Creative Ministries Offering Committee of Presbyterian Women designated $200,000 of the 1993 Birthday Offering toward Phase I of the construction project at Sangla Hill and to assist the United Presbyterian Education Board in Pakistan to sustain its longstanding commitment to female education by giving a new start to an old project.

Young Pakistani Women, Kinnaird College

In an era when higher education was frowned upon, the churches in Pakistan, particularly the Presbyterians, played a vital role in opening new frontiers by establishing, in 1913, Kinnaird College in the city of Lahore. Even today, in all of Pakistan, less than 1 percent of the women are in higher education. Now, with 1,750 enrolled and a constant demand for more admissions, Kinnaird, a Christian college for women, continues to maintain its longstanding tradition of excellence as Pakistan's leading educational institution for women. The students score in the highest percentile in state examinations and have a record of achievement in the life of the country.

In 1972, the government nationalized the college and then gave it autonomy in 1990. By 1993, the college was in need of a hostel, or dormitory, to serve its growing student body. After converting even storage space into dorm space, the college could house only one hundred students. The hostels at Kinnaird, despite nationalization, remain under the management of the churches and are run and supervised by Christian staff. The reputation of well-run hostels travels fast, resulting in requests from parents from troubled areas in Pakistan, the Middle East, and elsewhere to accept their daughters for enrollment in this safe environment. The hostels serve as a witness to the Lord by providing a safe, secure, and caring atmosphere for young women of all backgrounds.

Plans are under way to build a new hostel to accommodate one hundred students. Built of red brick, the hostel will have adequate kitchen, laundry, and toilet facilities. The layout is planned to ensure a sound security system. On the eightieth anniversary of the founding of the college, the Creative Ministries Offering Committee of Presbyterian Women designated $200,000 of the 1993 offering to help underwrite the construction of a new hostel at Kinnaird College. Thus, Presbyterian Women made a significant contribution to the building of the hostel and to the education of women in Pakistan.

Native American Church Leaders (*For other projects that benefitted Native Americans, see also 1926, 1938, 1954, 1964, 1966, transfer of funds—1976, 1982*)

National Indian Training & Research of Tempe, Arizona, under the sponsorship of the Native American Consulting Committee, submitted a proposal to Presbyterian Women for a portion of the 1993 Birthday Offering.

> Currently in the Presbyterian Church (USA) there are 115 Native American congregations. Of these 115 congregations, only twenty have Native American pastors. . . . Another six Native Americans are currently studying for ordination. The remaining 95 congregations are

serviced by non-Native Americans. In the past twenty years there hasn't been a single continuing education seminar or event designed especially for Native American leadership development.

The proposal continued by pointing out that attention needed to be given to identification, enlistment, and development of Native American pastoral and lay leadership. Some of the areas that were highlighted as ones needing attention were 1) workshops that focus on Native American spirituality, 2) training events for non-Native American pastors serving in Native communities, and 3) lay leadership development that updates leaders in ministerial duties and mission outreach.

The Native American Consulting Committee wrote that recruiting persons (focusing on women) to enter seminary is vital. They indicated that congregations do not understand or support the candidates in the process leading to ordination. They proposed organizing youth conferences, seminars, and workshops that address these issues and advise about scholarships and internships. The proposal pointed out the need for seminary professors to receive cultural-education training and for seminaries to offer courses that focus on Native American issues, tribal lore, spirituality, legal issues, and concerns.

In response to the proposal for funds to assist Native American seminary students, the Creative Ministries Offering Committee of Presbyterian Women designated $250,000 for the project. In a conversation in April 1996 with Harrell Davis, staff person in Louisville, he shared that it was expected originally that the grant would be used to work with the Nez Perce in leader development. However, the project was broadened to include eight synods and the program broadened to include youth, networking, and evangelism.

The eight synods that are involved in the project are Northeast, Sun, Lakes and Prairies, Rocky Mountains, Southwest, Alaska/Northwest, Southern California/Hawaii, and Pacific. The program is self-determining under the direction of the Native American Consulting Committee, with one representative from each of the eight synods and eight at-large members. The emphasis has been for the people in these regions to decide for themselves what the needs are. Youth have been involved in a significant way and the American Indian Youth Council has been involved.

Seven of the synods have identified needs and received seed money for projects that address these needs. Two synods—Lakes and Prairies and Rocky Mountains—joined together in an innovative effort called

"Wind over the Prairies." The emphasis of many of the synods has been youth involvement and congregational development. The Self-Development of People Program has been involved in supporting the program.

Presbyterian Women, through the Birthday Offering, have given gifts of reconciliation and hope to Native Americans in the community of the church.

1994

Reach Out, Protect the Children—Palestine Children in Dheisheh Refuge Camp, Israel

In 1994, a total of $800,000 was given to four projects to protect the lives of children—those living on the streets of Brazil and in the refugee camps of Palestine, those who have been abused in southern Appalachia, and international victims of torture now living in the United States. In the promotional material, Presbyterian Women were told, "No better investment exists than to help children and their mothers live into the fullness of life that Christ brings."

Project Green Life—Brazilian Street Children, Three Stage Project

The proposal for a grant from the 1994 Presbyterian Women Birthday Offering began:

> When we walk down the streets of our cities, we despair. Out of a population of 140 million people, 36 million children live in abject poverty. Since 1988, over 8000 children have been 'exterminated' by thugs, vigilante groups and the police. Brazil ranks third in the world in the number of documented AIDS cases. Only ten percent of the population visits a dentist regularly. Project 'Green Life' is an ecumenical program which seeks to plant the seed of hope in the lives of children, adolescents and women who have been marginalized and abandoned by family and society.

In the city of Sao Paulo, 600,000 children live on the streets. Street children are not angels. They steal, use drugs, fight, and kill people. In turn they are preyed upon, and annually 1,600 kids are purposefully killed.

In response to this appeal, the Creative Ministries Offering Committee of Presbyterian Women allocated $250,000 to Project Green Life. The

The Reverend Bev Swayze with street child, Sao Paulo, Brazil. (Courtesy—Ron Rice.)

project was carefully planned in three phases to address this gigantic problem, and it was envisioned that these projects would be a model to the city of Sao Paulo, which would be imitated throughout the city and the country.

Phase I is Project Emmaus, an educational shelter for twenty street children between ages seven and fourteen. In this safe place, the project planned to seek authorization from the state to be the permanent guardians of the children. At the same time, all aspects of the children's lives are to be cared for through good shelter, food, hygiene, and education. Part of the plan was for attempts to be made to change their habits and prepare them to be responsible citizens who can earn a living. In creative ways, the children will be told the Good News of a friend who never leaves or forsakes them, namely Jesus Christ.

Phase II is Project Morning Dew, a home for abandoned women and children with AIDS. In a planned caring environment, the residents

Favela family, Sao Paulo. (Courtesy—Ron Rice.)

would have a secure place to eat, to be clothed, to have daily activities, and to receive medical attention in the spirit of the Christ.

Phase III, Project Boca Bonita (Radiant Smile), was part of a plan for a fully equipped dental office to cater to the dental needs of these children and mothers and to reach others in a district of Sao Paulo where 20,000 children and adolescents. live.

Project Green Life is an ecumenical, cooperative effort of the Independent Presbyterian Church of Brazil, the United Presbyterian Church of Brazil, and the Independent Baptist Church of Brazil. Two members of each of the congregations, plus one mission coworker from the Presbyterian Church (USA), serve on the board. In addition, one of these persons serves as treasurer. (The PCUSA relates to three Presbyterian entities in Brazil—the Presbyterian Church of Brazil [IPB], the largest of the three; the Independent Presbyterian Church of Brazil [IPI], which split off from the IPB early in the century; and the United Presbyterian Church of Brazil [IPU], the smallest of the three.)

In a follow-up report in 1995, Knox and Bev Swayze, mission coworkers, wrote about progress in the first two phases of Project Green Life. The "Ex-Street Kid House" had two women doing an internship, one full-time, one part-time, with an experienced group of people who work on the streets with the kids. A home, in an excellent location, has been given to the project. It is close to bus lines and an excellent night school. The house must be remodeled, but it was estimated it would open in early 1996. One boy had already been recruited for the house. At the end of 1995, the Swayzes wrote that they were, at that time, working with twenty kids who live in a metro/train station and that work was progressing on renovation of the house.

In July 1995, a farm in Sorocaba, about an hour's drive from Sao Paulo, had been rented with hopes of eventually buying it. The Children of Bethlehem House, a home for children with HIV, is located in Sorocaba. Due to changing needs, the home is available for children up to age five who were born with AIDS. Project Green Life has been working very closely with the Evangelical Hospital in Sorocaba as well as several Presbyterian churches. All of the furniture and most of the equipment was donated by the local Rotary Club. The YMCA had also gotten involved. In the report at the end of 1995, the Swayzes wrote that:

> The community of Sorocaba has really begun to support the house, from donations of fresh bread given daily by a local bakery to money being given by the local telephone company to buy an industrial strength dryer. Along with paid staff, two retired nurses are volunteering.

There are plans to build a wing for those children and their families who are receiving treatment for AIDS at the Evangelical Hospital but cannot afford to stay at the hospital.

Project Boca Bonita had not been implemented as of July 1995. However, in the report at the end of 1995, the Swayzes reported the exciting news that an equipped dental office had been donated!

Project Green Life is working to alleviate in some small way the misery of Brazilian women and children, leading them to the knowledge and wholeness found in Christ, and is serving in a powerful way as witnesses to the kind of servant lives Christians are called to live.

Victims of Torture (Africa, Middle East, Asia, Central and South America, Eastern Europe), Minneapolis, Minnesota

In the January/February issue of *Horizons* magazine we read:

> On River Road in Minneapolis is a big, tawny house with a wide welcoming front porch. Inside, among the inviting greenery, bookcases and Hmong hangings, is a haven for victims of torture who come to Minnesota from Africa, the Middle East, Asia, Central and South America and most recently, from Central Europe.

The Center for Victims of Torture (CVT) opened in 1985, and in the decade following, about 420 men, women, and children received treatment for torture-related injuries. Survivors of torture live with the ongoing physical and psychological horror of brutality intentionally inflicted by repressive governments. These governments have long been skilled at using torture to destroy the morale and lives of individuals and their communities. Only in recent years has significant energy been focused on learning how to care for and heal the emotional, mental, and physical scars of the survivors.

The Center for Victims of Torture appealed to Presbyterian Women for a portion of the 1994 Birthday Offering. The Creative Ministries Offering Committee responded by allocating $200,000 of the offering in support of two initiatives proposed by CVT—The Child Survivor Project: Creating a Service Model for Child Survivors of Torture and International Training to Support New Treatment Centers for Torture Survivors in Nations of Recent or Active Repression.

The Child Survivor Project resulted from an analysis of current CVT clients and changing demographic trends. Some of the facts given were as follows: Nearly 20 percent of CVT clients were tortured as children, usually as a weapon against their parents; and an increasing number of clients (now more than 30 percent) have children living with them, many

Minneapolis Center for Victims of Torture provides medical and psychological treatment.

of whom were forced to witness the torture of their parents. In working with children who were either primary or secondary victims of torture, CVT staff have documented disruption of the developmental processes as well as special difficulties involved with the rehabilitative process. In addition, an increasing number of children in American schools are refugees, and, according to CVT, it is a near certainty that for each of these children, either they or a family member directly suffered some kind of human-rights-related trauma.

The proposed solution to these problems was to develop a model addressing the special needs of these young people with four objectives: 1) to explore the needs of primary and secondary child and adolescent victims of torture, 2) to design appropriate intervention and treatment strategies to support their healing, 3) to build links with other agencies serving refugee children in order to enhance CVT's referral capacity and provide training to the other agencies, and 4) to disseminate the results of CVT's work to key constituencies that can aid child survivors.

The second project, training for new treatment centers, results from the urgent need to promote the creation or support the growth of treatment centers in areas of repression around the world. More than one hundred governments either practice or condone the use of torture. According to CVT, fully sixty governments actively invest in the technology of torture. Additional specialized treatment centers are needed as sources of learning for health-care professionals, as symbols of hope and recovery to communities, and as places of safety and healing for survivors. CVT proposes to provide specialized training from health-care professionals to emerging treatment groups in at least five nations of active or recent repression. CVT also proposes to assist the emerging treatment groups with organization building and community support concepts in order to assist their long-term institutional growth and effectiveness and to link the emerging treatment groups to international support in order to monitor and protect their safety.

Appalachian Abused Women's Resource Center, Southern West Virginia *(For related projects, see also 1990, 1995, 1996, 1997)*

Since 1983, when the doors of the Women's Resource Center in Beckley, West Virginia, were opened as a shelter for survivors of domestic violence, local businesses and civic groups have rallied together with churches to maintain the refuge for battered women from seven counties in Appalachia. In a period of twelve months from June 1992, more than

Appalachia Abused Women's Resource Center serves seven counties.

200 adults and 290 children received help. The center is located in Raleigh County, a rural area in the heart of Appalachia. The Women's Resource Center (WRC) takes care of twenty-four percent of all sheltered domestic cases in the entire state of West Virginia.

The current facility at the time the proposal was submitted (June 1993) could house up to thirty-six individuals in nine nine-feet-by-eleven-feet dormitory-style rooms. The dining area was so small that residents often had to eat in shifts. The lounge area, which was thirteen feet by fifteen feet had to suffice for all residents. The need to expand was urgent, and WRC applied for a portion of the 1994 Birthday Offering. The Creative Ministries Offering Committee of Presbyterian Women, in response, designated $250,000 for the project.

In addition to housing residents, the shelter program includes individual counseling, group counseling, parenting classes, art therapy, homebound school for all school-aged children, adult basic education, client advocacy, children's structured activities, medical care, and administrative functions. All of this was done in two small offices, one meeting room, a reception area, and a playroom. Four to eight staff members and volunteers had to negotiate the use of the space on a daily basis. The adult basic education teacher used a storage room for teaching her clients. WRC had clearly outgrown its facilities.

The objective of the project was to build a new addition to the existing structure that would house shelter residents comfortably. These persons need a quiet, private space in which to make important decisions that will affect the lives of their families. In addition, the project called for renovation of the existing building to expand office and meeting room space and for a modern kitchen and dining area large enough to accommodate all shelter residents.

Presbyterian Women were not the only ones who joined in supporting this ambitious program. In a follow-up letter dated February 16, 1994, the WRC Executive Director wrote that to date $513,000, including the grant from Presbyterian Women, had been committed. These pledges included gifts and grants from the West Virginia Homeless Shelters Program, the West Virginia Housing Development Fund, the Beckley Area Foundation, the Benedum Foundation, the Episcopal Church United Thank Offering, and the UPS Foundation.

At the time the letter was written, final plans had been approved and approval was pending from the state architect, after which advertising for bidding and selection of a contractor would be made by the Raleigh County Commission. "Because the project is funded in part by federal funds, it must be administered through a unit of government." The plan was to break ground by the end of March. No further report was in the files.

With the help of Presbyterian Women, WRC is making a difference in the lives of survivors of domestic violence and abuse.

Palestinian Children in Dheisheh Refuge Camp—Multi-Purpose Child Guidance Center

The Dheisheh Refugee Camp lies on the road between Jerusalem and Hebron. Living in the enclosed camp are 1,574 families, a total of 7,795 persons. Since the beginning of the Intifada, or organized resistance, in December 1987, the camp has been a center for Arab confrontation of Israeli occupational forces. As a result, it has been a target for Israeli military and economic blockade. The children of Dheisheh live in an extremely hostile and economically deprived environment, which negatively affects their emotional, psychological, and social well-being. In February 1993, when the proposal for the Birthday Offering was written, schools and other public services and gathering places had been closed.

What happens to children who not only see repression and violence firsthand but also experience it themselves? Children for whom there is

Dheisheh Refugee Camp provides safe haven for children in war-torn Israel.

no safe place, not even their meager homes? They, of course, get caught up in the conflict. The only games they play are war games. They lose interest in learning. They become timid and fearful about playing outdoors, or they become aggressive and unruly. Their childhood is lost.

The Jerusalem-based Women's International League for Peace and Freedom established the Dheisheh Multi-Purpose Child Guidance Care Center with several objectives: 1) to provide comprehensive assessment and treatment of children who suffer psychological and physical damage as a result of living in a war zone, 2) to provide psychological support and training for families of these children, and 3) to enable children to respond to treatment and make a healthy contribution to their own future and to the Palestinian people. The expected outcome is that children will be able to express their anger and pain in an appropriate environment, that individualized programs of counseling and treatment will bring about a positive change in the child's behavior and help the child to cope in an insecure and hostile environment, and that children will receive follow-up care and support in the community.

The Creative Ministries Offering Committee of Presbyterian Women selected this project as one of the recipients of the 1994 Birthday Offering and designated $100,000 for the center, praying that with the help of the offering, the children may recapture a little of their lost childhood.

1995

Listen to your Brothers and Sisters in Africa (Cameroon, Ghana, Kenya), in North America (Huntsville, Alabama, and Chicago, Illinois), in Asia (Cambodia), and in the Caribbean (Dominican Republic)

The Creative Ministries Offering Committee of Presbyterian Women chose five widely scattered projects for the 1995 offering. A total offering of $800,000 was received for the five objectives.

Africa's Christian Women Working for Health, Peace, and Repatriation of Refugees, Cameroon, Ghana, Kenya

"The Women's organizations in many African partner churches of the Presbyterian Church (USA) are making vital, indispensable and unique contributions to their churches' ministries of healing, reconciliation and human fulfillment," according to an opening statement from the Worldwide Ministries Division of the PCUSA, Louisville, in an application for the 1995 Birthday Offering. "Three such projects are exemplary examples of the new leadership in ministry that women are giving to church and society." The Creative Ministries Offering Committee of Presbyterian Women chose to give $200,000 of the offering in support of the three projects.

The first was a new project in Cameroon, "Evangelization through Primary Health Care." The project already had organized one-week training sessions where women learn that health is spiritual (faith in Jesus Christ) and physical (family, hygiene, nutrition, and disease prevention and detection) as well as social and mental (harmony with family and community). As a result of training, women in seven communities have organized church-based health-care committees. The women's organization of the Eglise Presbyterienne Camerounaise and the Christian Women's Health Organization are working closely with Dorothy Brewster-Lee, MD, mission coworker physician, to develop this innovative leadership program.

The second project for Christian-Muslim relations in Africa is located in Ghana and works to foster understanding and cooperation between Christians and Muslims. With mission coworker the Rev. Janice Nessibou as coordinator, the women's program is expanding to include interfaith marriage counseling, family planning, and conflict resolution. Women in several other Central and West African nations will learn peacemaking skills as the program spreads through the network of Christian women's organizations.

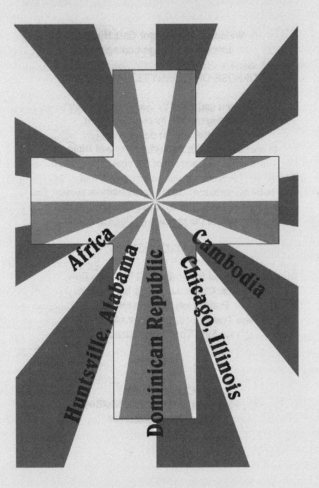

Birthday Offering brochure, 1995.

In Kenya, where the third project is being undertaken, the women's program of the ecumenical, international All Africa Conference of Churches (AACC) is challenging the difficulties women face in many parts of the continent. Of particular concern is the tremendous number of refugees—mostly women and children—fleeing into countries like Kenya, Angola, and Mozambique. Their governments, even with the help of humanitarian agencies, have few resources for meeting any but the most basic needs. The AACC is helping women refugees identify, prioritize and work on their family's survival needs. Even so, when the needs are identified and prioritized, there are still economic implications. Seed money from the Birthday Offering of Presbyterian Women will establish self-help projects that will enable repatriated refugee women to play a key role in their country's reconstruction when they return to their farms and villages.

Through support of these three projects, Presbyterian Women join with their Christian sisters in Africa in working for health, peace, and repatriation of refugees.

Khemara Rural Development Program for Women Farmers in Cambodia

Women make up sixty-five percent of the population in Cambodia and have been particularly hard hit by the changes in Cambodia over the past twenty years. A legacy of war and repression has devastated the country's population and infrastructure and left 6 to 10 million land mines in the national territory, posing an ongoing hidden threat to rural development. Rural poverty has long served the Khmer Rouge in their efforts to organize among Cambodia's poorest, so rural development is key to Cambodia's hopes for a peaceful future.

In an effort to organize Cambodians to work together to resolve problems and to mend the social fabric of a country where personal mistrust runs high in the wake of severe repression, Khemara was founded in 1991 as Cambodia's first native nongovernmental organization (NGO). Khemara has trained its all Khmer staff in community development and provides similar training to other Cambodian NGOs, seeking to strengthen the abilities of Cambodians to shape their own future and rebuild their nation. Khemara has worked with two communities in Phnom Penh, enabling women to assume successfully multiple roles as single heads of households, mothers, and primary breadwinners.

For the first time, Khemara is seeking to expand its program into rural areas. With a program focusing on technical training to improve women farmers' skills in agriculture, animal husbandry, literacy, simple arithmetic, and business skills, Khemara plans to support women whose livelihood depends on their skills as farmers. Long-term objectives are to install safe and reliable water sources for agriculture, drinking, and household use; to build community-based centers that provide health care, child care, and access to school for all school-aged children; and to increase the living standards of households headed by women farmers. The process for accomplishing these objectives is to establish a village committee and social support network in each village; to provide training to women farmers in agriculture, animal husbandry, basic mathematics, literacy and business management; and to develop a credit program to purchase supplies like seeds, fertilizer, and livestock.

Oxfam America has been funding Khemara's work since 1991. Oxfam is a nonprofit international agency that funds grassroots groups in poor countries in Africa, Asia, the Americas, and the Caribbean. Oxfam seeks to empower people to promote change from the "bottom up." The name *Oxfam* comes from the Oxford Committee for Famine Relief, founded in England in 1942. Oxfam America, based in Boston, was established in 1970 and is one of seven autonomous Oxfams around the world.

The Khemara Rural Development Program, through Oxfam America and the Presbytery of Boston (Synod of the Northeast) made application for the 1995 Birthday Offering. The Creative Ministries Offering Committee of Presbyterian Women designated $100,000 for Khemara, thus helping the poorest of the poor—Cambodia's rural women—to begin to rebuild their families, culture, and community.

Health Education, and Preventive Medicine Center, Dominican Republic

The title of the application for assistance with the health project in the Dominican Republic was "Building a Healthier Future in Paradise." Paraiso is an isolated, coastal town in Barahona, Dominican Republic. Approximately 22,000 Dominicans and Haitians live there and in the surrounding mountain villages. With no permanent medical facilities, people often die from treatable illnesses and injuries such as cuts, asthma, and diarrhea. For women, the leading cause of death is lack of care during childbirth. Babies are born underweight and malnourished.

In an effort to unite with Dominicans in providing for basic health needs, caring Christians in the United States and Dominican Republic have dedicated themselves to bringing affordable health care to Paraiso. They have formed the Paraiso Health Assistance Program, which made

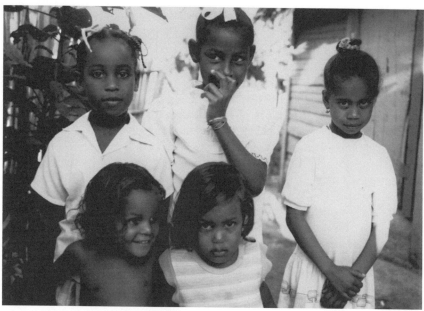

The children of Paraiso, Dominican Republic.

application for a portion of the 1995 Birthday Offering. The Creative Ministries Offering Committee of Presbyterian Women responded by allocating $150,000 for the program. With the help of the offering and a construction team provided by the Dominican government, they intend to build a Health Education and Preventive Medicine Center. Thirty-five neighborhood health promoters, already providing short-term first aid, will be trained at the center as lay medical workers in their communities. A radio communications system will link them to the center.

Once the center is built and the health-education program under way, the University of Santo Domingo and American universities have agreed to provide medical consultants and educators for a wide variety of basic courses on nutrition, sanitation, substance abuse, pre- and postnatal care, and many other topics. Marcia J. Lewis, a member of First Presbyterian Church, Avenel, New Jersey, has through her church's sponsorship worked full-time since 1992 in the Dominican Republic to bring the Paraiso Health Assistance Program into being. She says, "We have experienced great successes as a result of our hard work and faith. . . . Education offers the community the tools to attend to their own needs, empowering them to look for their own solutions to crises. . . . It's in God's hands now."

The Birthday Offering supports medical clinics like this one in Paraiso, Dominican Republic.

(Information for this project came from the January/February issue of *Horizons* magazine. No information or proposal or application forms were in the folders.)

Mother Advocates Program, Huntsville, Alabama *(For related projects, see also 1991, 1994, 1996, 1997)*

"Implementing and Replicating a Mother Advocates Program" was the project title chosen by the National Children's Advocacy Center (NCAC) of Huntsville, Alabama, on their proposal for a portion of the 1995 Birthday Offering. The NCAC, a nonprofit organization, is dedicated to preventing, intervening in, and educating the public about child abuse and neglect. The intervention component, addressing primarily sexual or severe physical abuse, provides child-sensitive interviewing and therapy, support through the prosecution process, and case monitoring. To ensure that no child's case is mishandled, child protection workers, police investigators, counselors, prosecutors, and a pediatrician meet weekly to review active cases. Individual counseling and support groups are offered for child victims, their nonoffending family members and adult survivors. In its ten-year existence, the NCAC has helped 200 other communities develop similar programs based on the Huntsville model.

Since the NCAC's Clinical Department was formed six years ago, practice, experience, and research have shown that the two most important factors in helping child victims recover from abuse are early intervention and support of the nonoffending parent.

The NCAC is proposing another program that will help abused children by giving support to the nonoffending parent. Since most often the nonoffending parent is the mother, this project will target mothers. The nonoffending parent is a secondary victim of the abuser's betrayal. After disclosure, the mother is faced with making life-changing decisions that may conflict with her most cherished ideals about marriage or relationships, or about her sense of competence as a spouse or parent. She is often forced to choose between her spouse and children and even between children. The nonoffending mother experiences severe trauma herself and needs clinical services and other resources to assist her in meeting her own and her children's needs. "It is imperative," in the words of NCAC, "that a mother's ability to provide protection for the child victim be assessed and supported." As a part of the project, the Clinical Department will utilize and train caregivers to minister to mothers of child victims.

The NCAC requested funds from the Birthday Offering to implement a two-year Mother Advocates Program. The Creative Ministries Offering Committee of Presbyterian Women chose this project as one of the five to receive a portion of the offering, $150,000. The program will be administered by the NCAC Clinical Director and a program coordinator. Six Mother Advocates will be employed and trained to provide support information, services, advocacy, referrals, etc., for the mother and her family. In its ten-year existence, the NCAC has helped 200 other communities develop similar programs based on the Huntsville model.

The Mother Advocates Program has the potential to improve the lives of families of abused children, and Presbyterian Women are quick to listen to the hurting cries of children and the despair of our sisters, the secondary victims.

Teen Mothers Residence, Chicago, Illinois

Through its Creative Ministries Offering Committee, Presbyterian Women united with Chicago's Community Services West to provide a homelike residence for teen mothers. The committee chose to designate $200,000 of the Presbyterian Women Birthday Offering to this project. Community Services West is an administrative organization for three community and church-based African-American agencies with a track record of working with the strengths of the people served to make a positive difference in difficult situations. They offer role models who provide discipline, evaluation and loving support to young women making an effort to change their lives.

According to a task force appointed by the Governor of Illinois, there are conservatively 21,535 homeless youth, ages fourteen to twenty, in Illinois. Among these youth, the report suggests that 7,900 had been rejected by their parents, 9,000 were sexually exploited while on the streets, and more than 7,000 became pregnant or were parenting teen mothers. Homeless youth live in constant danger, fear, hunger, and exhaustion. In Chicago, Community Services West is offering a glimmer of hope to homeless youth. Already it provides two state-approved high schools for dropouts and at-risk youth. But homelessness causes severe disruption of the educational process. With the help of the Birthday Offering, Community Services West plans to add a homelike residence that will house twenty-five teen mothers and their thirty-one children.

Life is especially hard for the children of homeless teens. They are almost always behind their peers physically and cognitively. For some of these teens and their children, there is a glimmer of hope waiting in a welcoming residence, thanks, in part, to Presbyterian Women.

1996

Multi-Cultural Child Development Center, Preschool Building, Santa Rosa, California

The West Santa Rosa Local Action Council, Inc., presented a proposal to Presbyterian Women for a portion of the 1996 Birthday Offering. The Council is a nonprofit organization with a board of directors. In response to the request, the Creative Ministries Offering Committee designated $100,000 to be used as partial funding for a new preschool building at the multicultural project.

Sixty-two multiethnic children from low-income, ethnically diverse families will benefit from the brand-new building. Three- to five-year-olds attend preschool at the center at no cost through an operations grant from the California Office of Education. The new facility will allow the center to continue and expand current direct services, which include parent education and a comprehensive nutrition program serving two meals daily. With a new building, the number of children served can be increased, an adult literacy program can be established, hours of service

Birthday Offering brochure, 1996.

extended, and a much-needed day-care program inaugurated (not possible in present limited facilities).

For twenty-one years, Knox Presbyterian Church subsidized the program by keeping the lease agreement well below market rates, but the church now needed the space for its own growing congregation and ministries. The center's operating budget precludes using any of the money for purchase of a building. Knox Presbyterian Church and Redwoods Presbytery set aside the needed land for a new building. The Santa Rosa Rotary Club will assist in fund raising, provide a pro bono legal and architectural services, as well as in-kind donations. Land values are extremely high, and suitable property is very scarce and expensive. The Knox Church location is ideally near low-income housing and is accessible by public transportation. The urgent need was for funding for construction of the building, estimated to cost $460,000.

Families served by the program are all below poverty-level income, including homeless families, single parents, parents in college, or other training programs, or simply families working for very low wages. Many of the families are refugees from Southeast Asia or Eritria and immigrants from Latin America. The center's program provides English language skills, mainstreams children with special education needs, and builds self-esteem and confidence. The curriculum promotes cultural awareness and teaches racial tolerance.

Presbyterian Women, through money contributed throughout the country, are thankful to be partners in providing a safe, healthy, educational environment that meets children's needs.

Mobile Dental Clinic, Asheville, North Carolina

The Creative Ministries Offering Committee of Presbyterian Women allocated $100,000 for this project, a mobile dental clinic. *Horizons* magazine reported on the project in the January/February 1996 issue:

> "Picture it! A 40-foot dental office on wheels, traveling the hills and coves of southern Appalachia, five days a week, forty-eight weeks a year, rain or shine! Think how it could reach children living in this rugged terrain who would otherwise never see a dentist. A mobile clinic could go where the children are—schools, strip malls, churches, playgrounds."

> Olson Huff, pediatrician, Presbyterian elder, and Medical Director of the Ruth and Billy Graham Children's Center, Memorial Mission Hospital,

The ToothBus, a mobile dental clinic supported by Birthday Offerings.

Asheville, North Carolina, "has been working with regional agencies to identify their unmet health needs in the 8,000-mile area served by Memorial Mission hospital. A statewide survey showed that children in this region have a great need for preventive and restorative dental care. Dr. Huff sees the clinic van as the answer because it can be available weekends and evenings. And by going where Appalachian families are, the program has a chance to overcome traditional reluctance to seek out health care for their children.

No information was available on how the ongoing work of the project will be financed, the cost of personnel, or cost of operations.

Our House, New Birth for Violent-Free Living, Greenville, Mississippi
(For related projects, see also 1987, 1990, 1994, 1995, 1997)
The Bible verse used on the brochure distributed by Our House speaks to the purpose of the ministry—new birth for violent-free living: *"'Therefore, we do not lose heart. Though outwardly we are wasting away, yet inwardly we are being renewed day by day' (2 Corinthians 4:16)."* This project is situated in the geographic area known as Mississippi's Mid-Delta, an eight-county rural community, one of the nation's most disadvantaged and impoverished regions. Out of a population of 245,000, 60 percent is

minority. Many are caught in a web of poverty, lack of education, and domestic strife.

For nine years, an ecumenical group of women of color ran a shelter for raped and battered women. In addition to providing food, clothing, shelter, and counseling to survivors, they reached out to 50,000 people through innovative, award-winning programs. These include Mississippi's first domestic-violence conference; a Christian youth choir for youth suffering from exposure to violence; a statewide networking event for victims, care providers, social workers, and law enforcers; a nine-county high school conference on date rape and violence, empowerment, and self-esteem; and interactive law-enforcement training for officers and judges.

The needs to be met by Our House, according to the staff, are threefold: 1) to enhance and expand direct (shelter care, counseling, advocacy) and preventive (education and public awareness) services for abused persons and to institute a new program to aid persons victimized by rape; 2) to empower a group of talented Christian women who are care providers to work in this important mission free from consistent, unbearable sexism and racism, with a sense of ownership and pride; and 3) to provide adequate, comfortable living and recovery space for the growing number of domestic violence victims through the purchase of a primary safe house.

The four objectives for this project as spelled out in the proposal are 1) to expand immediate temporary care through innovative, volunteer run safe houses in each of the eight targeted counties (three are being serviced by the current shelter program); 2) to initiate primary prevention through increased public awareness via special presentations, literature, and creative activities for youth and adults in the Mississippi Delta; 3) to coordinate, for the first time, court-ordered treatment programs for offenders; and 4) to launch a new crisis program to aid victims of rape.

The staff of the project determined that in order to expand and provide the services needed, the project needed a separate facility and independence in management. The proposal to Presbyterian Women for a portion of the 1996 Birthday Offering was for a grant to assist with purchasing or building a new facility, Our House, Inc., a domestic violence and rape crisis center. The Creative Ministries Offering Committee approved the request and made a grant of $350,000 for the new center. Federal, state, and local grants will continue to provide program funds. Presbyterian Women join hands with this committed, resourceful team of women as they continue to develop imaginative new approaches for preventing the wounds of domestic violence.

Women's Health in Haiti

Through a new program, women and their families in Haiti will benefit from a clinic and training provided by two highly respected, established organizations, MADRE, a multiracial, cross-class agency in New York City, and its sister organization in Haiti, SOFA (Solidarity with Haitian Women). The need for such a program is great. The 1991 *coup d'etat* drove Haiti, the poorest country in the Western Hemisphere, into total economic collapse. Even with the restoration of democratically elected President Jean-Bertrand Aristide, the economy remains crippled and services nonexistent. Malnutrition and disease, and, of course, AIDS are rampant. Furthermore, the country continues to recover from three years of brutal, repressive military rule and state-sponsored terrorism that included the violation of women. Women who attempted any resistance, regardless of their community or age group, ran the risk of being raped, gang raped, or otherwise tortured by the military and their civilian supporters.

Women's and children's clinic provides health care and immunizations in Haiti.

MADRE program provides supplies to Haitian school children.

MADRE and SOFA are working to meet the long- and short-term needs of Haitian women rape victims and their families. Three goals have been set: 1) to establish a clinic that will provide gynecology and health services, with special attention given to victims of rape. This involves seeking funds to rent, paint, furnish, and prepare the clinic; pay salaries for a staff of four, including one physician; and provide waiting rooms, medical equipment, supplies, medicines, and shipping costs; 2) to provide personnel from MADRE to travel to Haiti to train workers in rape counseling. MADRE has developed an extensive network of volunteer health-care professionals who can provide SOFA with training and technical support; and 3) to record the testimonies of raped women to be used in a petition to the Organization of American States Inter-American Commission on Human Rights. An attorney with the Harvard Law Project is in charge of training MADRE and members of SOFA in the techniques required for legal documentation, thus leading to prosecution of the rapes as war crimes.

The Creative Ministries Offering Committee chose this project as one of five to receive the 1996 Birthday Offering of Presbyterian Women and awarded $100,000 for Women's Health in Haiti.

Project Vida Demonstration Day Care Center, El Paso, Texas

Project Vida (Life) is a comprehensive, community-based Presbyterian program that works with community residents in responding to community needs. Project Vida serves a very low-income Hispanic barrio two blocks from the Juarez border in El Paso. Median salary is less than $7,000 for a family of four. Sixty-five percent of adults have less than a ninth-grade education. Housing is seriously overcrowded and dilapidated. The area has triple the violent crime rate of the rest of the city. The community is medically underserved and has the second highest number of teen pregnancies in El Paso County. The community has a very large number of low birth weight babies and mothers delivering without prenatal care.

As you can see, parenting and child care are serious problems. There is a waiting list of over 2,000 families for day-care slots. Many children are left in the care of older children during the day while a parent works. Infants and small children are kept as quiet as possible to avoid waking or disturbing others in very tight quarters. Young parents are unsure of themselves, and stress leads to cases of physical abuse or neglect.

Project Vida has developed a primary care clinic, housing programs, nutrition programs, as well as education and gang prevention programs. But the services are not adequate to meet the needs. An annual community congress (representatives of more than 850 registered families in the community) has proposed a three-pronged approach to improving both parenting and available child care:

1. Project Vida will develop a demonstration day care center for thirty children that will involve and train six community residents as staff and eight community residents as volunteers to develop a learning center for day care providers working in their homes.

2. Project Vida will provide training opportunities and contacts for fifty persons providing child care in their homes.

3. Project Vida will provide parenting support and training, as well as case management as needed, for parents wanting support or who are determined to be at-risk for child abuse and neglect. Project Vida estimates that they will work with 65 to 75 families each year at this level.

An article in the May 1995 issue of the *Journal of American Medical Association*, by Andrew A. Skolnick, begins:

> People who live in Zip Code 79905 are among the poorest of the poor in the fourth-most impoverished city in the U.S. The population of this

Texas community, which butts up against the U.S./Mexico border in eastern El Paso, consists mostly of native-born Mexican Americans and documented and undocumented Mexican immigrants.

Until the establishment of a community clinic in 1990 run by a Presbyterian ministry called Project Vida, most members of this neighborhood had few options when they became ill. . . . The project's clinic provides health services to more than a thousand families who live in one of the nation's most underserved communities.

An article in the El Paso *Herald-Post* on March 10, 1995, reads:

Through its medical and social services, project Vida has become the backbone of a run-down South Central El Paso community that often ranks among the poorest in the city. Five years ago the nonprofit organization established by the Presbyterian Church moved into a tiny building at 3607 Riviera Ave. The clinic, which offers family-practice services, was one of the first programs Project Vida got off the ground. Project Vida serves about 850 families with median household income of $7,000 for a family of four. There are classes for English and citizenship courses, a gang-prevention program, and a housing project. Another popular program is Food Care, which allows participants to buy about $30 worth of food at a discounted price of $13 in cash, food stamps or service credits acquired through volunteer service. Those who attend two hours of health presentations are also given service credits that may be used for the purchases.

Such is the positive publicity that Project Vida has received. Much of the success of the programs is due to the dedicated leadership and hard work of codirectors Rev. Bill Schlesinger and Carol Schlesinger. In response to a proposal for a portion of the 1996 Presbyterian Women Birthday Offering, the Creative Ministries Offering Committee designated $170,000 for Project Vida—Project Life (see also 1986).

In a communication from the Schlesingers on March 14, 1997, an update is given:

The Birthday Offering allowed us to begin the program at the Early Childhood Development Center. About 30 children are in the program daily and there is a waiting list. Parents enroll in parenting for at least two sessions a month. The parenting [is having] as much of an impact as the direct work with children.

The following story, which they shared, is worth repeating:

Juan (not his real name) had been raised with cuffs and harsh words. He was to be a strong male; crying was not allowed. He was in his early twenties, and increasingly frustrated with his hyper-active child who seemed to ignore both harsh words and cuffs. In the parenting group he began to talk through his own frustration and how his discipline methods didn't work. He and his wife were able to talk about different ways to work with their child, to distract rather than demand and to delight in the good things their three year old had to offer. Over several months Juan agreed to stop hitting his child, and began to relax about his own role as a father. He and his wife reported real improvement in both their child's behavior and their own relationship. After a long period with wrestling [with the decision], they agreed to have a developmental pediatrician review their son's development.

Juan's child, José, was a bright and energetic three year old. He had no fear and would gleefully demolish other children's projects. Totally out of hand, he showed little restraint or resentment of punishment. Early Childhood Development Classes were his first structured experience. Gradually the routine of the class gave him a sense of limits. Over a period of three months he became more interested in the activities of the class than in knocking over tables and chairs. He is still energetic, creative and impulsive, but has a sense of belonging to a group and being able to accomplish tasks.

1997

This book went to print before the 1997 Birthday Offering of Presbyterian Women was received, but the goal was $800,000, and if past history is an indication, that goal will, once again, be realized. There were five objectives chosen by the Creative Ministries Offering Committee for this seventy-fifth anniversary year. The amount assigned to each objective is dependent on reaching the total goal of the 1997 objectives.

The Duvall Home, Meeting Needs of Disabled Women, Glenwood, Florida

For fifty-two years the Duvall Home has been meeting the long-term residential care needs of mentally challenged children. The Duvall Home

Duvall Home serves more than 250 mentally challenged adults in a campus-like setting.

now proposes to increase its program of services by constructing a family-type group home specifically designed to meet the special needs and abilities of mentally challenged women. This group home will be handicapped accessible and be evaluated by Florida licensing agencies. It will be operated and staffed twenty-four hours a day. By incorporating group homes into the program of services, the Duvall Home will provide opportunities for residents to become a part of the mainstream and provide solutions for families faced with special needs. The goal for this objective, as determined by the Creative Ministries Offering Committee, is $125,000.

Rural Ministry, Giving Poor Children a Chance, Johns Island, South Carolina

The second recipient of the 1997 Presbyterian Women Birthday Offering is the Facilities Improvement for Rural Mission, Inc., Johns Island, South Carolina. A new multiuse facility will allow the mission to focus on an array of social and humanitarian services and ministries. The facility will house a Headstart Center and provide areas for drug- and substance-abuse programs, expanded activities for the elderly, the disadvantaged at-risk island youth, and the migrant and Hispanic community. This ministry will provide important services for the children of the migrant workers (mostly Hispanic), who labor in the vegetable fields, and the children of the resident black population. The goal for this project is $200,000.

The Years since Merger

Villa International, Atlanta, Georgia *(See also 1941, 1970)*

Villa International, Atlanta, is an ecumenical ministry of housing and hospitality for international visitors, operated by seven denominations: United Methodist, Episcopal, United Church of Christ, Disciples of Christ, Roman Catholic, Evangelical Lutheran, and Presbyterian (USA). Villa provides affordable housing and genuine hospitality to professionals from around the globe who are studying primarily at the Center for Disease Control (CDC) and Emory University. Villa is a five-minute walk from CDC and a twelve-minute walk from Emory. From time to time, Villa International also offers its facilities for private retreats.

In 1970, the entire Women of the Church Birthday Offering, $312,430, went to construct Villa International. A little know fact is that a second gift went to Villa International in 1972. An endowment fund of $10,000 was originally given in 1941 for the upkeep of Collegiate Hall in Montreat. After the property was sold in the late fifties, the fund was kept intact until 1972, when the Board of Women's Work voted to redesignate the entire endowment, $10,000, plus interest that had accrued for nearly

Villa International provides housing for international visitors and visiting professionals.

twenty-five years, to Villa International for furnishings in the new building. In 1997, the Creative Ministries Offering Committee of Presbyterian Women designated $125,000 for Villa International to help meet the goals of Phase I of a $1-million capital fund campaign.

A letter of March 12, 1997, was received from the Executive Director of Villa International, Harry F. Petersen, along with a video, the latest brochures, and promotional materials. He wrote that all of the 1997 offering will be used in Phase I of the Capital Fund Campaign, which has a goal of $404,000 and covers the period 1996–1998. Some of the items listed in Phase I are a new elevator, two public rest rooms, two indoor storage areas, an expansion of the dining room, an office addition, sound proofing of the library, a new drainage system, and widening of main entrance. Presbyterian Women's contribution of $125,000 will provide for almost a third of these items.

Some of the statistics from the latest brochures that Mr. Petersen kindly furnished help the reader to grasp the breadth of this ministry. Villa annually hosts more than 1,050 internationals from 110 countries. The average stay is twenty-five days. There are thirty-three bedrooms in the facility. Since 1972, Villa has welcomed more than 17,000 "strangers in our midst" from 140 nations. Doctors and medical researchers come to Villa to live while they study, do research, and learn new techniques at CDC. Other professionals study at Emory University or other institutions.

Faith exchange occurs during conversation or at the weekly prayer service in Villa's chapel, which is open to all interested guests. Together the residents learn through the amazing mosaic of cultures that the human family is truly rich and diverse in its makeup. Through this interaction, the participants take a few steps closer to the dream of a reconciled humanity.

Animal Husbandry Project—Cameroon Women for Enterprise and Environment (CAMWEE)

CAMWEE is a means of helping the hungry help themselves. This program will initiate thirty new livestock-development projects with women's groups identified by the Presbyterian Church of Cameroon. Under the auspices of Heifer Project International, each of the thirty projects will provide training and livestock for ten to twenty families. These families, in turn, will pass on animal offspring to other needy families in the community. The pass-on obligation continues with each new family, so the animals serve as living loans.

Through this program three women will be trained as agricultural extension agents. These women will in turn provide training in ecologically sound agriculture, planting locally appropriate feed sources, and building shelters with local resources. It is envisioned that the project will empower women; sustain good nutrition for children, women, and the community as a whole; increase family and community income; and bring stronger family unity.

The Creative Ministries Offering Committee of Presbyterian Women allocated $200,000 for this project.

Presbyterian Church (USA)—The Societal Violence Initiative Team
(For related projects, see also 1990, 1994, 1995, 1996)

The Societal Violence Initiative Team of the Presbyterian Church (USA), the Center for Sexual and Domestic Violence, Inc., in Seattle, and Presbyterian Women in Seattle Presbytery are partners in this project. The Creative Ministries Offering Committee of Presbyterian Women designated funds from the 1997 Birthday Offering, $150,000, to support development of a comprehensive program to address violence against women and children.

The two-part program will first develop a new national program of training and equipping Presbyterian leaders to respond to the needs of abused women and, second, develop and produce a series of educational videos designed specifically for youth ministries and for racially and ethnically diverse churches and service organizations. The videos will tell the stories of abused African-American and Hispanic women. The program will develop a network of trained leaders that can help congregations respond to victims and abusers.

Goals of this project are to equip church leaders to understand the needs of abused women and children, and to provide compassionate and meaningful care.

APPENDIXES

Messages of Reconciliation and Hope

*75 Years of Birthday Offerings
1922–1997*

APPENDIX A

Birthday Gifts through the Years
(1922–1997)

Arranged in Chronological Order

1922	Miss Dowd's School for Girls, Kochi, Japan (See also 1947, 1975)	$25,699
	Montreat Gate (See also 1936, 1941, 1948)	2,500
1923	Presbyterian School for Mexican Girls, Taft, Texas (Now Presbyterian Pan American School, Kingsville, Texas) (See also 1938, 1944, 1950)	52,928
1924	President's Home, Assembly's Training School (Now Presbyterian School of Christian Education) (See also 1948, 1956, 1958, 1977)	23,388
1925	Charlotte Kemper School, Lavras, Brazil	39,251
1926	Chair of Bible, Oklahoma Presbyterian College for Indian Girls, Durant, Oklahoma (Endowment transferred to Goodland Presbyterian Home Hugo, Oklahoma in 1966) (See also 1954, 1976)	42,574
1927	Winsborough Hall at the Jennie Speer School for Girls Kwangju, Korea (See also 1947)	58,875
1928	Emily Estes Snedecor Nurses Training School, Stillman College, Tuscaloosa, Alabama (See also 1938, 1942, 1952, 1960, 1972, 1988)	42,370

Year	Description	Amount
1929	Two schools for Mexican Girls, Chilpancingo and Zitacuaro, Mexico (See also 1957)	52,519
1930	Hallie Paxon Winsborough Foundation in the Endowment Fund for Ministerial Relief	55,695
1931	Girls Homes and Women's Work Buildings at Five African Mission Stations ($45,000) (See also 1939) Central School for Missionary Children, Lubondai, Congo (See also 1945)	50,836
1932	Christian Home Training in Two Mountain Schools in Appalachia (Stuart Robinson School and Highland Institute, Kentucky) (See also 1966, 1994)	42,652
1933	China Bible Institute; North Kiangsu and Mid-China Missions (See also 1947, 1972, 1991)	36,172
1934	Emergency Relief Fund for Home Mission Families, Retired and Deceased Ministers' Families	53,133
1935	Golden Castle School (Kinjo University), Nagoya, Japan (See also 1947, 1967)	41,965
1936	Fellowship Hall, Montreat, North Carolina (Since 1984 the Winsborough, Montreat Conference Center) (See also 1922, 1941, 1948)	31,810
1937	Agnes Erskine School, Recife, Brazil Work among the Caiua Indians, Durados, Brazil Training Christian Women and Girls for Service to Brazil	48,861
1938	Women and Girls of Other Races in the Homeland: Stillman College, Pres-Mex School, Ybor City Mission, Indian Presbyterial, Chinese Mission (New Orleans), Italian Mission (Kansas City) (See also 1923, 1928, 1942, 1946, 1952, 1956, 1960, 1972, 1988)	46,049
1939	Edmiston-Fearing Memorial Fund for Girls Homes, the Congo (See also 1931)	49,659

Appendix A

1940	Vacation Bible School Movement	47,306
1941	Pioneer Evangelistic Work, Brazil (Funds exhausted 1960) Collegiate Home, Montreat (This endowment fund was transferred to Villa International in 1972) (See also 1922, 1936, 1948, 1970)	60,419
1942	Training Christian Black Leaders for Work among Their Own Race (Funds transferred to Stillman, 1950)	51,634
1943	Christian Literature in Mexico	68,029
1944	Presbyterian School for Mexican Girls, Taft, Texas (Now Presbyterian Pan American School, Kingsville, Texas) (See also 1923, 1938, 1950) Defense Service Council	86,252
1945	Varied Work in the Congo Mission (Evangelistic, education, medical) (See also 1931)	110,033
1946	The Italian Mission, Kansas City, Missouri, (See also 1938) The Chinese Presbyterian Church, New Orleans (See also 1938, 1958) Relief of Christians and Reestablishment of Church Life in Europe and Asia ($57,608)	125,828
1947	Mission in the Orient—China, Japan, and Korea (See also 1922, 1927, 1933, 1935, 1947, 1967, 1975, 1984)	157,935
1948	Mountain Retreat Association, Montreat, North Carolina for the completion of Howerton Hall (Since 1977 owned by Montreat College) (See also 1922, 1936, 1941) Administration Building, Assembly's Training School, Richmond, Virginia (Now Presbyterian School of Christian Education (See also 1924, 1956, 1958, 1977)	136,732
1949	Varied Mission Work in Brazil The American Bible Society (See also 1972)	143,890
1950	Texas-Mexican Industrial Institute, Kingsville, Texas (now Presbyterian Pan American School, Kingsville) (See also 1923, 1938, 1944)	143,890

Year	Description	Amount
1950	Ecumenical and Training Opportunities for Students and Student Workers (Includes PSCE)	
1951	Chapels and Christian Centers, Congo	160,406
1952	Chair of Bible, Stillman College (See also 1928, 1938, 1942, 1960, 1972, 1988) Sunday School Extension Work	156,127
1953	Furlough Homes for Missionaries	181,800
1954	Evangelistic Work among Appalachian Coal Camps Goodland Presbyterian Children's Home, Hugo, Oklahoma The Protestant Radio and TV Center, Atlanta, Georgia	179,042 26, 1976
1955	Yodogawa Christian Hospital, Osaka, Japan	208,577
1956	Ybor City Mission Expansion, Tampa, Florida (See also 1938) Area Laboratory Schools for Training Church School Leaders (Includes PSCE)	185,214
1957	Medical Work in Korea (See also 1965) Student Homes in Mexico (See also 1929)	215,230
1958	Oklahoma Presbyterian College—Janie McGaughey Scholarship Fund (Transferred to Presbyterian School of Christian Education, Richmond, Virginia, in 1966) The Chinese Presbyterian Church, New Orleans (See also 1938, 1946)	193,887
1959	Lay Training Center, Brasilia, Brazil	206,200
1960	Classroom-Administration Building, Stillman College (See also 1928, 1938, 1942, 1952, 1972, 1988)	182,596
1961	Presbyterian Bible School, Hsinchu, Taiwan Christian Literature in Congo	219,094
1962	Presbyterian Guidance Program (Career and Counseling Service)	168,479

Appendix A

1963	Medical Work in Mexico Churches and Evangelistic Work in Brazil along BR-14 (See also 1973)	315,142
1964	Training Workers for Presbyterian Homes Evergreen Presbyterian Vocational School, Minden, Louisiana (See also 1974)	256,233
1965	Presbyterian Medical Center, Chunju, Korea, (See also 1957) Taejon Presbyterian College, Taejon, Korea	523,680
1966	Eastern Kentucky Lees College, Jackson (See also 1932) Note: Lees College is now owned and operated by the University of Kentucky Christian Service Ministry, Appalachia (See also 1994)	326,536
1967	Christian Higher Education in Japan Kinjo University, Nagoya (See also 1935, 1947) Shikoku Christian College, Zentsuji	316,734
1968	To Train Leaders to Proclaim God's Word Today's Way (TRAV)	261,097
1969	Good Shepherd Hospital, Tshikaji, Congo Reconciliation Ecumenical Conference Center, Figueira, Portugal	469,534
1970	Villa International, Atlanta, Georgia (See also 1941, 1997)	312,430
1971	Christian Family Service Centers in Congo, Korea, and Taiwan	335,391
1972	Chair of Business and Scholarships for Students, Stillman College (See also 1928, 1938, 1942, 1952, 1960, 1988) American Bible Society (See also 1949)	320,519
1973	Opportunity Unlimited: Amazon Breakthrough (See also 1962) Hunger Mobilization	570,677

1974	New Ventures in Christian Services at Evergreen Presbyterian Vocational School, Minden, Louisiana (See also 1964) New Ventures in Christian Discipleship (Women Leadership)	370,106
1975	Focus on Asia: Preparing Christian Leaders in Korea and Japan (Seiwa School, Japan; Hanil University and Ho Nam Seminary, Korea)	424,079
1976	Christian Service Ministry Unit in Transylvania Presbytery, Kentucky Goodland Presbyterian Children's Home, Hugo, Oklahoma (See also 1926, 1954) Bangladesh Christian Health Care Team Ministry Project	467,640
1977	Center for Ministry with the Aging, PSCE, Richmond, Virginia (See also 1924, 1948, 1956, 1958) Task Force on Criminal Justice (See also 1988) Countries of Southern Africa	428,268
1978	Mexican-American Coordinating Council, San Antonio, Texas (Now Hispanic American Ministry Council) St. Columba Ministries, Norfolk, Virginia	459,515
1979	Mission through Education: Christian Higher Education Ministries Ecumenical Institute, Bossey, Switzerland	357,959
1980	Tithe of Life (Youth in Service)	518,833
1981	God's World PCUS Seminaries	508,087
1982	Edmarc Hospice for Children, Suffolk, Virginia Pembroke Area Presbyterian Ministry, North Carolina	596,226
1983	White Cross Shipping Fund	555,681
1984	Third World Church Leadership Center, Seoul, Korea	539,125
1985	Gift of a Lifetime: Enabling the Ministry of Older People	530,592
1986	Border Ministry, Mexico-USA (See also 1996) Theological Libraries, France	556,310

Appendix A   223

1987	Communities of Hope and Caring: Khayelitsha Community Centers, South Africa Shelter for Families of Burn Victims, Greenville, Mississippi	594,084
1988	Volunteer Emergency Foster Care, Richmond, Virginia Stillman College (See also 1928, 1938, 1942, 1952, 1960, 1972) Ministries to Women in Prison, Atlanta, Georgia (See also 1977)	505,114
1989	Child Advocacy (Developed and administered through the Women's Ministry Unit and the Social Justice and Peacemaking Unit) Manos de Cristo, Austin, Texas Concerns Rising over Prostitution, Philippines	811,000
1990	Africa's Children (Program to be developed by the Global Mission Ministry Unit in partnership with churches in Africa Menaul School, Albuquerque, New Mexico A Faith Response to Abused Women and Children, Seattle, Washington (See also 1994, 1995, 1996, 1997)	957,449
1991	Intermountain Children's Home, Helena, Montana Mother and Toddler Group, Belfast, Ireland Solidarity with Chinese Theological Students, Nanjing, China (See also 1933, 1947)	962,777
1992	Boggs Rural Life Center, Burke County, Georgia San Francisco Network Ministries: Family Housing Women's Ordination for Ministry in Egypt and the Nile Valley (WOMEN)	891,210
1993	Inner-City Youth, New York City, New York Young Pakistani Women (New residence hall at Christian Girls Hostel and High School Hostel for Kinnaird College Native American Church Leaders	884,151
1994	Brazilian Street Children Victims of Torture (From Africa, Middle East, Asia, Central and South America, Eastern Europe) Minneapolis, Minnesota	850,000

1994   Appalachian Abused Women's Resource Center,
            West Virginia (See also 1990, 1995, 1996, 1997)
        Palestinian Children in Dheisheh Refugee

1995   African Christian Women (Working for health, peace,   800,000
            and repatriation of refugees in Cameroon, Ghana,
            and Kenya, Africa)
        Cambodia Women Farmers
        Health Education and Preventive Medicine Center,
            Dominican Republic
        Mother Advocates, Huntsville, Alabama (See also 1990,
            1994, 1996, 1997)
        Teen Mothers Residence, Chicago, Illinois

1996   Mobile Dental Clinic, Asheville, North Carolina   820,000
        The Multi-Cultural Child Development Center,
            Santa Rosa, California
        Our House (For abused women) Greenville, Mississippi
            (See also 1990, 1994, 1995, 1997)
        Women's Health in Haiti (Administered through
            MADRE in New York City and SOFA in Haiti)
        Demonstration Day Care Center (Project Vida),
            El Paso, Texas (See also 1986)

1997   The Duvall Home (For mentally challenged women)   800,000
            Glenwood, Florida
        Rural Ministry, Johns Island, South Carolina
        Villa International, Atlanta, Georgia
            (See also 1941, 1970)
        Cameroon Women for Enterprise and Environment
            (CAMWEE), Cameroon, West Africa
        The Societal Violence Initiative (The Societal Violence
            Initiative Team of the Presbyterian Church (U.S.A.),
            Louisville, the Center for Sexual and Domestic Violence,
            Seattle, and Presbyterian Women, Seattle, are partners
            in this project.) (See also 1990, 1994, 1995, 1996)

Total—$23,381,685

Note: When this book went to press, Birthday Gifts for 1997 had not been received. The goal for the five 1997 projects is $800,000.

APPENDIX B

Birthday Gifts through the Years
(1922–1997)
Arranged by Destination/Recipients

GIFTS AT HOME

Africa
- 1931 Girls Homes and Women's Work Buildings at Five African (Congo) Mission Stations
- 1931 Edmiston-Fearing Memorial Fund for Girls Homes
- 1945 Varied Work in the Congo Mission (Evangelistic, educational, medical)
- 1951 Chapels and Christian Centers in Urban Areas (Luluabourg, now Kananga; Bakwanga, now Mbujimayi; Muene Ditu; Luhuta; Tshimbulu; Mweka; Kasha; Kakenge)
- 1961 Christian Literature in Congo
- 1960 Good Shepherd Hospital, Tshikaji, Congo
- 1971 Christian Family Service Centers (Matete, area of Kinshasa; Mbujimayi; Kananga; see also Korea and Taiwan)
- 1977 Countries of Southern Africa (Primarily Mozambique and Zaire)
- 1987 Khayelitsha Community Centers, South Africa
- 1990 Africa's Abused Children (Partnership in Mission Office, Louisville, Kentucky
- 1994 Victims of Torture (See also Middle East, Asia, Central and South America, Eastern Europe)
- 1995 Africa's Christian Women—Cameroon, Ghana, Kenya (Worldwide Ministries Division, Louisville, Kentucky)
- 1997 Cameroon Women for Enterprise and Environment, CAMWEE (Heifer Project)

Asia
- 1946 Relief of Christians and Reestablishment of Church Life in Europe and Asia (Through the General Assembly's Permanent Committee on War Relief; see also Europe)

1994   Victims of Torture (See also Africa, Middle East, Central and South America, Eastern Europe)

Bangladesh
1976   Bangladesh Christian Health Care Team Ministry Project

Brazil
1925   Charlotte Kemper School, Lavras
1937   Agnes Erskine School, Recife
1937   Work among the Caiua Indians, Dourados
1937   Training Christian Women and Girls for Service in Brazil
1941   Pioneer Evangelistic Work
1949   Varied Mission Work in Brazil, including the Presbyterian Seminary of the North *and* the Bible Institute of the North
1959   Lay Training Center, Brasilia (Joint with UPW—Thank Offering)
1963   Churches and Evangelistic Work along the Belem-Brasilia Highway (BR-14)
1973   Churches and Work along the Trans-Amazon Highway
1994   Brazilian Street Children
1994   Project Green Life

Cambodia
1995   Women Farmers in Cambodia

Cameroon
1995   Africa's Christian Women (See also Ghana and Kenya)
1997   Cameroon Women for Enterprise and Environment (Heifer Project)

Central America
1994   Victims of Torture (See also Africa, Middle East, Asia, South America, Eastern Europe)

China
1933   China Bible Institute *and* North Kiangsu and Mid-China Missions
1947   Mission in the Orient (See also Japan and Korea)
1991   Theological Students (Nanjing Seminary)

Dominican Republic
1995   Health Education Center

Egypt
1992   Women's Ordination for Ministry in Egypt and the Nile Valley, WOMEN

Appendix B   227

Europe
1946   Relief of Christians and Reestablishment of Church Life in Europe and Asia (Through the General Assembly's Permanent Committee on War Life; see also Asia)

Eastern Europe
1994   Victims of Torture (See also Africa, Middle East, Asia, Central and South America)

France
1986   Theological Libraries

Ghana
1995   Africa's Christian Women (See Cameroon and Kenya)

Haiti
1996   Women's Health in Haiti (MADRE, New York City)

Ireland
1991   Mother and Toddler Group

Japan
1922   Miss Dowd's School (Seiwa School), Kochi
1935   Kinjo University (Golden Castle School), Nagoya (See also 1967)
1947   Mission in the Orient (See also China and Korea)
1947   Seiwa School and Kinjo University
1955   Yodogawa Christian Hospital, Osaka
1967   Chapel and Religious Center, Kinjo University (See also 1935) *and* Shikoku Christian College
1975   Focus on Asia: Preparing Christian Leaders in Korea and Japan (See also Korea)
1975   Seiwa School (Miss Dowd's School)

Kenya
1995   Africa's Christian Women (See also Cameroon and Kenya)

Korea
1927   Jennie Speer School for Girls, Kwangju
1947   Mission in the Orient (See also China and Japan)
1947   Jennie Speer School
1947   Bible Schools (Neel Bible School and Ada Hamilton Clark Bible School, Choong Nam, Soonchun, and Mokpo)
1957   Medical Work in Korea, especially in Kwangju
1965   Chunju Medical Center and Taejon Presbyterian College

1971 Christian Family Service Centers, Seoul (See also Africa and Taiwan)
1975 Focus on Asia: Preparing Christian Leaders in Korea and Japan (See also Japan)
1975 Hanil Women's Seminary, Chunju
1975 Ho Nam Theological Seminary, Kwangju
1984 Third World Church Leadership Center, Seoul

Mexico
1929 Two Schools for Mexican Girls, Chilpancingo and Zitacuaro
1943 Christian Literature in Mexico
1957 Student Homes for Girls
1963 Medical Work in Mexico
1986 Border Ministry, Mexico-U.S.A.

Middle East
1994 Victims of Torture (See also Africa, Asia, Central and South America, Eastern Europe)

Pakistan
1993 Young Pakistani Women (Kinnaird College Hostel Fund and Christian Girls Hostel and High School)

Palestine
1994 Palestinian Children in Refugee Camps (Dheisheh Multi-Purpose Child GuidanceCenter)

Philippines
1989 Concerns Rising Over Prostitution (CROP)

Portugal
1969 Reconciliation Ecumenical Conference Center, Figueira

South America
1994 Victims of Torture (See also Africa, Middle East, Asia, Central America, Eastern Europe)

Switzerland
1979 Ecumenical Institute, Bossey (WCC)

Taiwan
1961 The Presbyterian Bible School, Hsinchu
1971 Christian Family Centers (See also Africa and Korea)

White Cross Shipping Endowment Fund
1983 Endowment for Shipping Health Ministries and Medical Supplies

GIFTS AT HOME
Appalachia
1932 Christian Home Training Departments in Two Mountain Schools, Kentucky (Stuart Robinson School and Highland Institute)
1954 Evangelistic Work among Apalachian Coal Camps
1966 Lees College
1966 Christian Service Ministry in Appalachia
1976 Christian Service Ministry Unit
1994 Appalachian Abused Women's Resource Center (Southern West Virginia)

Christian Education and Training
1940 Vacation Bible School Movement
1950 Ecumenical and Training Opportunities for Students and Student Workers (Includes PSCE)
1952 Sunday School Extension Work
1956 Area laboratory Schools for Training Church School Leaders
1962 Presbyterian Guidance Program (Name changed to Career and Personal Counseling Service)
1964 Training Workers for Presbyterian Homes

Colleges, Schools, and Seminaries
Assembly's Training School [Renamed Presbyterian School of Christian Education], Richmond
1924 President's Home
1948 Administration Building
1966 Transfer of Janie McGaughey Endowment Scholarship Fund from Defunct Oklahoma Presbyterian College
1977 Center for Ministry with the Aging
Lee's College, Kentucky [Now part of University of Kentucky system]
1932 Successor Institution to Two Presbyterian Mountain Schools
1966 Endowed Chair of Appalachian Sociology
Menaul School
1990 Classrooms and Laboratory Project
Mission through Education: Christian Higher Education Ministries
1979 Campus Ministries
Oklahoma Presbyterian College
1926 Mary Semple Hotchkin Endowed Chair of Bible (Transferred to Goodland Home in 1966)
1958 Janie McGaughey Endowed Scholarship fund ($111,000 transferred to PSCE in 1966)
Presbyterian School for Mexican Girls, Taft, Texas
Presbyterian Pan American School, Kingsville, Texas (After merger in 1955 with Texas-Mexican Industrial Institute)
1923 Established the Presbyterian School for Mexican Girls in Taft, Texas

1938   Renovation, Painting, Refurbishing
1944   To Construct Kindergarten/Nursery, Library, Recreational Facilities
Presbyterian School of Christian Education (See Assembly's Training School)
Stillman College
1928   Emily Estes Snedecor Nurses Training School
1938   John Knox Hall (Home for Nurses)
1942   Reserve Fund—Training Black Leaders for Work among Their Own Race (Earmarked for Stillman College)
1948   Money from Reserve Fund to Convert Knox Hall to Men's Residence
1950   Money from Reserve Fund to Help Construct Birthright Hall
1952   Janie W. McGaughey Endowed Chair of Bible
1960   Alexander Batchelor Administration and Classroom Building
1972   Endowed Chair of Business
1988   Endowed Scholarship Fund
Texas-Mexican Industrial Institute for Mexican Boys
1950   Endowed Chair of Bible
Mission through Education: Christian Higher Education Ministries
1979   Campus Ministries

Communications
1949   American Bible Society (To further international work of ABS)
1954   Protestant Radio and TV Center, Atlanta, Georgia
1968   TRAV (The television, radio, and audio-visual agency of the PCUS)
1972   American Bible Society (New Testaments for "Cherokee and Navajo Indians" and Scriptures in Spanish for migrant workers)

Criminal Justice
1977   Task Force on Criminal Justice
1988   Ministries to Women in Prison

Ecumenical*
1970   Villa International (See 1941 for transfer of additional gift in 1972)
1978   St. Columba Ministries, Norfolk, Virginia
1990   Abused Women and Children, Seattle, Washington
1997   Villa International, Atlanta, Georgia
*Many of the offerings in recent years have gone to projects that have ecumenical participation; this is not a definitive list.

Homes
1954   Goodland Presbyterian Children's Home (Formerly Goodland Indian Orphanage)
1964   Evergreen Presbyterian Vocational School
1966   Goodland Presbyterian Children's Home (Transfer of endowment from OPC)

Appendix B   231

1974   Evergreen Presbyterian Ministries, Inc.
1976   Goodland Presbyterian Children's Home
1991   Intermountain Children's Home, Helena, Montana
1997   Duvall Home, Glenwood, Florida

Montreat Conference Center (Mountain Retreat Association)
1922   Entrance Gate (Memorial Gate for birthplace in 1912 of Woman's Auxiliary)
1936   Fellowship Hall (Now the Winsborough)
1941   Collegiate Home (Sold and endowment money transferred to Villa International in 1972; see also 1970)
1948   Howerton Hall (Sold to Montreat-Anderson College in 1977)

Racial/Ethnic Causes
1938   Chinese Mission, New Orleans
1938   Indian Presbyterial
1938   Italian Mission, Kansas City, Missouri
1938   Women and Girls of Other Races in the Homeland
1938   Ybor City Mission, Tampa (Hispanic)
1942   Training Black Leaders for Work among Their Own Race (Funds transferred to Stillman College in 1950)
1946   The Chinese Presbyterian Church, New Orleans
1946   The Italian Mission, Kansas City, Missouri
1956   Ybor City Mission Expansion
1958   The Chinese Presbyterian Church, New Orleans
1978   Mexican-American Coordinating Council (Now Hispanic American Ministry Council)
1982   Pembroke Area Presbyterian Ministry, Pembroke, North Carolina
1989   Manos de Cristo—a Servi-Iglesia Ministry, Austin, Texas
1992   Boggs Rural Life Center, Burke County, Georgia
1993   Native American Church Leaders
1996   Project Vida—Demonstration Day Care Center (El Paso, Texas)

Relief Funds (Depression Years)
1930   Hallie Paxson Winsborough Foundation in the Endowment Fund for Ministerial Relief
1934   Emergency Relief Fund for Home Mission Families, Retired and Deceased Ministers' Families

Seminaries, Presbyterian Church, U.S. (Austin, Columbia, Louisville, Union in Richmond)
1953   Furlough Homes for Missionaries
1981   God's World—To Stimulate Global Awareness and Involvement

Service (General)
1980 "Tithe of Life" (Youth in Service)
1985 Gift of a Lifetime: Enabling the Ministry of Older People

War Years
1944 Defense Service Council

Women, Children, and Families
1973 Hunger Mobilization
1974 New Ventures in Discipleship (Women Leadership)
1982 Edmarc Home for Children, Inc.
1987 Shelter for Burn Victims, Greenville, Mississippi
1988 Volunteer Emergency Foster Care, Virginia
1989 Child Advocacy (PCUSA, Louisville, Kentucky)
1990 A Faith Response to Abused Women and Children, Seattle, Washington
1991 Construction of Intermountain Children's Home, Helena, Montana
1992 San Francisco Network Ministries: Family Housing
1993 Inner-City Youth, New York City
1994 Appalachian Abused Women's Resource Center (Beckley, West Virginia)
1995 Residential Home for Homeless Teen Parents, Chicago, Illinois
1995 Mothers Advocates Program, Huntsville, Alabama
1996 Demonstration Day Care Center, El Paso, Texas
1996 "Our House"—A Domestic Violence and Rape Crisis Center, Greenville, Mississippi
1996 Ruth and Billy Graham Children's Health Center, Mobile Dental Clinic, Asheville, North Carolina
1996 Preschool Building for Multi-Cultural Child Development Center, Santa Rosa, California
1997 Confronting Violence Against Women, Societal Violence Initiative (PCUSA, Louisville, Kentucky)
1997 Home for Mentally Retarded Women (Duvall Home, Glenwood, Florida)
1997 Rural Ministry, Johns Island, South Carolina

APPENDIX C

Board of Church Extension (PCUS) Correspondence
(1966)

BOARD OF CHURCH EXTENSION *Presbyterian Church In The United States*

341 PONCE DE LEON AVENUE, NORTHEAST • ATLANTA, GEORGIA 30308 • 875-8921

JOHN F ANDERSON, JR., EXECUTIVE SECRETARY

DIVISION OF FIF... ...ICES
CLAUDE H. PR... ...tary

August 29, 1966

Mr. James W. Gabbie
Goodland Presbyterian Children's Home
Hugo, Oklahoma 74743

My dear Mr. Gabbie:

    Our Board at its meeting in Montreat on August 11th, following the Church Extension Conference, concurred heartily in the following recommendations of the Board of Women's Work regarding the further use of the income from the Mary Semple Hotchkin Bible Chair Endowment Fund and the Janie W. McGaughey Scholarship Fund, and pledged itself to carry out these recommendations to the best of its ability:

        That the income from the Mary Semple Hotchkin Bible Chair Endowment Fund, the 1926 Birthday offering, be designated to provide a Christian education worker on the campus of Goodland Presbyterian Children's Home, Hugo, Oklahoma.

        That the income from the Janie W. McGaughey Scholarship Fund, the 1956 Birthday offering, be designated to be used by Presbyterian School of Christian Education, Richmond, Virginia, to provide scholarships for students from minority ethnic groups in the United States and/or international students.

        That unexpended cash balance of income on hand from the above-mentioned Birthday offerings be made available at the discretion of the Secretary of the Division of Field Services, Board of Church Extension, to be used to provide aid to OPC students who need help toward the completion of their college education.

    In accordance with this action of our Board, the income from the Mary Semple Hotchkin Bible Chair Endowment Fund will become available for the support of a Christian education worker at Goodland Presbyterian Children's Home. Our monthly appropriation from the income from this endowment fund will be made to Goodland Presbyterian Children's Home through the Church Extension Committee of the Synod of Oklahoma. When the Synod's Church Extension Committee forwards its monthly application for our Board's salary appropriation (which becomes due and payable on the 15th of each month) requests will also be made by the Synod's Committee for the monthly appropriation for the support of the Christian education worker at Goodland. The treasurer of the Synod's Committee will forward immediately to you the monthly amount received from our Board for the

Mr. James W. Gabbie
August 29, 1966
Page 2

support of the Christian education worker. This matter has been cleared with the Synod's Church Extension Committee.

I was much interested to learn that Miss Luisa Rodriguez had accepted work at Goodland as Director of Christian Education effective September 1. You are fortunate indeed to have her join your staff to serve in this capacity. As yet we have not received from you any information as to the salary which Miss Rodriguez will receive. The income from the Mary Semple Hotchkin Bible Chair Endowment Fund during 1965 amounted to $3,259.28. We have no way of knowing just what the income from this fund will be during 1966. In view of the current fluctuations in the investment world it would seem wise, on the basis of the available income in 1965, to set the monthly payments from September 1st to the end of this year at $250.00. Since we do not have the monthly salary figure of your arrangement for Miss Rodriguez we have no way of knowing whether the monthly amount suggested will be sufficient to provide her salary in full.

At the present time, there is an income balance in the Mary Semple Hotchkin Bible Chair Endowment Fund of $5,143.80 but in view of the recommendation of the Board of Women's Work as set forth in the third paragraph of their recommendations (as quoted above) this balance is to be made available to aid OPC students who need help toward the completion of their college education. If all of this balance should not be needed for this purpose, the remainder could no doubt be made available for the support of the Director of Christian Education at Goodland. For the time being, however, none of this balance would be available for that purpose.

Two further actions were taken by our Board which will be of interest to you and future Goodland graduates. The first of these actions dealt with the possible use of the two remaining OPC funds held by our Board. The action of our Board with regard to these two funds was as follows:

> That the Youth Fellowship Scholarship Fund and the income from the Thomas P. Townsend Indian Scholarship Fund be made available to OPC students and high school graduates of Goodland Presbyterian Children's Home, upon recommendation of the scholarship committee appointed by the OPC Board and channeled to our Board through the Synod's Church Extension Committee.

The second action dealt with the method of making scholarship recommendations for Indian students to our Board. The action was as follows:

> The proposal that the scholarship committee appointed by the OPC Board make its recommendations to our Board through the Synod's Church Extension Committee regarding OPC students and Goodland graduates needing scholarship aid was approved. The scholarship committee as appointed by the OPC Board consists of Dr.

Mr. James W. Gabbie
August 29, 1966
Page 3

James D. Morrison, Dean of Southeastern State College, Durant, Mr. George Carter of Durant and Mrs. Louis Dollarhide of Oklahoma City.

If and when there are Goodland graduates who need scholarship aid to enable them to go to college or to pursue graduate education for full-time Christian services at recognized Presbyterian institutions, the names of such students should be submitted to this scholarship committee for consideration.

I trust that I have covered these matters in sufficient detail to set them clearly before you. If, however, there are questions about any of these matters, please do not hesitate to ask them.

It was certainly good to see you and Mrs. Gabbie at Montreat. I wish you could have stayed with us for the entire conference period. Let me thank you for your letter of the 25th which reached my desk this morning just as I was preparing to write this letter to you. Some of the delay in getting this letter off to you has been occasioned by vacations in the treasury department.

With very best wishes and warm personal regards, I am

Cordially yours,

Claude H. Pritchard
CLAUDE H. PRITCHARD

CHP:sj
cc: Rev. J. F. Austin
    Rev. Palmer W. Deloteus
    Mr. Walter McMullen
    Dr. Evelyn L. Green
    Dr. John F. Anderson
    Mr. Gordon A. Hanson

APPENDIX D

Board of Women's Work (PCUS) Excerpts from Minutes
(1972–1973)

Minutes - Board of Women's Work - October 1972   EXHIBIT C   11.

REPORT OF EXECUTIVE COMMITTEE
BOARD OF WOMEN'S WORK
October 1, 1972

The Executive Committee recommends:

1. That the Board of Women's Work communicate to the Board of World Missions our decision made in February 1972 that the Birthday Objective Committee (three officers of Women's Advisory Council and three officers and Executive Secretary of Board of Women's Work) be charged with the responsibility of re-designating unused Birthday Offerings, with Board of Women's Work and Women's Advisory Council approval, and that we invite the Board of World Missions to consult with this Committee regarding the unused portions of the 1933 and the 1947 Offerings.

Minutes - Board of Women's Work - October 23-24, 1973   3.

    Wednesday, October 24, 1973

    The Board reconvened in the auditorium of the Presbyterian Center at 9:00 A. M. with the same members of Board and Staff present with the exception of Board Member, Ms. Sidney Claire West.

WORSHIP Following the Call to Order by the Chairman the Worship Service on Change was conducted by Mrs. C. A. McArthur, Jr., and concluded with a prayer litany for the Church.

USE OF 1973 BIRTHDAY OFFERING Dr. James Cogswell, of the GEB, reported to the Board on the projected Hunger Program to be financed by the 1973 Birthday Offering. Half of the money will be used to set up a network of Hunger Action Enablers, one half for Hunger Action Projects around the world.

REDESIGNATION OF BIRTHDAY FUNDS A letter from the Board of World Missions relative to the redesignation of unused Birthday Funds by concurring actions of their Board and the Board of Women's Work was read. The Board of Women's Work voted,

    That the undesignated Birthday Offering plus accrued interest be used to supplement the 1973 Birthday Objective. The Chairman was requested to write a cover letter explaining the action of the Board with a copy to go to Dr. Brown.

APPENDIX E

Board of World Missions (PCUS) Excerpts from Minutes
(1972–1973)

Board of World Missions, Minutes, July 1972   p. 119

72-7-204 Redesignation of Women's Birthday Offering for China

Two Women's Birthday Offerings of prior years were designated for work in Mainland China. Current balances of the fund are as follows:

1933 Birthday Offering "for China Bible Institutes" $115,118.80

1947 Birthday Offering "for Missions in the Orient"   34,475.22

Minutes continued, p. 120

120

VOTED:

1. That the funds remaining from the 1933 and 1947 Women's Birthday Offering be consolidated as a Fund for Christian Mission among the Chinese People.

2. That the Fund for Christian Mission among the Chinese receive the average annual interest of the total portfolio to accrue to the Fund in December of each year.

3. That the aforesaid interest may be utilized for projects among Chinese people throughout the world, such projects to be administered through the Program Administration Division.

4. That the principal of the Fund for the Christian Mission among the Chinese people, augmented by un-utilized interest which shall have accrued thereto, shall remain intact until such time as opportunity may arise for its use in Christian Mission on the Mainland of China, at which time all or part of the principal of the fund may be used for this purpose.

Board of World Missions, Minutes, August 1973   p. 161

73-8-108   Mrs. Marion Reynolds, Chairman, Board of Women's Work -
           Redesignation Birthday Gifts for China 1933 and 1947 -

Mrs. Marion Reynolds, Chairman of the Board of Women's Work, had requested to be present to discuss the redesignation of the 1933 and 1947 Birthday Gifts for China. Mrs. Reynolds was presented by the Vice-Chairman, Dr. Todd.

VOTED:

1. That the Board of World Missions approve any redesignation of these funds made by the Board of Women's Work. The Board of World Missions at its October Board meeting will suggest projects for the redesignated funds but the final decision as to the project will rest with the Board of Women's Work.

2. That the Board of World Missions express its conviction for the tremendous meaning for the overseas work that has come through these Birthday Offerings since 1922 and that the Board recommend to the General Executive Board that such Offerings be continued.

Board of World Missions, Minutes, October, 1973   p. 189, 190

73-10-404   Redesignation of Women's Birthday Gifts for China - 1933 and 1947

At the request of Mrs. Marion Reynolds, Chairman of the Board of Women's Work, the Board of World Missions has agreed to suggest projects for consideration by the Board of Women's Work in its redesignation of the residue of Birthday Offering funds given in prior years for work on the mainland of China. The principal sum involved is $149,549.02.

VOTED: that the Board of World Missions recommend to the Board of Women's Work that the entire residue of the 1933 and 1947 Women's Birthday Offerings be redesignated exclusively for Christian work overseas, in support of the following projects and in the following proportions:

a. One-third of the total for capital improvements at Seiwa Girls' Jr.-Sr. High School in Kochi, Japan.

b. One-third of the total to the Board of Honam Theological Seminary in Korea, for the training of women in Christian Education (Hanil Women's Seminary).

c. One-third of the total for the purchase or construction of missionary and/or pastoral residences in connection with the Transamazonas pioneer program in Brazil.

APPENDIX F

Board of World Missions (PCUS) Correspondence
(1973)

BOARD OF WORLD MISSIONS
Post Office Box 330
Nashville, Tennessee 37202

PROGRAM ADMINISTRATION
DIVISION

REC'D. OCT 30 1973 2155
FILE _____
CR _____

October 29, 1973

Miss Janie McCutchen,
Board of Women's Work,
341 Ponce de Leon Ave., N. E.,
Atlanta, Ga. 30308

Dear Janie:

My secretary gave me the report of your telephone conversation this morning, and we are, therefore, enclosing herewith our check in the amount of $155,665.00, which is the balance in the combined Birthday Offerings of 1933 and 1947 as of October 31, 1973.

With all the best, I am

                      Cordially yours,

                      J. A. Halverstadt.

JAH:l
Enclosure
cc/ Rev. William F. Henning, Jr.
cc/ Dr. David W. A. Taylor
cc/ Dr. T. Watson Street
cc/ Mr. W. P. Partenheimer

Telephone: (615) 298-3351   Office location: 2400 Twenty-first Avenue South   Cable "Liberate"

APPENDIX G

Creative Ministries Offering Committee

Carrying on the tradition of Birthday Gifts (see "How Did It Begin?" page xv), the Birthday Offerings are predetermined projects selected by the Creative Ministries Offering Committee of Presbyterian Women. No more than five projects are selected annually. The offerings are for programs not included in ongoing General Assembly mission support. Objectives are chosen on the basis of meeting the needs of hurting people and with the faith that adequate money to fund them will be received.

Projects are funded proportionately according to the requests made, the goal assigned to each, and actual offerings. The offerings are an extension of and separate from Presbyterian Women's mission pledge support.

The committee is made up of nine persons, six from the Churchwide Coordinating Team of Presbyterian Women and one each from the three divisions listed below of General Assembly Council:

Vice Moderator for Issues, Presbyterian Women Churchwide Coordinating Team, Chair of Creative Ministries Offering Committee

Financial Secretary, Presbyterian Women Churchwide Coordinating Team

Four others from Presbyterian Women Churchwide Coordinating Team

One elected representative from the Division of Congregational Ministries

One elected representative from the Division of National Ministries

One elected representative from the Division of Worldwide Ministries

Committee members serve one three-year term and are rotated for continuity.

The Associate for Mission Participation, Presbyterian Women, is the staff person for the Creative Ministries Offering Committee.

The deadline for submission of proposals for Birthday Offerings is June 15.

APPENDIX H

Criteria for Birthday Offering Proposals

Criteria for Birthday Offering and Thank Offering (including Health Ministries) Proposals

These two offerings have a long tradition with Presbyterian Women (PW)

In order for projects to be funded, the offering must

1. **Have a clearly defined purpose that meets a crucial need for persons who are hurting or be judged of critical importance, in accordance with mission concerns and policies of the Presbyterian Church (U.S.A.)**
2. Provide some form of aid that relates directly to the persons served
3. **Be a new program or a new thrust of an existing program**
4. Offer indication of the changes, either long-term or short-term, that may take place as a result of funding the project
5. Identify the possibilities the project has for working with women, children and racial-ethnic persons to improve conditions of life for them
6. Be seeking a one-time grant, although the project may not necessarily be completed in a single year
7. Not be included in the regular budget for which supplementary funds are being sought
8. Not be used in payment of debt or to fund a permanent endowment
9. Give evidence of other funding sources being explored, indicating amount requested from each source and amount received
10. Describe how the program will continue when this one-time grant (if received) is depleted
11. Describe the process to be used for evaluation and accountability
12. **Provide written endorsement of a Presbyterian Church (U.S.A.) synod or presbytery— if outside U.S.A., provide written endorsement of indigenous church**
13. Be under way for the purpose designated within five years for Birthday Offering grants or three years for Thank Offering (including Health Ministries) grants
14. Note: SIGNATURE OF PROPOSAL WRITER IS REQUIRED.

Time Line			
	Filing Date	**Decision**	**Funding**
Birthday Offering	March 15–June 15	January of the following year	October
Thank Offering	June 15–Sept. 15	April of the following year	May

Resources

Bedinger, Robert Dabney. "Althea Brown Edmiston," In *Glorious Living: Informal Sketches of Seven Women Missionaries of the PCUS*, compiled by Hallie P. Winsborough and edited by Sarah Lee Vincent Timmons. Atlanta: Committee on Women's Work, PCUS, 1937.

Edmiston, Althea Brown. "Maria Fearing, " In *Glorious Living: Informal Sketches of Seven Women Missionaries of the PCUS*, compiled by Hallie P. Winsborough and edited by Sarah Lee Vincent Timmons. Atlanta: Committee on Women's Work, PCUS, 1937.

Erickson, Lois Johnson. "Annie Henrietta Dowd," In *Glorious Living: Informal Sketches of Seven Women Missionaries of the PCUS*, compiled by Hallie P. Winsborough and edited by Sarah Lee Vincent Timmons. Atlanta: Committee on Women's Work, PCUS, 1937.

Irvine, Mary D., and Alice L. Eastwood. *Pioneer Women of the Presbyterian Church*. Richmond, Va.: Presbyterian Committee of Publication, 1927.

McGaughey, Janie W. *On the Crest of the Present*. Atlanta: Board of Women's Work, PCUS, 1961.

Presbyterian Church in the United States. *Presbyterian Survey*. Atlanta: Presbyterian Church in the United States (various issues 1974–1988, from the department of history, Montreat, N.C.).

Presbyterian Church (U.S.A.). *Horizons Magazine.* Louisville: Presbyterian Women, Presbyterian Church (U.S.A.), (January–February 1989, 1990, 1991, 1992, 1993, 1994, 1995, 1996, 1997).

Simmons, Henry C. "Presbyterian School of Christian Education: Center on Aging." In *Gerontology in Theological Education,* edited by Payne and Brewer, 75–87. New York: The Haworth Press, 1989.

Simmons and Peters. *With God's Oldest Friends: Pastoral Visiting in the Nursing Home.* New York: Paulist Press, 1996.

Simpson, Eva. "The Changing Face of Mission," *Presbyterians Today.* Louisville: Presbyterian Church (U.S.A.), (April 1997).

Sprinkle, Patricia Houck. *The Birthday Book, First 50 Years.* Atlanta: Board of Women's Work, PCUS, 1972.

Swann, Vera P., ed. and comp., *Lest We Forget—Racial Ethnic Profiles.* Atlanta: Presbyterian Publishing House, 1987.

Sydenstricker, Myrtle Stosberg, "Charlotte Kemper," In *Glorious Living: Informal Sketches of Seven Women Missionaries of the PCUS,* compiled by Hallie P. Winsborough and edited by Sarah Lee Vincent Timmons. Atlanta: Committee on Women's Work, PCUS, 1937.

Index

Photo page numbers are in bold type.

Abrego, Angela, 112–13, 142
Ada Hamilton Clark Bible School, Chunju, Korea, 34, 90–91. *See also* Hanil University
Affum, Beatrice, 126
Africa's Children, 161
Agnes Erskine School for Girls, Recife, Brazil, 22
Agnes Scott College, 20
Alba Hotel, Montreat, N.C., 35
Alliance Against Institutionalized Dehumanization, 161
American Bible Society, 36, 54, 68–69
American Board of Counseling Services, 54
American Indian Youth Council, 183
Amick, Dr., 43
Aristide, Haitian President Jean Bertrand, 205
Anapu Center, Agropolis, 77
Animal Husbandry Project—Cameroon, 212–13
Antwi, Daniel, 126
Appalachian Abused Women's Resource Center, Beckley, W.Va., 189–90, **190**, 191
Arnold, Frank, 74–75, 78
Arnold, Hope, 74, 78
Assembly Hall, Ybor City Presbyterian Mission, 24
Austin Presbyterian Theological Seminary, Austin, Texas, 40–42, 112–13, 122–24, 160; Mission Ranch, 41–42
Ayad, Fawzia F., 178
Bacon, Silas, 45, 95–96
Bangladesh Christian Health Care Team Ministry Project, 99–100
Bangladesh Village Health Care and Agricultural Development, 100–102, 104
Barnard, Dottie, 86
Battle, David, 159–60
Beckley Area Foundation, 191
Benedum Foundation, 191
Bible Institute of the North, Garanhuns, Brazil, 36
Bible School, Mokpo and Soonchun, Korea, 34

Birthright, Mr. and Mrs. Charles, 29
Boggs Academy, Burke County, Ga., 174–75
Boggs Rural Life Center, Burke County, Ga., 174, **174,** 175
Border Ministry, Mexico-U.S.A., 140, **141,** 158; Christ's Frontier, 142; *Frontera de Christo,* 141; Project *Amistad,* 140, 142; Project *Verdad,* 141; *Puentes de Cristo,* 140, 142; *Pueblos Hermanos,* 141–42
Boyce, James R. and Marguerite, 55
Boy Scouts, 94, 97
BR-14 Highway project, Brazil, 56, 73–74
Brethren Service Center, New Windsor, Md., 134
Brewster-Lee, Dorothy, 193
Bridgman, Mr. and Mrs. Stewart, 104
Brown, Bill and Isabel, 43
Brown, G. Thompson, 90, 92
Carpenter, Marj, 20
Carrie MacMillan Home, Kochi, Japan, xv, 3–5, **5**. *See also* Seiwa School
Casa de Publicaciones El FARO, S.S., 20
Cathedral Community Services, Belfast, Ireland, 170
Catholic Relief Services, 101–2
Center for Disease Control, Atlanta, Ga., 65, 211–12
Center for the Prevention of Sexual and Domestic Violence, Seattle, Wash., 163, 166–67, 213
Centers of Hope, Sudan, Africa, 164
Central Presbyterian Church, Kansas City, Mo., 24
Central School for Missionary Children, Lubondai, Congo, 16, 17, 31–32
Charlotte Kemper School, Lavras, Brazil, 7, 23
Child Advocacy Project, 155, 156–57
Children of Bethlehem House, Sorocaba, Brazil, 187
Children's Hospital of the King's Daughters, 130

Child Survival Program, 164; Blantyre Synod, 164; Malawi, 164
China Bible Institute, North Kiangsu, China, 18
China Christian Council, 173
Chinese Presbyterian Church, New Orleans, La., 23, 32, 50–51
Choctaw County Genealogical Society, Okla., 97
Christian Council of Mozambique, 110
Christian Family Service Centers, Kananga, 67; Matete, 67; Mbujimayi, 67; Seoul, 67; Taiwan, 67
Christian Health and Agricultural Project, Alhadipur, 103
Christian Higher Education Ministries, 115, 117
Christian Service Ministry in Appalachia, 60–61, 93–95, 104; Home Repair Program, 94
Christian Women's Health Organization, 193
Christ Presbyterian Church, Kansas City, Mo., 32
Chung Dong Tuk, 68
Church World Service, xvii, 101, 132
Clark, Ada Hamilton, 90
Codington, Herbert, 49, 100, 103–4; family, 102
Cogswell, James A., 79–80
Columbia Theological Seminary, Decatur, Ga., 40–42, 118, 122–25, 160
Clothes Closet, 40;
Columbia Friendship Circle, 42; Mission Haven, 40–42; Samuel N. Lapsley Building, 40
Community Services West, Chicago, Ill., 199–200
Concerns Arising Over Prostitution Drop-In Center, Manila, Philippines, 155, 160–61
Congolese Girls School, Lubondai, Congo 17, 31
Coppedge, L. J., 55
Crane, Paul, 58–59
Crawford, John, 32
Crawford, Mary, 110
Cutler, Jean, 134
Davis, Harrell, 183
Davis, Mary, 68, **69**
Dearinger, David L., 96–98

Defense Service Council, 31
Dheisheh Refuge Camp, Israel, 184, 191, **192**;
Child Guidance Center, 191–92
Diaz, Frank, 111, 113
Dietrick, Ron, 49
Dimmock, Albert E., 105
Dowd, Annie Henrietta
Dowd, xvii, 3–4, **4**, 15, 89–90
Duvall Home, Glenwood, Fla., 209–10, **210**
Ecumenical Child Care Network, 157
Ecumenical Institute, Bossey Switzerland, 117–20
Ecumenical Training Center, Kite, Zambia, 53
Edmarc Hospice for Children, Inc., Tidewater, Va., 127–28, **128**, 129–130; Project M.A.G.I.C., 129–30
Edmiston, Alonzo, 26
Edmiston, Althea Brown, 16, 25–26, **26**
Eglise Presbyterienne Camerounaise, Cameroon, Africa, 193
El Buen Pastor Presby-terian Church, 158
El Divino Salvador Church, Dallas, Texas, 111
Ellinwood Church, 160
Emory University, 211–12
Evangelical Hospital, Sorocaba, Brazil, 187
Evangelical Presbyterian Church, Ghana, 126
Evergreen Presbyterian Vocational School (Evergreen Presbyterian Ministries, Inc.), Minden, La., 57, 81–82, **82**, 83, **83**, 84–85; Extended Care, 83
Ex-Street Kid House, Brazil, 186
Rural Mission, Inc., Johns Island, S.C., 210
Faculty of Reformed Theology of the Kasai, Congo, 32
Family Counseling Center, Taipei, 68
Favela family, **186**
Fearing, Maria, xvii, 15, 25–26, **26**
Ferguson, Duncan, 18
First Church of Kochi, Japan, 87
First Czecho-Slovakian Church, Prince George, Va., 23

251

First Presbyterian Church, Avenel, N.J., 197; Winston-Salem, N.C., 65; Hazard, Ky., 61; Houston, Tex., 62
Florida State University, 38
Foley, Tom, 56
Forbes, William Ross, 120
Fort Valley State College, 175
Friendship Hospital (Sanatorio de La Amistad), Ometepec, Mexico, 55
Friendship Press, 156
Friendship Student Circle, 20, 48
Frontier Housing, 95
Future Farmers of America, 98
Gammon Institute, Brazil, 7
Gannaway, Bruce, 163
Gantt, Lucy, 15
Gartrell, Bill and Fern Jennings, 74
German Evangelical Central Agency, 58–59
Gibson, Tameka, 148
Gift of a Lifetime, 137–39
Girls Scouts, 94
Glorious Living, 16
Goodland Presbyterian Children's Home (Goodland Dependent School; Good Land/Goodland Indian Orphanage; Good Land Mission and Day School; Goodland Orphanage School; Good Land School), Hugo, Okla., 9, 43, 44, **44**, 45, 50, 95–97, 97, 98–99, 99; Bacon Hall, 43–44, **44**, 45, 96; Bicentennial Funds, 97; Church, 95
Good Shepherd Hospital (Institut Medical Chrestien de Kasai), Tshikaji, Congo, 32, 64–65, 133
Gotcheb Clinic, Ethiopia, 164
Graham Tuberculosis Hospital, (General Hospital; Kwangju Christian Hospital), Kwangju, 49
Green, Evelyn, 79
Grosvenor Environmental Society, 170
Guerrant, Dr., 17
Hadsell, Heidi, 119
Hall, Nancy and Walter, 133
Halverstadt, J. A., 19
Hanil University (Hanil Women's Seminary), Chunju, Korea, 19, 34, 90–92

Han-Luan Chih, 126
Hannam University (Soong Jun University; Taejon Presbyterian College), Taejon, Korea, 59–60
Haymond Church, Haymond, Ky., 61
Headstart, 210
Health Education and Preventive Medicine Center, Dominican Republic, 197
Heifer Project, 212
Hestir, Bluford, 63
Highland Institute, Guerrant, Ky., 17. *See also* Lees College
Hogge, Marcus, 127–28
Ho Nam Theological Seminary, Kwangju, Korea, 19, 90–92
Hopper, Dorothy Longenecker, 17
Hopper, Joe, 17
Hospital la Salud, Mexico City, 55
Hospital of Light (Sanatorio La Luz), Morelia, Mexico, 55
Howard University, 92
Huff, Olson, 202
Hughes, Charles R. Jr., 73
Hugo High School, Hugo, Okla., 98
Hull Memorial Church, Hazard, Ky., 61
Hunger Mobilization (Action Program against World Hunger), 79
Inner City Church Council, San Francisco, Calif., 38
Institute Biblico Eduardo Lane, Brazil, 75
Intermountain Children's Home, Helena Montana, 167–68, **168**, 169
International Fund for Ireland, 170
International School, Kinshasa, Zaire, 17
Irvine, Mary, xvii
Japanese Imperial Calvary, 62–63
Jennie Speer School for Girls, Kwangju, Korea, 9–10, 34; Chair of Bible, 34; Winsborough Hall, 10, 33
John and Phyllis Todd Award for Excellence in Teaching, 39
Johnson, Bob and Corinne, 74
Jones, Neil, 39
Junkin, Nettie, 52
Kasai Rural Clinics Program, 133
Kemper, Charlotte, xvii, 7–8
Khayelitsha Community Centers, South Africa, 144–45

Khemara Rural Development Program, 195–96
Khulna Pioneer Village project, 101
King, Captain, 37
King, Henrietta, 37
Kinjo Gakuin (Golden Castle School; Kinjo University), Nagoya, Japan, 20-21, **21**, 33, 62, **62**; Ella Houston Hall, 62; Glory Hall, 20, 33; Kinjo Junior High School, 20; Kinjo Kindergarten, 20; Kinjo Senior High School, 20
Kinnaird College, Pakistan, 181, **181**, 182
Kinsler, Arthur W., 10
Kinsler, Arthur W., 34, 49, 59, 68, 91–92, 137
Kiwanis, 130
Kuhn, Dr. and Mrs., 103
Lane, Patty, 113
Lapsley, Samuel, 15
Lay Training Center (National Presbyterian Institute of Education), Brasilia, Brazil, 51
Lees College (Central University, Richmond, Va.; Lees Junior College), Jackson, Ky., 17–18, 61; Chair of Appalachian Sociology, 18, 61
Lewis, Marcia J., 197
Long, Brad, 53
Long, Paul and Merry, 74, 78
Louisville Presbyterian Theological Seminary, Louisville, Ky., 40, 42, 122–26; Endowed Chair in International Mission and Evangelism, 126; Furlough Home, 41
MADRE, New York, N.Y., 205–6, **206**
Magness, Alice, 85
Makemie Church, Accomac, Va., 20
Manjarrez, Eufemia, 48
Manos de Cristo (Hands of Christ), Austin, Texas, 155, 157–59
Marabá Center, Marabá, Brazil, 77
Mary Baldwin College (Mary Baldwin Seminary), 7
Mary Semple Hotchkin Endowment for Chair of Bible (Chair of Bible, Oklahoma Presbyterian College for Indian Girls), 8–9, 50, 99
Maxwell, Jack M., 123
McAlpine, R. E., 20
McCall, Jessie Junkin, 53
McCormick Theological Seminary, Chicago, Ill., 113, 120

McCutchen, Janie, 19
McCutchen, Mrs. Leighton, 51
McGaughey, Janie W., 9, 30, 50
McLellan, Joe, 75
Medical Benevolence Foundation, 58
Memorial Mission Hospital, North Carolina, 202, 203
Menaul School, Albuquerque, N.Mex., 161, 164–65, **165**, 166, **166**; Rendon Hall (Classroom and Laboratory Project; Renovation Project), 164–65, **65**, 66
Mexican-American Coordinating Council (Hispanic American Ministry Council), San Antonio, Texas, 111–13
Milk Cow project, 78
Miller, Jean Guy, 135–36
Miller, Louise, 28–29
Miller, Robert, 131
Ministries with Women in Prison, Inc., 148–49, **149**, 150
Ministry of Education, 63
Minneapolis Center for Victims of Torture, Minneapolis, Minn., 187–88, **188**, 189; Child Survivor Project, 188
Miss Fearing's Girls Homes, Africa, 14–16, **16**, 25, **26**, 31
Missionary Air Fellowship, 75
Mission Group on Persons in Special Need, 113
Mission Press at Luebo, Congo, 53
Mission through Education, 115, **116**
Mississippi Fire Fighters Memorial Burn Center, Greenville, Miss., 145. *See also* Shelter for Families of Burn Victims
Moak, Soon W., 136–37
Mobile Dental Clinic, Asheville, N.C., 202, **203**
Monsarrat, National Council President, 143
Montgomery, Margaret, 133
Montreat, N.C., xv, xvi, 6, 21, 22, 28–29, 35, 64, 211
Montreat College (Montreat-Anderson College), Montreat, N.C., 21, 35; Belk Campus Center, 22; Collegiate Home (Collegiate Hall; Hickory Lodge), 28, 67, 211; Fellowship Hall (Groseclose Hall; the

Index

Winsborough, Montreat Conference Center; World Fellowship Building), 21–22, 35; Gate (Memorial Gateway), 6; Howerton Dormitory and Cafeteria, 22, 35; Woman's Club, 28. *See also* Montreat
Moon, Cyrus H., 135
Mo-Ranch, 112
Moseley, Bill, 27, 74
Moseley, Sara B., 86
Moseme, Abiel Matitsoane, 126
Mother Advocates Program, Huntsville, Ala., 198–99
Mountain Retreat Association, 22, 35
Mulder, John, 42, 125–26
Multi-Cultural Child Development Center, Santa Rosa, Calif., 200, 202
Myers, Marcia, 18
Myramyr, 119
Nanjing Theological Seminary, Nanjing, China, 125, 172–73, **173**
National Children's Advocacy Center, Huntsville, Ala., 198
National Christian Council of Churches, 103, 143, 156–57, 161
National Indian Training & Research, Tempe, Az., 182
National Women's Union of the Evangelical Church of Egypt, 178
Neel, Lois, 90
Neel Bible School, Kwangju, 34, 90–91. *See also* Hanil University
Nelson, C. Ellis, 123
Nessibou, Janice, 193
Nonweiler, Mr. and Mrs., 103
Norfolk Jaycees, Norfolk, Va., 130
Okamura, Tamiko, 20
Oklahoma Presbyterian College (Calvin Institute; Durant Presbyterian College; Oklahoma Presbyterian College for Indian Girls), Durant, Okla., 8–9, 50, 99
Old Dominion University, 114
Oldenburg, Douglas, 41, 125
Operation Exodus—Inner City, New York, N.Y., 179–80; Crossroads Africa, 38; Unlimited: Amazon Breakthrough, 73, **74**

Organization of American States Inter-American Commission on Human Rights, 206
Orr, Kenneth, 105
Our House, Greenville, Miss., 203–4
Oxfam America, 194
Page, Edward, 127–28
Paraiso Health Assistance Program, Paraiso, Dominican Republic, 196–97
Parkhill, Ralyn, 82
Passaigalia, Walter, 32
Payne, Carleen, 148
Pemberton, Olson, 75
Perce, Nez, 183
Perkins School of Theology, 113
Petersen, Harry F., 212
Peterson, Catherine (Kitty), 46, 87
Philips, J. Davison, 42, 123, 125
Pioneer Evangelistic Work in Brazil, 27
Presbyterian Bible School (Hsinchu Bible School), Hsinchu, Taiwan, 52–53
Presbyterian Guidance Program, 54–55
Presbyterian Historical Association, 28
Presbyterian Homes, 57
Presbyterian Medical Center (Chunju Medical Center; Jesus Hospital; *Yesoo Pyongwon*), Chunju, Korea, 49, 58–59
Presbyterian Medical Clinic, Bangladesh, 101
Presbyterian-Mexican School (Presbyterian School for Mexican Girls), Taft, Texas, 6, 24, 30-31
Presbyterian Pan American School, Kingsville, Texas, 37; Homer McMillan Dormitory, 37. *See also* Presbyterian-Mexican School *and* Texas-Mexican Industrial Institute
Presbyterian School of Christian Education (Assembly's Training School), Richmond, Va., 7, 9, 27, 35, 50, 105, 107, 113; Center for Ministry with the Aging (Graduate Center for Educational Ministry), 105, 107, 138; Mission Court, 40–41
Presbyterian Theological Seminary, Mexico City,

Mexico, 123; Recife, Brazil, 36; Seoul, Korea, 135–36
Presidente Medical Center, Brazil, 77
Pritchard, John, 109, 126
Project Green Life—Brazilian Street Children, 184–87; Project Emmaus, 185; Project Morning Dew, 185; Project Boca Bonita, 186–87
Project Green Thumb, Pembroke Area Presbyterian Ministry, 130–31; Nutrition Education Program, 130; Farmers' Market, 130–31; Food Supply Program, 130; Home Demonstration Clubs, 130
Project Vida—Project Life, 207–8; Demonstration Day Care Center (Early Childhood Development Center), El Paso, Texas, 207–8; Food Care, 208
Pruit, Virginia Gray, 17
Ralston, C. J., 8
Randolph, Annie E., 20
Reconciliation Ecumenical Conference Center, Figueira da Foz, Portugal, 65
Rescue Home, Luebo, Congo, 32
Ribeiro, Dr., 79
Rice, William, 100
Roberts Foundation, 176
Ronald McDonald Children's Services, 130
Ross, Hervey, 48
Rotary Club, 187, 202
Rule, Dr. and Mrs., 65
Ruth and Billy Graham Children's Center, Memorial Mission Hospital, Asheville, N.C., 202
Salvation Army Orphanage, Reynosa, Mexico, 142
San Francisco Network Ministries, 175–76; 555 Ellis Street Family Apartments, 176–77
San Francisco Theological Seminary, Calif., 113
Sangla Hill Girls School Hostel (Christian Girls Hostel, Middle and High School), Sangla Hill, Pakistan, 180–81
Santarém Chapel/ Church, Santarém, Brazil, 77

Santa Rosa Rotary Club, Santa Rosa, Calif., 202
Sapelo Island Research Foundation, Ga., 175
Schlesingers, Bill and Carol, 208–9
School for Mexican Girls, Chilpancingo/Zitacuaro, Mexico, 13–14; Student Home, 48
Seiwa School (Industrial School of Kochi; Miss Dowd's School; Seiwa Gakuen; Seiwa Junior Senior Girls High School), Kochi, Japan, xv, xvi, 3–4, **4**, 19, 33, 87, 89, **89**, 90, 132
Self-Development Program, 113, 184
Seminary in Lesotho, 126; Nanjing, China, 125
Senhati Pioneer Village, Bangladesh, 102
Service Men's Christian League, 31
Shelter for Families of Burn Victims, Greenville, Miss., 145–46
Shelton, Robert M., 42, 124
Sheperd, Dan, 133
Sheppard, William, 15
Shikoku Christian College, Zentsuiji, Japan, 62–63; New Life Gymnasium, 63; Zion Hall, 63
Simmons, Henry C., 107
Simmons, Lib McGregor, 118–19
Simpson, Eva, xvi
Sligh, Julie S., 129–30
Smith, Mr. and Mrs. Scott, 104
Smythe, Mary, 20
Snedecor, Emily Estes, 12
Societal Violence Initiative Team, 213
SOFA (Solidarity with Haitian Women), 205–6
Soongsil College, Seoul, Korea, 60
Southeastern Teachers College, Durant, Okla., 8
Southern Association of Colleges and Schools, 10, 29, 37, 39
Spach, Jule, 75, 78–79
Sprinkle, Patricia Houck, 3, 10, 17, 23, 39, 48, 53
St. Columba Ministries (St. Columba Ecumenical Ministries, Inc.), Norfolk, Va., 111, 113, 115; Community Ministries Fund, 114; Family Center Ministry, 114: Robin Hood Apartments, Norfolk, Va., 113–14

St. Columba Presbyterian Church, Norfolk, Va., 113–14
St. Johns Presbyterian Church, Tampa, Fla., 47
St. Peter's Parish, Belfast, Ireland, 169
Stacy, Jerry, 142–43
Stair, Fred R. Jr., 123
Stark, Mrs. Oliver Porter, 95
Stillman College (Stillman Institute), Tuscaloosa, Alabama, 10–12, 15, 24–25, 29, 39–40, 51–52, 68–69, **69**, 146, 148; Alexander Batchelor Building, 51–52; Birthright Hall, 29; Chair of Bible (Janie W. McGaughey Professor of Bible), 39; Chair of Business, 68; Emily Estes Snedecor Hall, 12, **12**, 13; Emily Estes Snedecor Nurses Training School, 10, 24–25; Hallie Paxson Winsborough Hall, Stillman College, 11, **11**, 29; John Knox Hall (Student Health Center), 25, **25**
Stuart Robinson School, Blackey, Kentucky, 17
Suffolk Presbyterian Church, Suffolk, Va., 127
Sursavage, Mr. and Mrs. "Butch," 100, 102, 103
Swann, Vera, 16
Swayze, Bev, **185**, 186–87
Swayze, Knox, 186–87
Sydnor, Charles, 43

Taft High School, Taft, Texas, 31
Tait, Mattie Ingold, 58
Taiwan Theological College, Taipei, Taiwan, 52
Tampa Presbyterian Planning Council, 47
Taylor, Alice, 114
Teen Mothers Residence, Chicago, Ill., 199
Texas-Mexican Industrial Institute, Kingsville, Texas, 37; Chair of Bible, 37–38
Third World Church Leadership Center, Seoul, Korea, 134, 136–38
Tithe of Life, 120, **139**
Tompkins, Jerry, 37–38
Tongi Clinic, Bangladesh, **102**
Townsend Street Presbyterian Church, Belfast, Ireland, 169; School, 171–72; Education and Training Center, 171; Mother and Toddler Group, 169–71; Social Outreach Centre, 169–70; Youth Club, 172
Trans-Amazon Highway, Brazil, 73, 75–76, 78
TRAV (Television, Radio, Audio-Visual Agency), 63–64
Trinity Theological, Lagon, Ghana, 126
Trull Foundation, 159
Tucker, Grayson L. Jr., 42, 125–26
U.S. AID, 101, 132, 134

U.S. Department of Health and Human Services, 175
Ueno, Hiroe, 5, 87, 89
Underwood, John T., 91
Union Theological Seminary, Richmond, Va., 7, 40–41, 108, 113, 122–24, 126–27; West Virginia Building, 40
United Theological School, Congo, 32. *See also* Faculty of Reformed Theology of the Kasai
United Way, 129, 160; Combined Campaigns, 129
University of Alabama, 12; Kentucky, 18, 61; Santo Domingo, 197; Texas, 41
Vail, Alice Longenecker, 17
Vass, Winifred Kellersberger, 53
Villa International Atlanta, Ga., 28, 45, 65, **66**, 67, 211, **211**, 212
Volunteer Emergency Foster Care, Richmond, Va., 150
Wagner, Bernard, 83–85
Weaver, Ellen, 95–96, 99
Weeks, Louis, 41, 126–27
Welch, Ruth and Doug, 164
Weller, Jack E., 94, 104
West Indies Theological Seminary, Jamaica, 125
West Santa Rosa Local Action Council, Inc., Santa Rosa, Calif., 200
West Virginia Homeless Shelters Program, 191

White, Bobbi, 119
White Cross Sewing, 131–34
Williams, Don and Laura, 74
Wilson Leprosy Colony, Soonchun, Korea, 49
Winsborough, Hallie Paxson, xv, 4, 11, 14, 132
Woman's Bible School, Kiangyin, China, 34
WOMEN (Women's Ordination for Ministry in Egypt and the Nile Valley), 177–78
Women in Action in Harris County Jail, Houston, Texas, 109
Women's International League for Peace and Freedom, 192
Women's Work in Brazil, 23
World Council of Churches, xvii, 120
Wynn, Cordell, 11, 13, 25, 29, 39, 51, 68, 148
Yakni Achukma preaching station, Hugo, Okla., 95
Yale University, 113
Yanjing Union Theological Seminary, North China, 172
Ybor City Presbyterian Church, Tampa, Fla., 47
YMCA, 187
Yodogawa Christian Hospital, Osaka, Japan, 45, 46, **46**, 47
Youth in Service, 120, **121**
Yushan Theological College, 126

About the Author

Catherine Stewart Vaughn is an active elder at the Black Mountain Presbyterian Church in North Carolina and is a member of the Presbytery of Western North Carolina's Committee on Ministry. Cathy was elected commissioner to the 209th General Assembly of the Presbyterian Church (U.S.A.) in 1997, serving on the Bills and Overtures Committee.

Cathy Vaughn received an Honorary Life Membership in Women of the Church (PCUS) in 1976 and in Presbyterian Women in 1988. She has held many leadership positions, including chair/president  at each level—local, presbytery, synod, general assembly, and ecumenical. Besides being a member and chair of the denomination's Birthday Selection Committee from 1984 to 1986, she has participated in forty-two years of "joyous" Birthday Celebrations. Her husband, Silas M. Vaughn, is past president of Montreat-Anderson College. They reside in Montreat, North Carolina.